A Language as Social Semiotic-Based Approach to Teaching and Learning in Higher Education

WILEY

Language Learning Monograph Series

Mary J. Schleppegrell, Series Editor
Nick C. Ellis, General Editor

Schumann:
The Neurobiology of Affect in Language

Bardovi-Harlig:
Tense and Aspect in Second Language Acquisition: Form, Meaning, and Use

Kasper and Rose:
Pragmatic Development in a Second Language

Seedhouse:
The International Architecture of the Language Classroom: A Conversation Analysis Perspective

McNamara and Roever:
Language Testing: The Social Dimension

Young:
Discursive Practice in Language Learning and Teaching

Bigelow:
Mogadishu on the Mississippi: Language, Racialized Identity, and Education in a New Land

Christie:
Language Education Throughout the School Years: A Functional Perspective

Coffin and Donohue:
A Language as Social Semiotic-Based Approach to Teaching and Learning in Higher Education

A Language as Social Semiotic-Based Approach to Teaching and Learning in Higher Education

Caroline Coffin *is Professor in English Language and Applied Linguistics at The Open University, UK, and co-convenor of the Language and Communication Research Unit. Since the early 1990s she has been using a language as social semiotic approach to investigate the role of language in learning in a range of contexts. Using the tools of systemic functional linguistics she has been particularly interested in investigating disciplinary knowledge and discourse including how it is taught and learned through computer mediated dialogue. Her research into language, education, and communication has been funded by a wide range of organizations including, in the UK, the EU, ESRC, HEA, DfeS, and, in Australia, the New South Wales (NSW) Department of Education, the NSW Education and Training Foundation, and the Department of Ethnic Affairs. For the last three years she was secretary of the Executive Committee of the British Association of Applied Linguistics (BAAL) and served on the UK Committee for Linguistics in Education. Published books include* Exploring English Grammar: From Formal to Functional *(Routledge, 2009, with Donohue and North),* Applied Linguistics Methods: A Reader *(Routledge, 2009, with Lillis and O'Halloran),* Historical Discourse: The Language of Time, Cause and Evaluation *(Continuum, 2006) and* Teaching Writing in Higher Education *(Routledge, 2003, with Curry, Goodman, Hewings, Lillis, and Swann). http://fels-staff.open.ac.uk/c.coffin*

Jim Donohue *is Head of OpenEnglish Language Teaching in the Department of Languages at The Open University UK, where he leads on the production of online and distance courses in English for Academic Purposes and works in collaborations with faculties across the university to develop language-based approaches to teaching and learning. He has researched extensively in the fields of academic and professional communication using systemic functional linguistics approaches and drawing on many years spent applying Paulo Freirean perspectives in adult and community education settings. He is particularly interested in how linguistics can be used to enhance learner-centered and experiential learning. He is currently secretary of the committee of the European Association of Teachers of Academic Writing. He has published in the* Journal of English for Academic Purposes *(and was co-editor with Coffin of the special issue,* English for Academic Purposes: Contributions from Systemic Functional Linguistics and Academic Literacies*),* Journal of Applied Linguistics and Professional Practice, English for Specific Purposes, *and* Writing & Pedagogy, *and is co-author of the book* Exploring English Grammar: From Formal to Functional *(Routledge, 2009, with Coffin and North). http://fels-staff.open.ac.uk/j.p.donohue*

Registered Office
John Wiley & Sons Ltd, The Atrium, Southern Gate, Chichester, West Sussex, PO19 8SQ, United Kingdom

Editorial Offices
350 Main Street, Malden, MA 02148-5020, USA
9600 Garsington Road, Oxford, OX4 2DQ, UK
The Atrium, Southern Gate, Chichester, West Sussex, PO19 8SQ, UK

For details of our global editorial offices, for customer services, and for information about how to apply for permission to reuse the copyright material in this book please see our website at www.wiley.com/wiley-blackwell.

Library of Congress Cataloging-in-Publication Data

Coffin, Caroline, 1958-
A language as social semiotic-based approach to teaching and learning in higher education / Caroline Coffin and Jim Donohue.
pages cm. – (Language learning monograph series)
Includes bibliographical references and index.
1. Language and languages–Study and teaching (Higher) 2. Semiotics–Social aspects. 3. Language arts (Higher)–Correlation with content subjects. 4. Interdisciplinary approach in education. I. Donohue, Jim (Linguist) II. Title.
P53.774.C64 2014
418.0071–dc23

2014010378

ISBN 978-1-118-92382-5

Set in 10/13 pt TimesNRPS by Aptara
Printed in the U.S.A. by The Sheridan Group

01—2014

A Language as Social Semiotic-Based Approach to Teaching and Learning in Higher Education

Contents

Language Learning ISSN 0023-8333

Series Editor's Foreword

This monograph offers research-based perspectives and linguistically informed approaches to supporting language and literacy development in higher education. In this way it continues a theme established in the previous *Language Learning* monograph, Frances Christie's (2012) exploration of the role of language in supporting children's learning across the school years. As did Christie, here Caroline Coffin and Jim Donohue see language as central to teaching and learning, but rarely a focus of attention in the instruction students receive. Their motivation for addressing this issue in the context of higher education is the growing population of university students from diverse backgrounds. They argue that the linguistic diversity among students that instructors are encountering across all of higher education means that in every field, support for engaging in the discourses of the discipline as they learn the content of the discipline is crucial for student success.

To address that need, the authors have brought together findings from research programs and instruction they have been engaged in at The Open University in Milton Keynes as well as in other university settings over the past several years that illustrate how the achievement of disciplinary learning goals can be enhanced through what they call a *language as social semiotic* approach to teaching and learning. This approach calls for making a connection between the *meanings* to be developed and the *forms of language* through which those meanings are enabled.

Like Christie, the authors of this monograph draw on systemic functional linguistics (SFL) (e.g., Halliday, 1978; 1994; Hasan, 2005) for their theoretical framework, as it enables them to approach the study of language in context with a rich set of analytic tools and constructs. In particular, the notion of *register* from SFL is central to their analysis, as they explore the ideational, interpersonal, and textual meanings that are at stake as students respond to the demands of the field, tenor, and mode of the discourse they are engaged with. The authors put this theory into dialogue with the sociologist Bernstein's (e.g., 1996) work on *critical socializing contexts* to establish the relevance and need for work on language learning in higher education. Additionally, they draw on the ethnographic approaches and orientation to ideology of academic literacies research (e.g., Lea & Street, 1998) and on the Vygostkian (e.g., 1978) notion of *semiotic mediation*, engaging with instructors and students, as well as engaging students and instructors with each other, in mutual inquiry and learning. This mutual learning, at the center of the process of inquiry they describe, results in robust findings that offer innovative insights to inform tertiary pedagogy.

This set of theories and methodologies enables them to adopt a new perspective on the challenges students face. They present data from interviews with students that show how students come to higher education differently positioned in the ways they recognize and respond to the contexts of learning; what Coffin and Donohue refer to as the students' *semantic orientations.* To support students with different semantic orientations, the authors illustrate how the linguistic demands of the disciplines can be made explicit for learners through *metasemiotic mediation,* explicit interaction about language that enables mutual understanding, and scaffolding of the new knowledge to be learned.

Following a chapter that provides an overview of the volume and sets up the issues to be addressed, Chapter 2 introduces student voices that establish the kind of variation this work addresses. We find here that both multilingual students of varied backgrounds as well as English-speaking students from contexts not previously served by courses in higher education are the focus of the volume. The concerns these students raise show the different semantic orientations instructors will encounter and set up the issues to be addressed. In this and the next chapter, the authors show how the theory they draw on has enabled them to study student learning in higher education in collaboration with subject specialists and the students themselves, suggesting new methodologies for gaining insights into ways of supporting students and generating new pedagogical approaches that enable students to learn language and disciplinary content simultaneously.

Each of the next three chapters then presents a research study in a different disciplinary field, providing data and discussion about students' orientations and ways of addressing their language learning needs in the context of rich disciplinary work. In Chapter 4, the context is a Film Studies course where we see students attempting to adopt the abstraction and distance needed to write a *taxonomic film analysis* in ways that will be valued in the discipline. Film Studies students come with experience with everyday ways of making meaning about films, but adopting the more technical stance that the field requires calls for them to learn to see film as an object of analysis. Coffin and Donohue identify the linguistic resources students need in order to accomplish this and provide recommendations from their research about how to enable students to develop those resources. The chapter includes illustrative materials from a syllabus developed in collaboration with subject specialists, and student outcomes provide evidence for the efficacy of this approach.

Chapter 5 turns the focus to Health and Social Care (HSC), where many students are returning to higher education from practical work in the field to enhance their credentials to move ahead. Students therefore bring much knowledge of the contexts of HSC, but often are not able to leverage that knowledge as they write arguments, often submitting work that does not make linguistic choices that enable their voices to be authoritative. While the research reported in this chapter was prompted by concerns from instructors about sentence-level writing issues, the authors show how those concerns could not be addressed in isolation from an understanding of the genre of argument that was expected. However, their research also found that students may resist adopting new stances they perceive as overly academic, so they developed an approach they call *mediated text analysis discussions* that engage students in conversations to reflect on the choices they made in their writing and consider alternative options. These discussions offer ways for instructors to gain insights into students' intentions, even when their writing is difficult to understand, and for the students to gain insights into the ways academic readers encounter their writing and what they expect. The authors show how students' different semantic orientations shape their written work, and their analysis of students' written texts and the changes that can be negotiated through the mediated text analysis discussions suggest new ways of addressing the writing of students unfamiliar with academic registers.

In Chapter 6, Coffin and Donohue address a very modern concern: how online and distance education can support students in their disciplinary meaning making. They analyze the genres and registers used by instructors and students in online forums, as well as interviews they conducted with instructors and students about their experiences in these contexts in Applied Linguistics and HSC courses. By conceiving of the online forum as a *macrogenre* with embedded genres of various types, this chapter offers insightful perspectives on new ways instructors can support students in online contexts. The authors show how the spontaneity, interactivity, and hybrid nature of online forums can be recruited by a skillful instructor to support students in moving from more contextualized, everyday ways of meaning making toward the more decontextualized ways of meaning making that are valued in academic writing.

The key contributions of the monograph are summarized in Chapter 7, where the authors make recommendations from their research for how language can be taught and learned in disciplinary contexts in higher education. This volume breaks new ground in bringing knowledge about language together with content learning in sophisticated and discipline-appropriate ways and offers creative new approaches to inform and inspire the provision of support for students' learning in higher education.

Mary J. Schleppegrell
University of Michigan, Ann Arbor

References

Christie, F. (2012). Language education throughout the school years: A functional perspective. [Language Learning Monograph Series]. *Language Learning 62*(Supplement 1).

Halliday, M.A.K. (1978). *Language as social semiotic*. London: Hodder-Arnold.

Halliday, M.A.K. (1994). *An introduction to functional grammar*. London: Edward Arnold.

Hasan, R. (2005). *Language, society and consciousness*. London: Equinox.

Lea, M. R., & Street, B. (1998). Student writing in higher education: An academic literacies approach. *Studies in Higher Education*, *23* (2) 157–172.

Vygotsky, L.S. (1978). *Mind in society: The development of higher psychological processes*. Cambridge, MA: Harvard University Press.

Acknowledgments

In this monograph we describe an approach to teaching and learning that could not exist without the paradigm-shifting work of Michael Halliday, Ruqaiya Hasan, and Jim Martin, alongside many other theorists and researchers within the systemic functional linguistic tradition. Their work has inspired our thinking, our research, and the applications of our research for the past 20 years and more.

We would also like to thank our functional linguistic colleagues around the world for their engagement with, and interest in, our work in higher education—particularly Helen Drury, Sheena Gardner, Janet Jones, Robin Melrose, and Emily Purser. Through the last decade or so The Open University colleagues (past and present) have also been an important source of intellectual support and stimulation. Equally, we would like to acknowledge the significance of the opportunities we have had to engage in dialogue and partnerships with colleagues in other disciplines, both at The Open University and beyond.

There are many other academics who have influenced us, but equally influential have been the students we have worked with and we would like to express our appreciation for their time, ideas, and their willingness to share their experience of the role of language in the teaching and learning relationship.

We would also like to thank Mary Schleppegrell, our editor, for all the encouragement, responsiveness, and understanding she has shown, which has smoothed our journey toward publication.

Finally, across the last two years, our writing of this monograph has sometimes absorbed more of our attention than has been good for us—or those around us. We would therefore like to give a special thanks to Roger and Zaza for semiotically mediating us back into the everyday world of contextualized living, particularly at various danger points when the decontextualized world of academic meaning making looked set to threaten our health, our humor, and our capacity to commune and make meaning in terms that others could make sense of!

Caroline Coffin & Jim Donohue
The Open University
June 2014

DOI: 10.1111/lang.12036

Language Learning ISSN 0023-8333

CHAPTER 1
Language, Teaching, and Learning: General Orientations

1.1 Language in Teaching and Learning

That language is central to teaching and learning at the university level is obvious, obscure, and open to dispute all at the same time. It is obvious in the books, course materials, computer screens, Web sites, lectures, seminars, and assignments that occupy students and teachers[1] throughout their time at university. And yet, except in a few subject areas, language is not the focus of attention; ideas are. Academic activity goes on through the medium of language but the nature of the medium is that it is transparent, that it can be seen 'through' to the ideas that it expresses. When language itself comes into focus, it is often because of the struggle to make sense by means of it or, less frequently, perhaps, because of the elegance or felicity displayed in its use.

To claim centrality for language is therefore counterintuitive. It is also contestable on other grounds. Bringing language into focus to see how it is performing rather than looking through language to the ideas that it is expressing could lead to a focus on form over substance. In the world of ideas that constitutes a university, this looks like the wrong order of priority. It could also be argued that bringing to conscious attention the unconscious workings of human communication will lead to a debilitating *self*-consciousness that will undermine communicative effectiveness. Then there is the burgeoning of other modes of communication alongside language in the new media age; in particular, the visual mode. Finally, there is the great range of other factors that play a role in the interactions of teaching and learning at university: cognitive, social, economic, affective, and physical ones.

Despite such challenges, we make the case for the centrality of language within the teaching and learning process. Furthermore, we argue that underestimating the power and role of language in higher education risks misunderstanding the very nature of teaching, learning, and intellectual development. The basis for our claim lies in the social semiotic approach to language and learning, which we adopt (drawing on Halliday, 1978; Hodge & Kress, 1988;

Language Learning 64:Suppl. 1, June 2014, pp. 1–10

DOI: 10.1111/lang.12037

Kress, 2013; Martin, 2009). In a social semiotic approach, language is seen as the powerhouse of meaning making, and language, teaching, and learning are therefore inseparable. Teaching and learning, in other words, hinge on the developing capacity of students and teachers to harness the meaning-making resources of language efficiently and effectively in relation to purpose and context and to expand their language and meaning-making repertoires as necessary. It is our opinion that success in teaching and learning can be enhanced by recognizing and responding to the implications of this view that language is central to the process.

1.2 The Diverse Linguistic Contexts of Higher Education

A feature of higher education that *is* bringing into focus the centrality of language in teaching and learning is the increasing diversity that characterizes contemporary universities. First, universities have become sites for globalized teaching and learning through the international movement of staff and students and the worldwide delivery of distance education programs and qualifications. Intensifying migration flows have also contributed to increasingly multilingual, national populations. Second, following a pattern long established in North America, widening participation recruitment strategies have opened universities up to students who would not previously have entered university in the United Kingdom, Europe, Australia, and elsewhere. Finally, an expanding range of professional curricula (e.g., nursing, social work, business) in the higher education sector means universities welcome in students with professional experience and expectations strikingly different from those of the younger school leavers who made up the student body a couple of decades ago. As a result of these changing contexts, universities are places in which varied styles of language, literacy, and learning jostle against each other as students, teachers, and administrators all seek to make sense of their experience of higher education.

The extent to which the changing linguistic contexts of teaching and learning and the diverse linguistic repertoires of students and teachers are seen as a valued resource and the extent to which they are perceived as a challenge varies. In the day-to-day pressures of managing teaching and learning in higher education, notions such as "language deficit," "first language interference," or "poor literacy skills" may come easily to hand. When they are taken up, such notions frequently obscure the relationship between language and learning. For example, universities may blame secondary education for failing students, thus repeating a pattern familiar in secondary schools where primary education is blamed for "deficiencies" in secondary school pupils' linguistic abilities.

As Christie points out, the overriding assumption is that students have acquired the necessary oral and literacy skills to deal with school knowledge in their early primary school years and that these skills are then simply and endlessly "recycled, as it were, to learn new information" (Christie, 2012, p. 3). The error in this assumption has been pointed out by many researchers (e.g., Christie, 2012; Christie & Martin, 2005; Christie & Derewianka, 2008; Coffin, 2006; Schleppegrell, 2004) who have demonstrated how the high levels of abstraction, judgment, evaluation, and interpretation demanded from late adolescence onward in schooled learning require very different uses of language than those of primary school. While some individuals may move seamlessly from a spoken, interactive, domestic world into one that is written and increasingly abstract, such a smooth trajectory is not the experience for all. For those moving from a non-English-speaking context into an English-medium education system, emerging knowledge of the English language system may further complicate the situation. For mature students coming to university for professional development purposes, the contrasts between their experience of language in the workplace and in the university may be pronounced and challenging.

There is a temptation for universities' responses to this complex situation to be either language and literacy based *or* subject teaching and learning based. It is common for institutions to invest in centers that focus on students' language or literacy as a problem, giving high visibility to it in, for example, writing centers or remedial language support. In other institutions, there is a focus on learning more generally in, for example, learning or study skills centers. Programs such as Language Across the Curriculum or Writing Across the Curriculum that appear to acknowledge the relationship between subject knowledge, language, and writing still place much of their attention on teaching language to students or teaching *about* language, paying less heed to what is taught and learned *through* language. In this work, we propose a response that treats learning language, learning about language, and learning through language as equally important aspects of the teaching and learning process and as a more effective response to the diversity in higher education that we have outlined above.

1.3 A Language as Social Semiotic (LASS) Approach to Teaching and Learning

In our view, academic knowledge does not consist of academic content and behaviors learned independently of language and literacy. Nor are language and literacy simply carriers of academic content and behaviors. Rather, knowledge, behaviors, and language develop symbiotically. We describe an approach to language, teaching, and learning that takes account of this. It is a Language as Social Semiotic LASS approach to teaching and learning. In a social semiotic perspective, language is seen as a resource for meaning making, drawn on by language users to create texts in the processes of communicating. These texts and their elements constitute *signs* and, as signs, inextricably fuse both form and meaning. In other words, making the *meanings* of university study and the *forms* of university texts are inseparable activities.

The LASS approach to teaching and learning we present has been developed through our research and teaching in face-to-face and distance education universities. It has led us to bring together what we view as three core perspectives on teaching and learning within higher education: semantic orientation, semiotic mediation, and language as a social semiotic.

First, focusing on the learner, we see higher education as an opportunity to expand one's capacity to make new meanings about the world and so develop new ways of being, seeing, thinking, and acting. This process of learning we see as influenced by four factors:

i) learners' immediate external circumstances: for example, the quality of the teaching they receive, the material resources they have access to, the availability of time to write an assignment, or their family commitments;
ii) their affective dispositions: the physical–emotional orientations that permeate and shape their experiences of the world and their responses to these;
iii) their previous knowledge of the subjects they are studying or of related subjects;
iv) the cognitive-linguistic dispositions which they have developed throughout their lifelong interaction with their educational, social, cultural, material, and economic contexts.

It is the last of these four factors that we focus on here, using the term *semantic orientation.*[2]

Second, focusing on the teacher, just as university students come with varied resources enabling them to engage in learning in different ways, their teachers also are positioned in different ways to respond to them. Working from these premises, a LASS approach to teaching and learning treats learning as semiotic (and therefore semantic) expansion and teaching as semiotic intervention designed to support that expansion. As we explain in Chapter 2, this means that both learners and teachers are engaged in processes of *semiotic mediation.*

Third, in order to approach language in teaching and learning as a social semiotic, we draw on *systemic functional linguistics* (SFL) theory (Halliday & Matthiessen, 2004, 2006; Martin, 1992). SFL-informed empirical research and pedagogic innovations conducted over the last 30 years provide us with our starting point. Throughout this work we foreground the need for such systematic research to underpin LASS pedagogic policy and practice. LASS is an approach that we would argue is applicable to all tertiary learning environments. In the chapters that follow, however, our focus is on fields of study that would typically be classified as "applied" (namely Health Studies, Education, Film Studies, and Business Studies), where students' nonacademic and professional experiences come into direct contact with the abstract, theoretical knowledge of university-level settings. We have chosen to focus on these areas because they are sites in which the practical, commonsense knowledge of students' everyday experience meets the uncommonsense knowledge of the world of scholarship in a pronounced form. As a result, these are "contact zones" (Pratt, 1998, p. 173), in which students' meaning-making repertoires may come under considerable pressure as they learn to bridge from one linguistic and cognitive domain to the other.

A LASS approach is a content- and language-integrated approach and is related to recent developments in Content and Language Integrated Learning (CLIL) in universities (see, e.g., Wilkinson, 2004; Wilkinson & Zegers, 2008). However, adopting a LASS perspective emphasizes the interaction of teachers and learners in processes of semiotic mediation and so we deliberately include the term "teaching" in a LASS-based approach to teaching and learning in recognition of this.

1.4 The Role of Written Language in Teaching and Learning in Higher Education

Our focus here is primarily on the role that written language plays in higher education. Written texts continue to be circulated as the primary currency of the educational economy, representing most of the knowledge that has been developed by academics and students alike. The *decontextualized* meanings that we see as characterizing academic activity have been, and continue to be, constructed largely through the medium of written text. Following Wallace (2003), we would argue that much of the spoken language used in university learning is deeply influenced by written academic discourse and can be regarded as essentially "literate" in nature. So, in our research, speaking and listening are treated as playing ancillary roles in the teaching and learning process, the core of which we regard as a reading-into-writing process. Our way into this reading-into-writing process has been through the writing that students do for assessment purposes and the teaching that precedes and succeeds that writing.

1.5 Language in a Digital World

Although we have proposed that our focus will be on the linguistic semiotic system, we are very aware that language is not the only semiotic resource and that, increasingly, all semiotic resources are digitally mediated. Semiotic resources can be visual, musical, gestural, mathematical: anything whose meaning can be interpreted constitutes an element in a semiotic system. Academic knowledge is shaped not only *in* and *through* and *with* language but *in* and *through* and *with* other semiotic resources. Nevertheless, our primary focus here is on language, the semiotic mode which can be most difficult to look at, because, as one of our informants, a university pro vice-chancellor, put it, "it's a transparent medium in which we swim."[3] In the rapidly developing multimodal world of contemporary universities, it becomes even easier to overlook written language amidst the other modes that technology is bringing to the fore. Yet the foundation skills of reading and writing still underpin the ability to deal with multimodal texts as these traditional skills come to be combined with skills in interpreting and producing other semiotic resources. Our goal here is to treat language as a social semiotic system in its own right and to consider the implications of this for university-level teaching and learning.

1.6 Preview of Chapters

Over the next six chapters, we will explain and demonstrate the LASS approach to teaching and learning that we are proposing.

Fundamentally, we address three questions:

- How can a theory of language as a social semiotic contribute to our understanding of the different ways professional academics and university students make meaning?
- How can a theory of language as a social semiotic contribute to our understanding of the ways teachers engage with students' meaning making in higher education?

- How do understandings from (i) and (ii) constitute a LASS-based approach for enhancing teaching and learning in higher education?

Chapter 2 introduces a LASS approach to teaching and learning, beginning with three students' accounts of their experience of language in university study. The students are clearly aware that language, particularly written language, is central to their success. But they vary in their level of adjustment to what they perceive as the demands of language and learning at university. The chapter considers the idea that this variation reflects differences in students' ways of using language, which are now deeply implicated in the ways students make meanings, and introduces the term semantic orientation. The chapter proposes a distinction between the contextualized language of everyday communication and the decontextualized language of academic communication, which may be key to the variation. This distinction will become one of the major themes of this monograph.

Moving on from these individual students, the chapter explores the role of language in teaching and learning more generally. Beginning from the premise that language is a semiotic system, that is, a system with which meanings can be made, teaching and learning are seen as processes of exploiting this meaning-making system. The term that describes these processes is *semiotic mediation*. By recognizing that teaching and learning are semiotic processes, a step is taken toward foregrounding the role of the semiotic system of language in those processes and countering the tendency for language to remain an invisible but highly influential element in students' and teachers' success. It is emphasized that semiotic mediation is a process in which teachers and students are equally active and not something that the teacher is solely responsible for.

This leaves the question of how to bring into focus the semiotic system of language. The chapter presents a brief review of the research into teaching and learning that has been carried out using SFL as the analytical framework. SFL is the theory that we argue provides the LASS approach that the chapter has suggested is needed (see Halliday & Mathiessen, 2004, 2006, for a detailed account of SFL theory, and Coffin, Donohue, & North, 2009, for an introductory account). Finally, returning to the diversity of student meaning-making processes introduced at the beginning of the chapter, it is proposed that ethnographic procedures should inform SFL research and teaching interventions in order for them to be responsive to variation among participants in the world of higher education.

In Chapter 3 we elaborate on some of the key theoretical tenets of SFL and explain and illustrate concepts and analytical tools central to LASS. Beginning from the premise that language use is a matter of making selections from across a linguistic *system* that has developed in response to the contexts that constitute social life for a language group, the chapter introduces the constructs of *genre* and *register*. We show how these constructs help to explain the way we make meaning through language (both *grammar* and *lexis*) in response to our communication goals and the social/academic contexts we find ourselves in. SFL provides tools and a metalanguage that are used throughout the rest of the book to describe the contexts of academic study, and, in particular, the nature of decontextualized meaning making and semiotic mediation introduced in Chapter 2.

Chapters 4–6 present research-based accounts of three LASS teaching and learning situations.

In Chapter 4, the focus is on Film Studies texts produced by students in response to a film viewing. Two students' responses are examined closely to uncover the different ways that the film is represented in each text. It is shown how one of the students exploits genre and a register of decontextualized language in order to turn the film into an object of study, applying a conceptual framework that she is acquiring through her participation in the Film Studies course. The other student's text reveals through its genre and register the student's strong orientation toward film production as opposed to film analysis. These two approaches to the film viewing are by no means equally valued in the semiotic mediation of the course and demonstrate how central to meaning making in higher education are the genre and register choices that students make. In order to support the semiotic mediation of both the students and the teacher in this context, a pedagogic strategy based on SFL analysis and known as *metasemiotic mediation* is described. Evidence of the impact of metasemiotic mediation on the teaching and learning processes is presented that suggests that, by paying explicit attention to how the semiotic resources that are available to participants are used, acquisition of subject knowledge is enhanced alongside the development of linguistic resources.

In Chapter 5 we look at the range of genres that Health and Social Care (HSC) students write, focusing on argumentation. Once again, differences in students' responses to the assignment are attributed to individual orientations toward making meaning and using language. The chapter introduces an ethnographic method for obtaining insights into students' semantic orientations. In these *mediated text analysis discussions*, differences in how students interpret assignment tasks and implement their interpretations of these tasks appear to reflect different stages of development in genre and register knowledge for academic meaning making. The close correlation between genre- and register-related linguistic features and the level of attainment reflected in the assignment grade and feedback provides strong evidence for the central argument of this monograph: that language and learning are intimately connected. Mediated text analysis discussion is proposed as not only a research method but also a teaching and learning procedure in which metasemiotic mediation—the deliberate and explicit bringing to awareness of the relation between language and learning—can enhance existing teaching and learning processes.

Chapter 6 considers the kind of teaching and learning that takes place in online discussion forums. It uses the concept of genre to describe the way in which virtual spaces are structured for academic exchange and uses the lens of register to look at the kinds of meaning making that occur through language—from the perspective of content (*ideational* meaning), relationship building (*interpersonal* meaning), and cohesion (*textual* meaning). Overall, we argue that there is considerable potential for online discussion forums to provide the kind of semiotic mediation that can support students in learning the language of their field of study and, in so doing, learning their field. This is achieved through the fusing or recontextualization of the more traditional academic activities of reading, writing, and speaking as a form of written dialogue. From a practical perspective, we will demonstrate the significance of practitioners understanding how online discussion forums are structured and how language functions in order to maximize the opportunities for semiotic mediation that these "third spaces" (Bhabha, 1990) offer.

Chapter 7 proposes ways in which a LASS approach to teaching and learning can be implemented in higher education institutions. Beginning with basic principles of a LASS approach, the chapter describes the research procedures that are important preliminaries to and continuing elements of its implementation. Evidence of how language and learning are related can be gathered from institutional data on student recruitment and performance as well as classroom observation and other forms of collaboration between language specialists, subject specialists, and students. This evidence can be used to promote the uptake and inform the implementation of a LASS approach in which metasemiotic mediation is used to enhance teaching and learning across the institution. Treating language as a social semiotic is an approach that can be adopted in one-to-one interactions between lecturers and students, in individual classrooms, in entire courses and programs, all the way up to the whole-institution level. For a university that is interested in enabling the engagement of all its members in the decontextualized meaning making of higher education, we argue that it is important to take advantage of the insights that a LASS approach offers into the relationship between three inextricably entailed entities: language, teaching, and learning.

Notes

1 In this book we use the general term, teacher, to refer to professors, tutors, lecturers, instructors, and indeed anyone involved in the teaching process.

2 Throughout the book, the first mention of a key term is italicized. Further references to these italicized terms will be found in the index.

3 Professor Alan Tait was Pro Vice-Chancellor (Academic) at The Open University from 2007-2012. He made this comment in an interview the authors held with him concerning language, learning, and institutional change. Because of its felicity for a LASS perspective on language we refer to it a number of times throughout the monograph.

CHAPTER 2
A LASS Approach to Teaching and Learning: Theoretical Foundations

2.1 Introduction

Life can be seen as a series of encounters with new contexts to communicate in, new topics to communicate about, and new people to communicate with. Engaging successfully in such encounters requires developing new ways of making meaning and thus new ways of using language. Doing this inevitably changes the way we categorize, interpret, and understand our natural and social world. As we argue in Chapter 1, language is central to the teaching–learning enterprise. And it is the purpose of this monograph to explore, from a linguistic perspective, some of the most significant aspects of the new contexts, topics, and people that constitute the higher education environment.

In this chapter, we start our exploration by providing a general orientation to language and learning within the context of higher education from the perspective of LASS. In turn, we further develop the concepts (briefly introduced in Chapter 1) of semantic orientation and variation, meaning making, decontextualization, and semiotic mediation, discussing how these have informed our LASS approach—both to teaching and learning and to the research that underpins and informs this. To lead into this more abstract discussion, we start with the actual voices of first-year university students, as it is responses to the challenges of higher education such as theirs that have motivated our linguistic exploration and informed our approach.

2.2 Student Experiences of Teaching and Learning

The higher education environment in which students study is characterized by conditions both of flux and continuity. There is flux in the population of learners, who come from increasingly diverse backgrounds of education, social class, ethnicity, language, and country. There is flux also in the environment: in the development of new university-level subjects (such as professionally oriented ones), new media (such as online and multimedia ones), new teaching and learning methods (such as open and distance learning and part-time study), and new institutional policies (such as widening participation,

Language Learning 64:Suppl. 1, June 2014, pp. 11–38

DOI: 10.1111/lang.12038

internationalization, and employability). Alongside these changes are continuities: in subjects (in many of which knowledge is still accumulated diachronically), pedagogy (where lectures and seminars continue as central modes of teaching in face-to-face universities, and online learning combines the didactic approach of lectures with the constructivist approach of seminars), and assessment (where essay assignments persist in the humanities and social sciences, and short-answer questions persist in the sciences).

In the following extracts, the three students whose words we present reveal some of the different responses to this context of teaching, learning, and assessment and, in particular, some of the complexities of how they navigate academic meaning making and what this means for their sense of self (their identity). These students were interviewed in the context of a research project discussed in greater detail in Chapter 5. At the time of the interviews, they were enrolled in an introductory course in Health and Social Care (HSC) at The Open University in the United Kingdom, one of the world's oldest established providers of distance education at the tertiary level. A brief background for each student is provided to contextualize their comments.

James

James is a nontraditional UK student from a White working-class background. His preuniversity qualification was a vocational diploma rather than the more traditional academic set of A-level qualifications. At the time of the interview, James was working as a member of a hospital-home rehabilitation team and therefore had professional experience relevant to the HSC course he was taking. Widening participation policies and the academicization of domains of knowledge and practice (such as nursing and the caring professions) that were once developed on the job means that James's profile fits that of many students who are now entering universities. The extracts we have taken from the interview highlight issues that are not unique to James. These include anxiety, mystification, and resistance in response to perceptions of university-imposed conventions of language and learning and assessment practices; tensions between personal, professional, and academic orientations to knowledge; and concern about the effects of academic study on his own and others' identity/ies. We have grouped the interview extracts below around these issues.[1]

Language, learning, and the assessment of knowledge

> ... I mean one of the horrors that was in the back of my mind when I took this course on was the writing. As I said before, I can go off on a tangent, but one of the concerns I had was not what I wrote but how I wrote it.

I've never done academic study, academic writing, and I have had run-ins with my tutor, on the basis of my last assignment, my last essay, I thought I'd put together a balanced argument. I had—52 was the score—which is a pass I know, it's over 40. But 48 marks knocked off for academic writing, or lack of, really annoyed me.

. . . That was annoying because he put on the feedback—and his feedback is good—but it was very much along the lines of, oh you know, "Your feedback: you've got lots of information in here, you've put lots of information together but you haven't done this, you haven't done that."

. . . Oh, we had quite a heated discussion on e-mail . . . . I thought I'd really done a lot of input with Lennox Castle [topic of assignment[2]]. It really hit a note. It hit a chord and a half. And I really felt that I'd gone into it. I researched it. It was very interesting, I had a lot of interest. I started many big discussions at work over Lennox Castle. I even met someone, funny enough, down the pub, a Glaswegian, who was born there and his mum come on the phone and spoke to me about Lennox Castle and I really put my . . . I really felt the referencing, I'd done the referencing as [the tutor] had asked me to do it. And to get a 52 and have 48 marks knocked off, it really, I'll tell you what, I was furious. I was really . . . and it knocked me back on this one.

. . . I worry that there is someone sitting there with certain notes, certain guidance, and that if you put anything extra in they either wouldn't know or would not know how to mark it.

Academic versus professional or personal discourse

. . . .And I prefer blatancy. I prefer layman's terms. I don't agree with the, you know, using big massive jargon. You walk into someone and speak to them about personalization they ain't got a clue what you're talking about.

. . . If academic writing was really that important why don't we use it at work now? That's a question.

Identity

. . . I've always been of the opinion that a lot of people that have done [the course], that have become qualified, and I've met people like this, have either become extremely overbearing, in which, again, you can't

> have a conversation with them without them trying to correct you every five minutes. "You can't say things like that." ... The course changes 'em, the way of thinking changes 'em to where they focus on things but don't seem to be able to make a decision. Whereas, from my point of view, I go and look at the problem. Address the problem, look at the problem, make a decision, you've got to do it. And that was another fear that I had when I came to the course, to do the course.
>
> I'm very much of the opinion that when I first looked at qualification, the idea of attending the course and doing it, I very much thought ... Oh, I spoke to a number of people and I said "If I change in any way give me a slap" and they laughed. And they said ... "No, you won't change." It's the challenging aspects as well, is something that I don't see in my colleagues who have done this course through different areas. Inability to challenge. It just doesn't seem right to me.

****

James begins with the "horrors" engendered by the writing required in studying the course and used in the assessment of his knowledge and understanding. His view is that there are ways of writing in university-level study that he has somehow not understood and the knowledge he has accumulated has gone unrecognized because of incomprehensible university standards for writing academically. For him, this is the wrong order of priorities, the privileging of form over substance. Part of his criticism comes from his recognition that, in his workplace, this academic discourse would be ineffective. He sees himself as someone who is decisive and practical. Academic communication appears to him to change individuals' capacity to act decisively or empathetically. There is thus a strong disconnection for James between form, substance, and value in the communication he is attempting to develop in pursuit of this academic qualification.

James's progress in university-level study will depend on how he continues to work with the disconnections he describes, how his teachers support him in doing so, and how the university as an institution creates the conditions in which both he and they can do this. These matters are not ancillary to James's learning. They go to the heart of what he is doing and what his teachers and the university as an institution are doing in their turn. In this respect, we do not agree with James's analysis of the situation as one of unnecessary disconnection prompted by incomprehensible and arbitrary academic standards of language and knowledge, though we recognize this as his authentic experience.

In our view, what James describes can be understood through a language-based approach to teaching and learning that sees university-level learning in terms of learning language and learning through language.

Andrea

The second learner to speak about her experience is Andrea, a Black student from a West African ex-Portuguese colony but primarily educated in Italy. She left school at age 17 and has no formal qualifications. Andrea is plurilingual, having grown up speaking Portuguese at home and using Italian as her main medium of study. She studied English as a foreign language in school in Italy but says it was only when she came to the United Kingdom 4 years ago and started to talk to people that she learned the language. Apart from studying the HSC course, she is studying for GCSEs[3] in math and English in order to meet the entry requirements for a degree in social work at a face-to-face UK university. At the time of writing, Andrea was working as a senior care worker in a residential care home. The interview extracts raise a set of issues different from those raised by James. They suggest that Andrea's global experiences have given her a facility and confidence with language(s) and, possibly related to this, a flexible view of learning and its professional value. In general, she expresses a confident and positive disposition toward reading and writing in her university studies. There is no reference directly to issues of identity because throughout the interview Andrea made it clear that she was quite relaxed about the transition from an Italian to a UK academic environment.

Language, learning and the assessment of knowledge

> I did two introductory courses, Opening courses, with The [Open University]. . . . Yeah, they taught me, you know, they put me on the way of understanding how to write an essay. Because how to write academically, you know, because before I was just freestyle writing essay and now they give me structure like introduction, main body and then conclusion, things like that.

> I think that we were discussing even with another friend of mine, . . . she's Italian as well, it's the complete different way that they are doing essay here and we used to do essay when we were at school. Because, for example, here they like a lot to put reference the book, to go back to what is in the book and make even some reference in the . . . Even, how do you call them? When you repeat exactly what's written in the book?

. . . A quote, exactly. So quoting the books and things like that. In Italy they don't do that. They will tell you, "Okay, study what you have to study from page to page and then do it with your own words. We don't want anything about the book. We want to read what you write and understand it without knowing that book. This is how did you write in Italy." Whereas I remember see now my first assignment did with the Opening course. She say "Yeah, it is very good, but this is not how you write it." So she was full of feedback. She was telling me "No, you need an introduction, a main body, a conclusion and you need to put the references and quotes and things." I was like "What!" It was a little bit challenging but now I am getting more used to it.

Academic versus professional or personal discourse

Yeah because I think you need, yeah, exactly, as I say, to take a theory to practice and see how it is work. You know the theory, ok, now show me that you know how it works in practice.

Yeah I think it's, yeah because once you understand the concepts you can even, as I say, if you understand the concept you can relate it to the practical part of the daily experiences and the study case, you know. So it would be easy to remember this one or to go back and think about other case studies that you studied before. I think in this particular case even the case of . . . Anwar [name of character in a different case study], yeah, I don't remember the name but the concept. I think, yeah, he used the mainstream services that were there . . . So I could have put the case of Anwar as contraposed to the case of Simon [name of character in this case study] . . .

. . . If I have a better choice of words when I'm writing my assignments it will be good to learn how to write it in care plan [for a service user in a care home]. Think about the practicity[4] of being a social worker. This is what it will be at the end.

When you are writing things you need to think what you are writing and the moment that you think what you are writing basically is what you're studying. So you get back to it, it gets in your mind more deeply, you know. Yeah, you understand it better by writing down things.

> ... Exactly. I think as I write, everything I write is more focused on my personal experience more than everything else because it will help me to understand what is there, you know.

****

As did James, Andrea brought cultural experience to her study that meant she was forced to reconsider deeply her ways of writing for academic study purposes. But this did not lead to the "horrors" that James reported. Andrea found the reorientation toward the university's conventions of language, literacy, and knowledge to be a rewarding and broadly satisfying one. What emerged in the interview and is indicated in the comments above is that she was able to relate discourse structured by concepts to her personal and professional experience and deepen her understanding of this experience as a result. In this respect, she was well adjusted, intellectually and emotionally, to a central feature of academic discourse and academic knowledge making: its abstract nature. Throughout this monograph, this quality of academic discourse (which we refer to as decontextualization) will emerge as a central concern of a LASS-based approach to teaching and learning.

Also noteworthy in Andrea's interview extracts is her seeming awareness of the role of language in knowledge making (and the inseparability of language and learning) and her articulation of the relationship between language and cognition:

> When you are writing things you need to think what you are writing and the moment that you think what you are writing basically is what you're studying. So you get back to it, it gets in your mind more deeply, you know. Yeah, you understand it better by writing down things.

This indicates an intuitive understanding, and perspective on, language as a meaning-making resource.

In sum, James and Andrea are exploiting the meaning-making resources they have brought to their engagement in learning in a university context, but mediating their engagement will call for different strategies by them and by their teachers.

Zuna

The third learner is Zuna, a Black, plurilingual student, educated in Nigeria but living in the United Kingdom for 9 years. Zuna grew up speaking Yoruba and English at home and studying at school and college through the medium of English. She did not complete her A-levels but has a diploma from a

Nigerian polytechnic. In Nigeria she ran a laundry business for some years before coming to the United Kingdom, where she studied for a National Vocational Qualification (NVQ2). At the time of the interview she was working as a residential carer with people with learning disabilities. Zuna shares some of Andrea's cross-cultural and cross-linguistic experiences but these have left her with uncertainties about what is expected in studying this course. Like James, she wants to know the discourse conventions of university-level study, but she does not share his ambivalence toward them.

Language, learning and the assessment of knowledge

> . . . Yeah, after reading the book and after making the notes from the book then I go on the internet again. I put the key words, like the project has said to us that we should do research on the website. I'm used to read because I look at it, I try to compare what I've read and that internet might even explain it even more than the book. And at times the book might even explain more than the internet. Then I put the two together. That is why he [the tutor] kept on saying "Reference, where did you get the reference?"

> I'm used to writing essays but because this is another different place so I want to know which area—because at first I was, the writing, I always go straight to the point because I thought essays you're not meant to even talk so much. Just go straight to the point. But in this situation now I know I have that conclusion and introduction is very important . . . Yeah and if I can know what are the things I'm not meant to do when I'm writing the essay.

> Because giving mark of 49 over 60 I don't know if I'm ok, I don't know what other people are reaching. I don't know what other . . . mine I don't know if it's the highest, I don't know if . . . yeah, which I want to know so that I can improve the mark.

****

Zuna is eager to understand and adopt university ways of writing and learning. However, despite her determination to respond to the course expectations, her tutor's feedback indicates there is a mismatch between her intentions and her achievements.

We chose to present the voices of James, Andrea, and Zuna because they represent some of the diversity of the language landscape of contemporary academic life and learning. Andrea and Zuna both have rich resources in their plurilingual repertoires. However, in both cases, they do not yet have the same control over some of the subsystems of English that would have been developed by speakers of English as a first language (L1) growing up in an "inner circle" (Kachru, 1985) English-speaking country. There are some indications of this in their use of the article and tense systems in the quotations above.

James, unlike Andrea and Zuna, is an L1 speaker and was bought up in England. Not surprisingly, he has control over the English language systems that Andrea and Zuna do not. Thus there are differences in the linguistic resources and backgrounds of the three students. What James does have in common with Andrea and Zuna, however, is that his use of the English language system for making academic meanings is still in development. How far such a system has already been developed in the other languages Andrea and Zuna speak is not clear. But what is clear is that all three students will be challenged to further develop their capacities to make academic meanings through English as they progress in their studies.

Over the next five chapters, we will outline how a LASS approach to teaching and learning (and the research that is integral to such an approach) can deepen our understanding of students' experiences of learning, challenges they and their teachers may face, and some of the solutions to these challenges.

The next few sections in this chapter outline three core concepts that underlie the language-based approach to learning, teaching, and researching that we are proposing:

- Semantic orientation and variation
- Language as a social semiotic
- Teaching and learning as semiotic mediation

We then provide a brief overview of prior work that has served as a foundation for our LASS approach. This serves as a useful reference point for those interested in exploring further some of the SFL insights developed to date in a range of tertiary contexts. Related to the foundational SFL research informing our approach is work conducted in a related field of studies referred to as *Academic Literacies* and therefore we highlight the relevance of its ethnographic methodology and ideological orientation to our approach.

2.3 Semantic Orientation and Semantic Variation

The previous section illustrated some of the diverse orientations to language, academic writing, and fundamentally to university-level learning and knowledge. Of particular interest for us has been the growing recognition that how individual students orient to academic learning and knowledge is in part tied to the linguistic resources they have available to them and that this, in turn, is influenced by their *linguistic socialization*. The concept of socialization is, of course, not new. Since its introduction as a central tenet in the work of the American functionalist tradition of sociology (e.g., Parsons & Bales, 1956) it has served to explain how social experiences constitute shaping influences on our identity and our participation in social processes (e.g., Giddens, 1979). However, by using the term *linguistic* socialization we are drawing attention to language as central to the process rather than simply being indexical of it.

It is the linguistic dimension of socialization that has been developed through the work, in particular, of the sociologist Bernstein (e.g., 1996) and by Halliday, the central architect of SFL (e.g., 2003, pp. 139–174) and by Hasan (2005). As Hasan puts it, our linguistic experiences throughout life position us and form and represent our identity, our consciousness, and our culture. The repertoire that represents an individual's access to the linguistic system is not simply a tendency to use language in particular ways (although it is that); it is a preference for making meaning in particular ways. This predisposition to make meaning in particular ways and, as a result, to use language in certain ways is referred to by Hasan as semantic orientation. This orientation is particularly influenced by *critical socializing contexts* in an individual's life. Hasan (2009, p. 415) gives the example of a mother–child interaction whereby, in the course of getting dressed to go out, the mother introduces the conceptual world of changing weather. For Bernstein, critical socializing contexts included regulative, instructional, and imaginative contexts of interaction between parents and children. Subsequent critical contexts occur in the course of schooling, where his theory proposes that previous orientations are reinforced. One of the most significant features of a semantic orientation in an academic learning context is an individual's orientation toward making abstract (decontextualized) meanings, what is referred to by James as "big massive jargon."

For Hasan, the significance of semantic orientation is played out through the identities of teachers and learners. Speaking about learners, she says:

> The central aspect of learner identity that should concern the educator has to do primarily with the learners' learning styles and the formation of these to a very large extent rests upon those conditions of semiotic mediation that the learner has experienced and is experiencing in his/her social life . . . [T]he primary point of interest for educators has to be the learner's "mental disposition"—the pathways of the brain used habitually

> for engaging with new information—because it is such "habits of mind" which will deal with the information presented as educational knowledge. Given this genesis of learner identity, variation is obviously inherent to the concept. It is in this sense that the complex concept of learner identity—or more appropriately identities—needs to inform every aspect of the educational process. (Hasan, 2011, p. xii)

The concept of semantic variation has been subject to much criticism, particularly for appearing to promote a deficit model of certain kinds of learners. Hasan, Halliday, and Bernstein have all made robust rebuttals of these critiques (e.g., Hasan, 2011, pp. 73–98). One point that Hasan makes is a fundamental premise of a language-based approach to teaching and learning. She says that "compared with the total language system each individual suffers from some kind of language deficit . . . language deficit is a universal condition for all speakers of any language" (Hasan, 2011, p. 87).

2.3.1 Contextualized and decontextualized meanings

Following Hasan, we see the abstractions that James and Andrea were referring to as *decontextualized* meanings. From what has been said so far about the relation between language and context, the idea of language that is decontextualized may sound contradictory. To explain it, we need to distinguish between types of context.

The relationships between language, meaning, and different types of context can be illustrated by thinking of a scientific experiment. There will be considerable contrast between the language used by the researchers conducting an experiment in the lab, their discussion at a later point in a research meeting, and a written lab report. There is a cline from a context where language is action that is integral to the carrying out of the experiment toward a context where language is used for detached reflection on the activity. The context for the reflective language of the lab report is quite different from the context for the action language of the researchers and lab assistants.

Of course, this reflective function is typical of much adult language use in which the immediate physical context of situation does not provide the topic for the language that is used. Out of this fact, decontextualized language emerges. We will see this if we go beyond the simple contrast between action and reflection and look at different types of reflection. Recounts of the experiment (which, in part, is what the lab report will be) refer directly to physical events even though that reality is not present or tangible anymore. In a different genre, for example, a written academic journal article, we are likely to see language that refers to an even less tangible reality. In one such article, the following noun groups occurred: *optimal visual attentional control* and *mediators of the relationship between challenge/threat evaluations and motor performance*. These are abstractions generated out of multiple details of material reality and very far removed from their physical contexts of situation. Hasan describes their referents as "virtual" reality (see Hasan, 2009, pp. 403–427).

Some of the most extensive work in SFL on the nature of decontextualized language has been done by Hasan (e.g., 2005, 2009, 2011) alongside Cloran (1994), building on the work of the sociologist, Bernstein (e.g., 1990, 1996). As mentioned above, Bernstein (1971, p. 181) proposed that development of decontextualized language is encouraged or discouraged during critical socializing interactions in an individual's life. The significance of this becomes clearer when we interpret language as a functional linguistic system that is drawn on by language users in contexts of situation in response to the situation—Bernstein calls this a *reservoir* (1999, p. 159)—and the parts of the linguistic system that the user has greatest facility with, which Bernstein refers to as the user's *repertoire* (1999, p. 159). Bernstein's proposal was that critical socializing events were crucial in developing an individual's repertoire and that a defining feature of linguistic repertoires was the degree of decontextualization they demonstrate. Hasan (e.g., 2005, 2009, 2011) and Cloran's (1994) work investigated whether this was the case. As decontextualization in academic meaning making is central to the LASS approach we are presenting, we will consider the relevance of what they found for higher education contexts.

In a LASS approach to teaching and learning, the concept of semantic variation promotes awareness of the differences in how participants interpret a context and the repertoire of resources they have available to act within the context. The point of recognizing this diversity is to seek to understand more fully what implications it has for semiotic mediation, particularly in relation to the linguistic semiotic system. This shifts the focus more toward participants and their experience than was the case with earlier SFL text analysis and aligns SFL based enquiry more strongly with the interest in students' and teachers' identities and experiences shown by some other approaches such as the academic literacies one that we discuss in Section 2.7.

2.4 A LASS Approach: Rethinking Language, Teaching, and Learning

In their comments, James, Andrea, and Zuna showed an intuitive awareness of the role of language, particularly written language, in learning. As mentioned earlier, this awareness seemed particularly acute for Andrea. But language is not necessarily the focus of teaching and learning in universities. Students and teachers are more likely to be concerned with *ideas*, with the subject matter that is communicated *through* the medium of language. Making a case for a language-based approach to teaching and learning depends on the view of language we adopt. Language is a medium in which we, as meaning makers, are constantly immersed. This can make it difficult to see language in ways that are not reductive. One such reductive perspective is to see language as a problem, where students are marked down for language errors that "interfere with communication." These can be comparatively superficial and therefore easily observable errors of spelling, clause grammar, or punctuation. While it is true that these language features interfere with communication to some extent, the relationship between language and communication is much more profound than these corrections imply. Meaning is being made at every level in all the assignments that teachers respond to. In order to respond to language use from this broader perspective of language as a meaning-making resource, a model of language of much greater complexity than one that focuses on formal error correction is called for.

Context of communication is key to a social semiotic perspective. The social situatedness of language is embodied in the *linguistic system* itself, the reservoir developed throughout the history of language use in the contexts that constitute a society. Social situatedness is also embodied in the language resources of an individual, the repertoire developed throughout the individual's personal history of language use in the contexts that have constituted the individual's own life experience. Social situatedness is also embodied in specific *instances* of language use that emerge in the ongoing interaction between language users in the contexts in which they are using language to make meanings.

Treating language as a social semiotic connects language with the notion of *semiotic mediation* (Hasan, 2005; Vygotsky, 1978, 1981, 1987, 1999), in which language is seen as a semiotic tool that enables conceptual development. Through their use of the semiotic system of language to represent and engage with physical, social, emotional, intellectual, and spiritual worlds a language user builds up their representations of these worlds and engages with them. Such semiotic mediation begins in childhood, in the home and community life. It takes on new dimensions in the context of formal education.

As James, Andrea, and Zuna testified, sites of semiotic mediation in a university environment are sites of knowledge construction but also of power struggle, identity formation, and relationship building. In this monograph, we will seek to uncover and demonstrate some of the implications of adopting such a semiotic perspective of teaching and learning at the university level.

2.5 Teaching and Learning as Semiotic Mediation

Throughout SFL research into language in school education, researchers have looked toward the Vygotskian notion of semiotic mediation in order to make sense of the teaching and learning processes (Gibbons, 2006; Hasan, 2005; Martin, 1999; Wells, 1981, 1986). Vygotsky (1978, 1981, 1987, 1999) proposed that conceptual development occurs through interaction in which concepts are articulated publicly in a *social* process of semiotic mediation between teacher and learner and are ultimately internalized by the learner through an *internal* process of semiotic mediation. In formal education, mediation by a teacher within what Vygotsky refers to as the learner's *zone of proximal development* enables (or *scaffolds*) a learner to make meanings that go beyond their current stage of conceptual development.

Although it is easy to slip into seeing the teaching–learning process as one in which the teacher semiotically mediates the learning of a student, this is not the whole picture. The term semiotic mediation refers to a process in which interactants employ semiotic tools; in education, the primary semiotic tool is language. The conceptual development referred to above comes from the engagement of the learner in the social interaction. The learner's engagement depends on how semiotic tools mediate meanings to the mind of the learner. Semiotic mediation is thus a joint enterprise between the teacher and the learner. As Hasan points out, "The emphasis of semiotic mediation is an 'achieved interpretation' which is the essential condition for the internalization of concepts and the relationship between them: it is the process we call understanding" (2011, p. 69). At this point, it should also be noted that "teacher" here is a term that refers not only to a person officially designated with the title of teacher, but also to socially produced semiotic artifacts like written (or multimodal) texts that also mediate meanings to the mind of the learner. In these cases, the agency of the learner in the semiotic mediation process may be more obvious.

An important insight that Hasan draws from the points made above is that semiotic mediation is not necessarily confined to the development of scientific or technical concepts in formal education (see, e.g., Hasan, 2005, p. 137). Because semiotic mediation refers to any use of language (or other semiotic tool), Hasan (2005, pp. 194–215) proposes a distinction between *visible* and *invisible semiotic mediation,* which we show in diagram form in Figure 2.1.

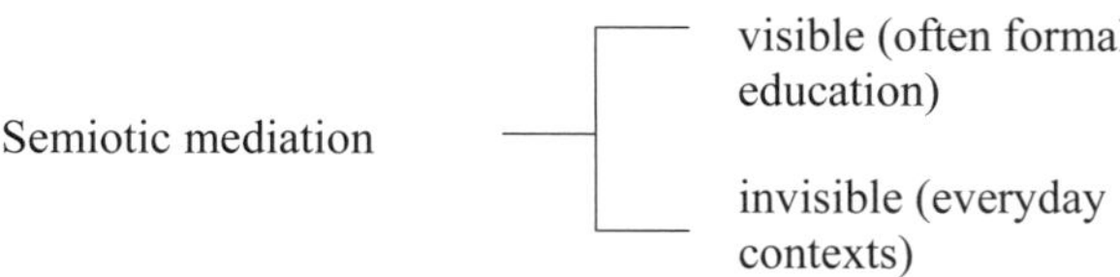

Figure 2.1 Types of semiotic mediation.

Invisible semiotic mediation is that which occurs in the ongoing interaction of everyday life, in the home, the community, in the interactions that are often regarded as so natural, familiar, and invisible that the fact of semiotic mediation is not recognized or commented on. In Cloran's (1994) and Hasan's terms, this is primarily the location of contextualized meaning making—of the meanings of here and now, of the tangible and sensuous environment. In Hasan's view, such invisible semiotic mediation lies at the heart of who we are as individuals and is the means by which culture is created and transmitted from generation to generation and from individual to individual. It is also the main mechanism in developing the individual semantic orientations and semantic variation discussed in Section 2.3. The semiotic modality[5] that mediates the bulk of such understanding is the spoken language.

In contrast, visible semiotic mediation is more deliberate and sets out intentionally to scaffold decontextualized understanding, primarily by means of language, and within formal educational contexts, often through written language (see Figure 2.2).

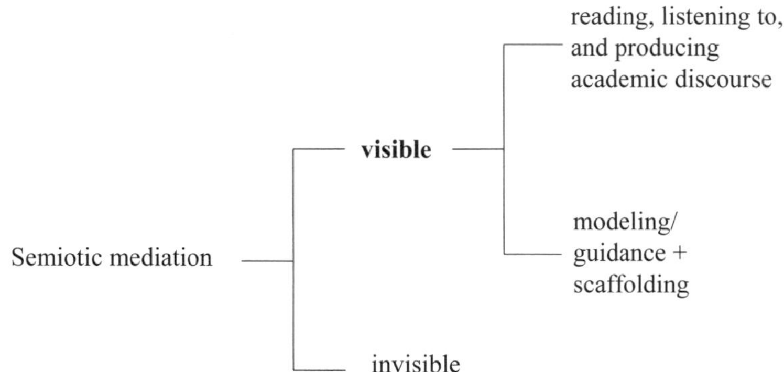

Figure 2.2 Types of visible semiotic mediation.

However, not all visible semiotic mediation takes place within formal educational contexts, nor through the semiotic modality of written language. Following Bernstein's theory about the role of critical socializing contexts in language development, Hasan's (e.g., 2005, 2009, 2011) and Cloran's (1994) research showed that decontextualized meaning making occurs in contexts outside formal education. An example that Hasan gives is of a mother and child discussion in which a comment on a moth dying leads to consideration by the mother and child of the ephemerality of animal life (Hasan, 2005, p. 207). Hasan proposes that children who have engaged frequently in such conversations where meanings become decontextualized from their immediate surroundings—in what Cloran (1994) calls symbolically based social processes—are advantageously positioned when they enter the increasingly decontextualized world of formal education.

Rose and Martin's (2012) account of SFL genre-based pedagogy in school (as opposed to university) education makes a strong commitment to teachers and learners developing awareness of the nature and role of language in learning. Their view of semiotic mediation is one in which educators and educational institutions adopt a strong influencing role of "guidance through interaction in the context of shared experience" (p. 307). They interpret schools as having as their fundamental goal the shaping of the "consciousness of students in terms of both the knowledge they acquire and their social identities as learners, workers, and citizens" (p. 314). This may not be a conscious or explicitly stated goal, however. While Rose and Martin's interpretation may indeed hold true for school education, the goals of the pedagogic practices of a university are more complex and paradoxical. In universities, critical and self-directed models of learning are espoused more fully (see, e.g., Hannan & Silver, 2000, p. 3; Laurillard, 2002, p. 25) and at first sight, this might suggest a difference in objectives to school pedagogy. The paradox is that these commitments to autonomy and independence in university-level pedagogy also shape the consciousness of students, though in different ways.

2.5.1 The pedagogic device, classification, and framing

The paradox mentioned above leads to some of the tensions referred to by the students at the beginning of this chapter. We will use some concepts from Bernstein's sociology of education to examine these tensions. The first concept is the *pedagogic device* (1996, pp. 39–53). This is Bernstein's term for the educational process, which he sees as made up of three parts, in which knowledge is:

i) created by university-level academics in their role as professionals,
ii) recontextualized for pedagogic purposes by academics in their role as teachers,
iii) and evaluated by academics in their role as evaluators.

Two further concepts from Bernstein can be used to develop the concept of the pedagogic device: *classification* and *framing* (1971, pp. 202–231). A university's curriculum amounts to the classification of academic knowledge into fields of study. Among these fields of study are subjects or disciplines around which the boundaries are very well established (physics and history are examples), and within these disciplines may be subdisciplines (such as nuclear physics and Ancient history); these are *strong* and *closed* classifications. There are also "regions" where boundaries are more permeable and where multiple disciplines may be drawn on in constructing the curriculum (the subjects we deal with in this monograph fall into this category: Business Studies, Education, and HSC); these are *weak* and *open* classifications. Pedagogy, which is the process by which the curriculum is realized as actual teaching and learning, is framed in terms of *instructional discourse* (i.e., the presentation of the content of the curriculum) and *regulatory discourse* (the management of the teaching and learning processes, particularly the evaluation of learning). The extent to which students are empowered in their university-level study depends in part on how classification and framing are managed by the educational institution, the teachers, and the learning materials, as well as by the students themselves.

It might be asked what is gained by rewording "teaching and learning processes" as "visible semiotic mediation." Our first answer is that it focuses attention on the fact that at the center of teaching and learning processes is the use of language to make meaning—that is, *semiosis*. Semiotic mediation is a process in which two (or more) participants are engaged in a meaning-making interaction by means of symbols that depend on the participants' interpretations for the meanings they create.[6] Hasan emphasizes the interactive nature of semiotic mediation by distinguishing between a mediator and a mediatee. This aligns with a view of semiotic mediation that emphasizes the scaffolding of the cognitive development of a less expert learner by a more expert teacher. However, as Hasan showed in the quotation we presented earlier, the mediatees also have mediation work to do. First, they have to engage in the social (*intermental*) interaction that constitutes the scaffolding, and second, they have to internalize the concepts that are expressed in the interaction (an *intramental* process). In effect, both mediator and mediatee are involved in a process in which the semiotic system mediates meanings to the mind. For this reason, we prefer to see *both* the teacher and the learner as mediators, as shown in Figure 2.3.

What distinguishes the teacher from the learner when they engage in acts of scaffolding in the zone of proximal development is that the teacher is a mediator *in an initiating role* and the learner is a mediator *in a responding role*. These roles can also be reversed. For example, when a teacher delivers

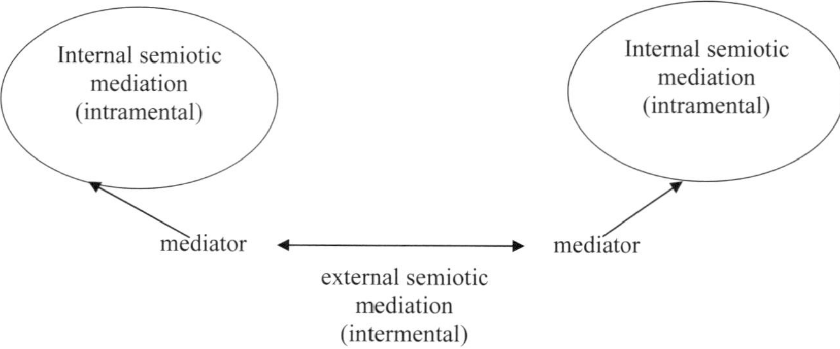

Figure 2.3 The process of semiotic mediation.

a lecture they are initiating semiotic mediation and a student is responding; when a student writes an assignment, they are initiating semiotic mediation (albeit in response to an assignment prompt from the teacher) and a teacher is responding. Following Hasan we can say that for both the teacher and the learner the shared objective of semiotic mediation is understanding. However, there is also a distinction in the objectives each has when engaged in acts of semiotic mediation. The teacher as semiotic initiator is seeking to enable the reconfiguration of the learner's conceptual structures; in other words, to support their learning. The convention in formal university-level education is that the learner as semiotic initiator is not seeking to reconfigure their teacher's conceptual structures, at least not until they have progressed some distance in their learning. In fact, students' semiotic activity is intended to reconfigure *their own* conceptual structures whether they are initiating or responding. This reflects the fact that they are the learner and the teacher is the authorized representative of a field of knowledge (see Figure 2.4). For this reason, the understanding

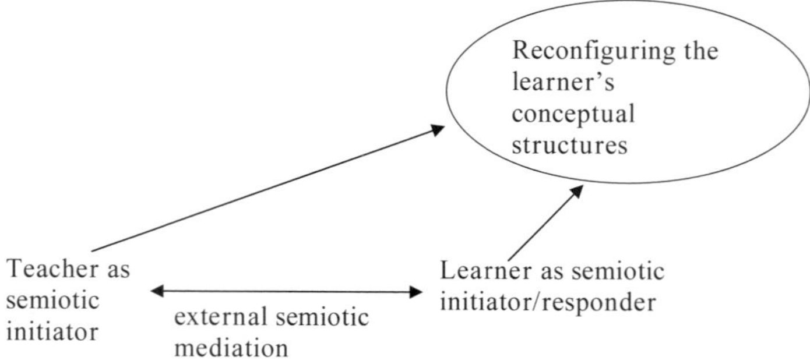

Figure 2.4 The roles in visible semiotic mediation: Teacher as initiator.

that is achieved by the teacher when responding to acts of semiotic mediation initiated by a learner (e.g., an assignment text) is used to evaluate the learner or to further scaffold the learning of the student rather than to reconfigure the teacher's own conceptual structures (as shown in Figure 2.5)—although such

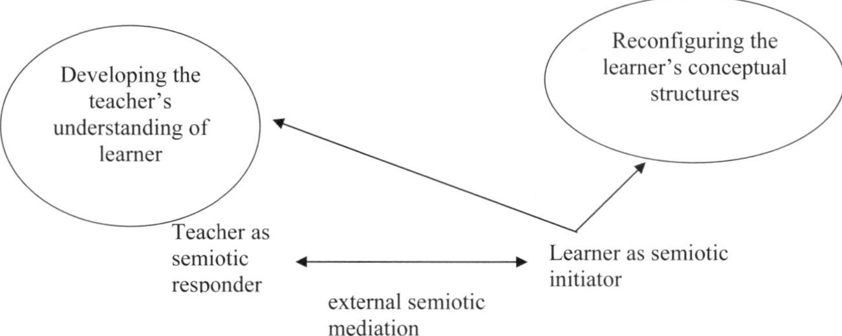

Figure 2.5 The roles in visible semiotic mediation: Learner as initiator.

reconfiguration is not impossible.

Not all models of teaching and learning accept this strong distinction between the teacher and learner. Community and adult education, for example, have long been influenced by the work of Paulo Freire and sought to place the student in as authoritative a role as the teacher and to place the teacher in a learning role (see, e.g., Freire, 1972; Ledwith, 2011). Such an approach has also had some influence on formal university-level teaching practices (see, e.g., Shor, 1987). However, the knowledge of formal education is authoritative knowledge and, however democratically the teacher structures the engagement of the learners with this knowledge, there will remain an authoritativeness in both the knowledge itself in relation to learners (i.e., in its classification) and also in the teacher, who usually also has an evaluating (i.e., regulatory) responsibility. It is by recognizing the agency of the learner in acts of semiotic mediation in the ways that we have proposed above that the agency of the learner remains grounded in the realities of university-level education. In these realities, the learner's engagement is undoubtedly motivated by making the learning their own but the authority of the learner in constructing the knowledge as their own is constrained by the socially constructed nature of the knowledge they are learning (its classification) and by the regulatory discourse of the institution in which they are seeking to learn.

Our second answer to the question we asked about the value of treating teaching and learning as semiotic mediation is that recognizing the centrality of meaning making (through language) in the process of teaching and learning promotes a recognition of the value of *metasemiotic awareness* to that process. Semiotic mediation can be carried out successfully by interactants who pay no conscious attention to the semiotic systems they are using in their interaction. On the other hand, conscious awareness of the existence of semiotic systems in interaction creates opportunities to enhance the exploitation of these systems. Conscious attention to how semiotic systems work is regarded as normal in the case of less familiar semiotic systems such as mathematics or film. Language, however, has become naturalized in many teaching–learning contexts and, as we suggested earlier, is often invisible. Because we are immersed in it and it permeates our consciousness, it is difficult to recognize that it too is a semiotic system—albeit a highly complex and multiple one. Our proposal is that semiotic mediation can benefit from conscious awareness of the semiotic systems and processes involved. When such awareness is articulated, it constitutes a meta-level to semiotic mediation and stands in contrast to modeling, guidance, and scaffolding and other types of mediation such as reading/writing (where there is no reference to the role of language in meaning making). This explication of semiosis can be referred to as *metasemiotic mediation,* as shown in Figure 2.6.

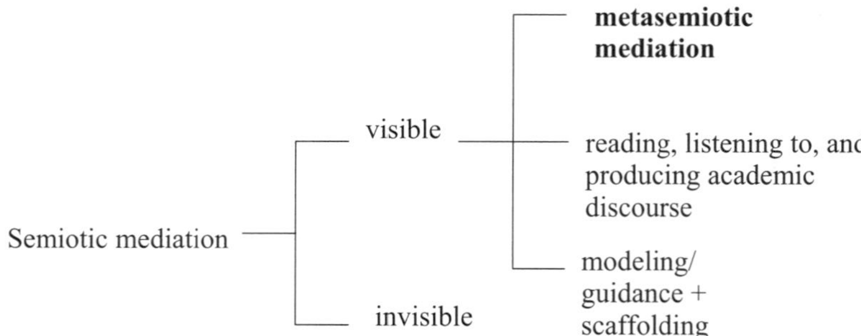

Figure 2.6 Metasemiotic mediation.

We see SFL as a theory that can, first, enhance semiotic mediation by promoting semiotic awareness and that can, second, enable metasemiotic mediation.

2.6 The Foundations for a LASS Approach to Teaching and Learning

The social semiotic theory of language that is applied throughout this monograph is SFL. SFL treats language as a resource for creating and understanding *texts in contexts*. It offers an interpretation and description of grammar that focuses less on grammatical structure (though this remains important) and more on meanings in texts in contexts. As Halliday proposes, we need "for educational purposes a grammar that is functional rather than formal, semantic rather than syntactic in focus, orientated towards discourse rather than towards sentences, and represents language as a flexible resource rather than a rigid set of rules" (2004, p. 323).

The analytical tools associated with SFL will be explained more fully in the next chapter. Here we will provide an overview of some of the areas that SFL researchers have investigated and that have contributed to the research foundation as well as the pedagogical aspects of a LASS approach to teaching and learning. Furthermore, we acknowledge the role played by the academic literacies research paradigm in informing our approach.

2.6.1 SFL research into academic meaning making

SFL has for the past 40 years been used in extensive investigations of academic discourse and associated pedagogy. Using the constructs of genre and register (discussed in Chapter 3), SFL research has produced rich descriptions of academic texts in terms of their purposes (such as explaining, reporting, or arguing) and their vocabulary and grammar, which are seen as inextricably connected with text purposes and contexts. Through investigating texts in their disciplinary contexts (e.g., history, science), SFL has challenged the widely held assumption that academic conventions are universal and independent of particular disciplines, an area that has generated wide debate in fields such as English for academic purposes (EAP) (e.g., Hyland & Hamp-Lyons, 2002, p. 6).

To date, SFL research has been carried out in a broad range of disciplines and subdisciplines as well as the more weakly classified regions. Texts constructed by professional academics and texts written by students as part of their undergraduate or postgraduate study have been explored. Areas include:

- Science (Drury, 2001; Halliday & Martin, 1993: Jones, 2007)
- Science and engineering (Drury, Aire, & O'Carroll, 2010; Drury, Langrish, & O'Carroll, 2006; Mort & Drury, 2012)
- History of science (North, 2005; North & Hewings, 2006)
- Biology (Hao & Humphrey, 2012; Humphrey & Hao, in press)
- Social sciences, including economics, sociology, and political science (Wignell, 2007)
- Geography (Hewings, 2004)
- History (Ravelli, 2004)
- Film Studies (Coffin, 2010; Donohue, 2012)

- HSC (Donohue & Coffin, 2012)
- Accountancy (Webb, English, & Bonnano, 1995)
- Management (Ravelli, 2004)
- Business (Portman, 2014; Shresthna, 2011)
- Education (Macken-Horarik, Devereux, Trimingham-Jack, & Wilson, 2006; Woodward-Kron, 2004, 2007, 2009)
- Applied Linguistics (Hood, 2004; Humphrey & Dreyfus, in press).

While SFL has been used extensively to map genres across the entire school curriculum (e.g., Coffin, 2006; Christie & Derewianka, 2008), within the tertiary educational sector, such extensive genre mapping has been a more challenging task. This is because of the range of disciplines and subdisciplines and the contested nature of knowledge making. However, drawing on SFL as an overall framework as well as corpus linguistics and Biber's non-SFL analysis of register, Nesi and Gardner (2012) have recently identified 13 *genre families* of undergraduate and postgraduate student writing across the arts and humanities, life sciences, physical sciences, and social sciences.[7] Their research drew on a corpus of 3,500 student texts (the British Academic Written English, or BAWE, corpus). Other BAWE corpus-related studies have begun to provide in-depth analysis of how grammar and lexis work to make meaning in different ways within specific disciplines (e.g., Gardner, 2008).

Central to many of the research studies listed above has been the use of abstract language in academic meaning making, that is, the use of decontextualized language as discussed in Section 2.3.1. Foundational SFL studies of abstract language were Halliday and Martin's *Writing Science* (1993) and (at the secondary level) Lemke's *Talking Science* (1990). Subsequent studies have focused, in particular, on the experience of L1 and second language speakers in developing technical, field-based *taxonomies* (Chen & Foley, 2004; Jones, 1991, 2004; Woodward-Kron, 2009). Complementing research in the construal of knowledge through abstract meaning making has been research into how learners position themselves in relation to such knowledge (e.g., in terms of endorsing or critiquing it). This brings into play the interpersonal, persuasive dimension of academic meaning making. Work in this area has been carried out by Coffin (2004), Coffin and Hewings (2005), Hood (2004, 2006, 2010), Lee (2010a, 2010b), Swain (2007), and Woodward-Kron (2002). Finally, there has also been extensive research into the textual organization of academic texts and messages (including work by Ravelli, 2004, and Hood, 2008).

In the last decade there has been a growing shift among some SFL researchers to draw on concepts from the sociology of education in order to develop new ways of theorizing knowledge, namely in terms of knowledge structures and knowers. A central influence on this research is the theorizing and empirical studies of Maton and colleagues (e.g., Maton, 2014; Maton, Hood, & Shay, in press). Maton has built on Bernstein's work in order to give greater attention to, and develop greater understanding of, relations *within* knowledge as opposed to relations *to* knowledge (e.g., of class, race, or gender), the latter being dominant in much of the sociology of knowledge and education literature. We have found that Maton's work has helpfully reinforced our own recognition of the importance of focusing on the "what" of learning in addition to the "how." Using complementary analytical concepts and tools, Maton has drawn attention to the structuring of intellectual fields and the pedagogical significance of this, namely the need to develop students' capacity in moving from contextualized to decontextualized meaning making and the need to support the expansion of their conceptual frameworks within a given field of study. Maton's concept of *semantic wave* is akin, though not identical, to the notion of the movement between contextualized and decontextualized meaning making that we discuss in this monograph.

2.6.2 SFL innovations in university-level pedagogy and associated research

The previous section provided an overview of how SFL researchers have used linguistic tools, at times in combination with sociological concepts, to gain insight into academic knowledge and meaning making as classified in university curricula. This section considers SFL innovations in pedagogy and related research investigating and reflecting on these pedagogic innovations, often in cycles of action research. The emphasis thus moves from classification to framing, specifically the presentation of the curriculum (instructional discourse) as well as the management of that presentation (regulatory discourse).

For some time there has been a strong tradition of SFL researchers and practitioners developing and designing language-based learning pedagogies. Using SFL descriptions of university-level disciplines (as well as academic meaning making in general) and informed by an understanding of the significance of semiotic and metasemiotic mediation, the aim has been to give greater attention to the role of language in the content areas of the university-level curricula and thus support students in "learning language, learning through language, and learning about language" (Halliday, 2004, pp. 308–326). One of the most influential teaching–learning innovations has been genre pedagogy including its adaptation for online contexts (e.g., Dreyfus & Martin, 2012; Dreyfus, Humphrey, Mahboob, & Martin, in press; Drury, 2004; Mort & Drury,

2012). One particularly effective instantiation of genre pedagogy is the *Reading to Learn* program initiated by Rose (Rose, Rose, Farrington, & Page, 2008), where there has been considerable work on developing techniques to support students' reading as a means of accessing relevant curricular knowledge.

Contexts for implementing and, in some cases, researching SFL-based pedagogies include mainstream degree programs that involve partnerships between linguistic and subject experts (e.g., Percy & Skillen, 2007; Taylor & Drury, 2007). Other contexts are specialized learning or study skills centers (e.g., Moore, 2007; Woodward-Kron, 2007) and academic writing programs. The role of technology in supporting students' language and learning development has also become an important focus for pedagogic innovation and investigation (e.g., Drury, 2004; Ellis, 2004; Mahboob et al., 2010; Mort & Drury, 2012) as well as SFL-based assessment procedures (e.g., Webb & Bonanno, 1995).

While, to date, the main focus in SFL educational work has been the development and design of language-based pedagogies, aspects of these pedagogies in action have begun to be systematically researched. An emerging interest lies in the kinds of dialogue that support the negotiation of meaning (Dreyfus, Macnaught, & Humphrey, 2011; Humphrey & Macnaught, 2011) and resonates with our own emphasis on the processes of semiotic mediation.

2.6.3 Ethnography and academic literacies: Their influences on a LASS approach to teaching and learning

Although our LASS approach builds primarily on SFL theorizing, research, and pedagogic innovation, it has also been informed by work conducted in a related field of study referred to as academic literacies (e.g., Lea, 2008; Lea & Street, 1998; Lillis, 2001). In this section, we discuss how its ethnographic methodology and ideological orientation to the role of academic writing in university-level teaching and learning have informed our approach (see also Coffin & Donohue, 2012; for an extended discussion).

As in the case of SFL, academic literacies traces its roots to the ethnographic work of Bronisław Malinowski (e.g., 1923). It looks to actual language in use for its data rather than to logic or introspection and the majority of its educationally oriented investigations involve researchers engaging (as participant observers) in the site and activities being analyzed. Academic literacies, as an ethnography-based approach, also places great emphasis on the participant/non-participant observation of the researcher. The focus and primary unit of analysis, however, is academic writing *practices* rather than texts and it particularly values insider (*emic*) perspectives on academic writing practices over a sustained period of time. Ivanič and Lea (2006, p. 7) argue that "the lived experience of teaching and learning—from both student and tutor perspectives—is central to understanding student writing."

There are various ways of obtaining insiders' perspectives, a common one of which is the in-depth semi-structured interview, focusing on literacy history and talk around text. In such interviews, the researcher elicits autobiographical accounts of language and academic literacy learning so that current practices and perspectives can be understood within the broader sociohistorical context of an individual's life experience. In talk around text, an approach devised by a key proponent of academic literacies (Lillis, 2001, 2003), the researcher encourages student writers to make comments and reflect on academic writing in ways not predefined by the researcher and by so doing establishes what is particularly relevant and significant to the student. In Chapter 5 we present research that was influenced by such a procedure, in which we carried out semi-structured interviews with students in a process of metasemiotic mediation we call *mediated text analysis discussion*.

There are differences between our ideology and approach and that of academic literacies researchers. Perhaps the most obvious is that the research underpinning the LASS approach to teaching and learning is text focused and employs an SFL framework in order to understand meaning making from a linguistic perspective; in other words, there is a strong *etic* dimension. The academic literacies research paradigm, in contrast, has a student-in-context focus and there is a strong commitment to an emic perspective.

Despite differences, we have combined elements of ethnography with the LASS approach. Furthermore, we consider that there is ideological overlap in the shared emphasis on developing students' capacity to be reflective and critical. In this we follow Hasan's (1996) proposal that, while students' chances of success in education are likely to be considerably enhanced if they are enabled to produce the sorts of discourse that are valued within the educational context, in order to participate in the production of knowledge they also need to develop the "ability to use language to reflect, to enquire and to analyze, which is the necessary basis for challenging what are seen as facts" (1996, p. 408). While primarily referring to school education and the genre pedagogy that was being implemented at the time, her call for what she refers to as *reflection literacy* has considerable resonance in higher education with its vision of independent, productive learners:

> If the pedagogy is successful it should ideally produce in the pupils a disposition to distrust doxic knowledge, that is, knowledge whose sole authority is the authority of someone in authority ... apart from

> questioning the norms of discourse and of knowledge, a literacy of this kind would seek to examine the norms of education itself. (Hasan, 1996, p. 412)

Hasan's proposal resonates with Lillis's (2003) call to move away from "monologic" approaches to meaning making, which encourage students' uncritical reproduction of official discourses of knowledge. At the same time, we should emphasize that, as previously discussed, a LASS approach also recognizes that, while a learner's engagement is undoubtedly motivated by making the learning their own, the authority of the learner in constructing the knowledge as their own is constrained by the socially constructed nature of the knowledge they are learning (its classification) and by the regulatory discourse of the institution in which they are seeking to learn. To pretend otherwise would be disingenuous. While some might claim that, on this basis, a LASS approach is less radical than other critical approaches to education, we, like Rose and Martin (2012), see it as socially subversive. This is because its central goal is to give all students access to institutionally powerful knowledge and in so doing change relations between social groups, in other words, "democratize education."

2.7 A LASS Approach to Teaching and Learning

We began this chapter with three students' experiences of teaching and learning in a university setting. In talking about their experience of learning, all three students were extremely aware that they were exploiting meaning-making resources and that the university environment they were in required meaning-making resources that they had not necessarily arrived with. Two of the students were not yet comfortable with what they thought was being asked of them; one, on the other hand, was apparently thriving in the situation and experienced her learning as successful. For her, there was an additional payoff in that she could see immediate applicability of the knowledge she was learning to her work life, despite—or, in fact, because of—the decontextualized nature of that knowledge.

The decontextualized discourse of knowledge was experienced by one student as of doubtful relevance to his workplace and also as some threat to his identity. He feared that academic study would disempower him through its abstractions and leave him in a world of indecisiveness. We believe he was right to wonder about the impact academic learning would have because it was highly likely that his semiotic engagement with the module materials and with his tutor would induce real change in his thinking and his being. Language is not an innocent conduit of information: it is an engagement with a context consisting of subject matter, interpersonal interaction, and textual forms, that is, it is an engagement with meaning. And because interaction is the context in which meanings are exchanged, interactants' interpretations of context and the nature of the resources that they bring to their engagement with those contexts constitute the meanings that are made.

As we observed at the beginning of the chapter, no one can expect to enter a context totally prepared for the meaning making that will be entailed. What the students describe is how they make the most of the situation, drawing on the semiotic resources they have. The differences they display are differences in semantic orientation: these are not only differences in the areas of the linguistic system previous experience has made them most familiar with using but differences in the kinds of meaning previous experience has made them most familiar with making. University-level study entails expansion of meanings and of meaning-making resources. University-level teaching is intended to support this process. The interaction amounts to semiotic mediation for both parties. In view of the semantic variation that exists between different participants, if students are to be meaningfully taught, then their semantic orientations, which lie at the heart of their identities and cultural experiences, are relevant to teachers. Without such awareness, semiotic mediation risks becoming a one-way process, which, in the worst case, can lead to uncritical engagement.

All forms of scaffolding of knowledge creation are forms of semiotic mediation. Because language is the main semiotic system for such mediation, it is the argument of this monograph that an understanding of language will contribute to the success of teaching and learning in universities. SFL is the theory of language that we are proposing as a vehicle for developing such understanding. SFL provides the tools for metasemiotic mediation, that is, the exercise of conscious awareness of how the semiotic system (of language in this case) is operating to make meanings.

Because of differences in previous experiences of semiotic mediation (and metasemiotic mediation) among mediators (teachers and students), there are differences in the semiotic repertoires of mediators and, consequently, in their semantic orientations. We see the value of drawing on the ethnographic tradition in SFL in researching semantic variation. By means of an ethnographically informed SFL approach to research informing pedagogic innovation, we propose that it is possible to engage meaningfully with the issues of power, identity, and knowledge that characterize university-level (and all) education. In this

LASS approach, the crucial observation is that language is always language in context. If learning is approached from a language in context perspective, then learning can be seen as learning language, learning through language, and learning about language (Halliday, 2004, pp. 308–326).

Notes

1 All interview extracts are transcribed verbatim, including grammar and vocabulary that may not be standard English. In order to indicate where we have omitted sections of the transcript we have used ellipses (. . .) to indicate this.
2 Lennox Castle was a residential institution for people with mental health issues.
3 These are public exams normally taken by UK school students at the age of 16.
4 Where Andrea uses the term "practicity," it is likely that the target standard English word would be practicality; in keeping with our treatment of interview extracts, we have preserved her usage.
5 Note that we are using the term "modality" here rather than the more common term "mode" in order to avoid confusion with the SFL technical term *mode,* which relates to register. Both register and mode are discussed in detail in Chapter 3.
6 Where we refer to participant we do not assume participants are necessarily physically co-present. For example, in the case of a student reading a book we see the author of the book as a participant.
7 The following genre families are set out in full in Gardner and Nesi (2013, pp. 37–40): case study, critique, design specification, empathy writing, essay, exercise, explanation, literature survey, methodology recount, narrative recount, problem question, proposal, and research report.

Language Learning ISSN 0023-8333

CHAPTER 3
A LASS Approach to Teaching and Learning: Analytical Tools

3.1 Introduction

This chapter sets out in detail the theory of language—SFL—that informs our LASS approach to teaching and learning. We discuss how SFL is a theory of language in context whose premises and analytical tools entail a radically different way of looking at language compared to more traditional, structural approaches (see Coffin et al., 2009, for a discussion of these differences). We also show how its orientation to language as a meaning-making resource entails, and its analytical tools enable, a fundamental shift in how we conceptualize the relationship between language and learning. Whereas in psychological cognitive approaches to learning, language occupies a relatively marginal role and is not explicated in any detail, this chapter argues that it is in fact the *detail* of language use that provides powerful insights into students' learning and into the teaching and learning contexts of higher education. Moreover, as subsequent chapters demonstrate, empirical research into how language works in learning contexts provides the necessary basis for a LASS approach to teaching and learning, the approach which underpins our research and teaching and which we illustrate throughout Chapters 4–6, bringing everything together from the perspective of institutional implementation in Chapter 7.

This chapter begins with a basic tenet of SFL that language use is language *choice* and that a *system-instance* perspective deepens understanding of meaning making. The next section introduces the construct of genre from this perspective. Genre theory and analysis (as developed within an SFL framework) is then further developed in the following section, showing how genre and context are related in terms of social purpose. Section 3.4 introduces the concept of register, which serves to link context (as theorized from a linguistic perspective) to language function, meaning, and use. It is in this section that we introduce tools for the analysis of language resources at the clause and text levels.

For some readers this chapter may serve as a reference resource that can be returned to at a point of need. Therefore, in subsequent chapters, we will indicate

DOI: 10.1111/lang.12039

where it may be useful to revisit aspects of the theoretical framework and analytical tools presented here. There are also a number of publications that serve as introductions to SFL theory (e.g., Bloor & Bloor, 2013; Coffin et al., 2009; Derewianka, 2011; Eggins, 2005; Thompson, 2014; Martin & Rose, 2007).

3.2 Language as Choice: A System-Instance Perspective

Each time a student or teacher uses language in a teaching and learning activity, they make a choice. There are always different ways of engaging in semiotic mediation and there are always alternative responses to a teacher's question or to an assignment task. In this section, we provide an overview of a key theoretical principle underpinning SFL in order to show how it informs our way of looking at language and our method of investigating and illuminating the relationship between language use and learning. Specifically, we discuss how a *system* perspective of language influences the way SFL analysts interpret the meaning of each individual clause or text as an instance both of an overall language system such as English and a specific domain of English use such as a university course in Business Studies.

Choices are made at various levels, from clause to whole text. Taking the clause first, below is a short response to work submitted by a student, followed by two possible alternative responses:

A. You need to present your argument more clearly.
B. (Alternative) Can you present your argument more clearly?
C. (Alternative) Next time present your argument more clearly.

Analyzed from the perspective of their formal structure, each follows a different structural order or *mood*:

A. *You need to present your argument more clearly.*

The subject *you* is followed by the verbal group *need to present* (declarative mood).

B. *Can you present your argument more clearly?*

The auxiliary, *can* is followed by the subject *you* (interrogative mood).

C. *Next time present your argument more clearly.*

The verbal group *present* is followed by the object, *your argument* (imperative mood).

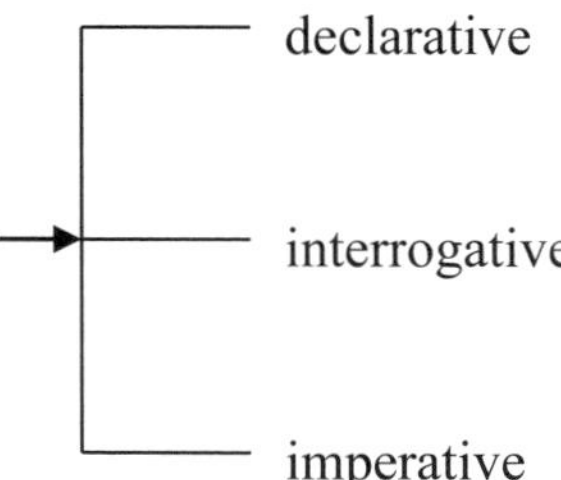

Figure 3.1 Clause types as a set of options.

Each of the clauses above can also be considered from the perspective of the set of clause types available in the English language, noting which type was chosen against the set of possible options. Thus, in example A the teacher giving assessment feedback chose to use a declarative clause but could equally have chosen an interrogative or imperative structure. Setting out or *mapping* the set of options available in any given language provides a system perspective. Figure 3.1 illustrates the graphical conventions that are used in this type of mapping. The arrow represents the entry point into the system and the brackets show that there are three choices available: *declarative*, *interrogative*, and *imperative*. Taking a system perspective and asking the question "Why this clause type and not another?" may reveal important differences in how teachers and students understand and interpret a learning context.

Whereas the initial approach to the examples above provided a *syntagmatic* perspective (i.e., by focusing on the sequential ordering of elements in each of the clauses), Figure 3.1 offers a *paradigmatic* perspective by setting out, and drawing attention to, the options available. Traditional formal approaches to language tend to take a syntagmatic perspective, whereas systemic functional linguists hold the view that both perspectives are important in order to fully understand meaning making.

A key point here is that language choices are usually made unconsciously: they are often reflexes of how we habitually orient to, and interpret, the contexts around us. Taking the example above to illustrate this point, we can propose that, while there may be a variety of factors affecting the choice of imperative in Example C, it is likely to be interpreted as a more authoritarian, old-school pedagogic approach to assignment feedback than that of the softer, mitigating interrogative structure of Example B.

Clause type (mood) is, of course, only one example of language choice, and it is clusters or syndromes of choices (across many texts) that build up a more in-depth and reliable sense of the different orientations of speakers and writers (their semantic orientations, as discussed in Chapter 2). As a further example, let us consider the introductory paragraphs to an assignment written by two different Business Studies students, Alena and Svetla, and consider the patterns of linguistic features in each. To aid the discussion we have underlined the subjects (or *Participants*) and the elements in initial position (*Theme*)[1] in each clause (at times Subject and Theme are conflated, but not always). The assignment task (or prompt) was as follows:

> Wal-Mart is a U.S.-based multinational corporation. Critically discuss the likely costs and benefits of its takeover of Asda, a UK-based company.

> **Alena's introduction**

> A multinational corporation (MNC) is a company that owns or controls subsidiaries in more than one country (Suneja, 2000).[2] Wal-Mart, a US-based company and its largest retailer, is an example of a large MNC with foreign subsidiaries in ten countries and a turnover of 2% of US GDP. On 26 July 1999 Wal-Mart acquired a UK-based supermarket chain Asda, with its 229 stores located mainly in the south of England. The following essay represents a critical discussion of the likely costs and benefits of the merger.

> **Svetla's introduction**

> In this assignment I will critically look on[3] the benefits and the costs of the US-based multinational corporation which overtook a UK-based company. At the beginning I will discuss a history of the Wal-Mart, US company and it's expand into the other countries as well as why companies and businesses which go multinational.

As the underlining makes prominent, Alena's choice of subjects and initial elements foreground the concept of *multinational corporations*, *Wal-Mart,* and *essay,* as well as chronology (*on 26 July 1999)*. On the other hand, Svetla's use of *I* gives attention to herself as writer, alongside the location of her writing activity (*in this assignment, at the beginning)*. There is a further related contrast in their different choices of verbs in the main clauses: largely relational Processes[4] of being are used in Alena's assignment (*is, is, represents*) compared to mental (*look*) and verbal Processes (*discuss*) in Svetla's. The consequences of clusters of choices such as these are explored more fully in later chapters. It is interesting to note at this point, however, that the students' different orientations in their introductions set the ground for continuing differences, with Alena working primarily with abstract concepts and Svetla tending to focus on Wal-Mart as a material entity. The final marks allocated to the students showed Alena's assignment (with a score of 89%) was more highly valued by her teacher than Svetla's (55%). While Alena's use of abstract concepts rather than material entities is not the only reason for her text being more highly valued, it plays an important role in demonstrating her engagement with the conceptual formation of the fields. Svetla, on the other hand, orients more to the less highly valued concrete actions of what the company Wal-Mart did.

Choice applies to text structure as well as to grammar. In the following section we introduce the SFL perspective on *genre* showing how genre has a particular analytical place and purpose within the SFL framework. Essentially, genre serves as an analytical tool for mapping choices in how communities and individuals structure and design whole texts as part of their meaning-making processes.

3.2.2 Mapping Choices in Text Structure: The Concept of Genre

In SFL, the term *genre* has been adopted to refer to the way in which we construct spoken and written texts in similar and recognizable (though rarely identical) ways in response to recurrent communicative purposes or goals. These goals shape the different *stages* (moves within a genre) individuals move through and, over time, in pursuing these recurrent social (communicative) purposes, societies and communities build up communal systems of text structures. Two major categories of genres can be distinguished: (i) *story genres,* which are event-oriented and organized in time, and (ii) *conceptual genres,* which are conceptually oriented and organized and comprise systems of genres for describing, explaining, and arguing about social and natural phenomena. As Chapters 4–6 will reveal, both types play a role in teaching and learning contexts.

3.2.2.1 Story Genres

Within all cultures, people's need and desire to narrate events and tell stories has led to the development of systems of story genres. These provide a communal reservoir (see Chapter 2, Section 2.3) of designed structures from which members of a culture can choose, often adapting and tweaking the prototype structures in line with their individual communicative purposes and social contexts. In English-speaking cultures, SFL research to date (Martin & Rose,

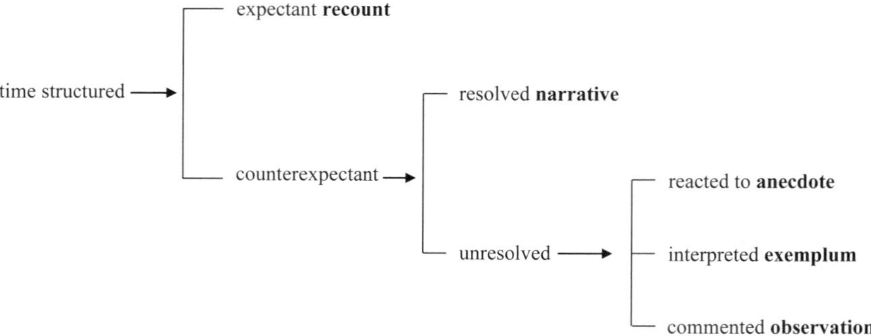

Figure 3.2 Choices in story genre: A system perspective (adapted from Martin & Rose, 2008, pg. 101).

2008) suggests that there are five main story genres to choose from, each with a distinct purpose and a different set of stages configured through a distinct set of lexico-grammatical resources (we will discuss genre stages in more detail in Section 3.3.1). Figure 3.2 shows the story choices as a system network.

Figure 3.2 shows that the first major choice in story telling is dependent on whether the speaker or writer's purpose is either to recount a temporal succession of relatively predictable events (a recount genre) or to narrate a set of unexpected problematic events that disrupt the usual state of affairs (glossed as counterexpectant).

Below is an example (instance) of each type, showing the major functional stages (in italics) that a writer/speaker would typically move through. Both are taken from higher education courses that use computer mediated discussion forums as part of their teaching-learning process. Typically online forums are organized around discussion tasks designed to prompt debate relevant to students' prior reading and future assessment tasks. In the applied contexts from which the following two forum extracts are taken, students are being encouraged to reflect on and discuss the relationship between theoretical knowledge and the real-world context of health provision (in Karalena's story) and of classroom teaching (in Fiona's story).

The first forum extract, Fiona's story, is from a master's course in Applied Linguistics. The second, Karalena's story, is taken from a third-level undergraduate course, *Perspectives on Complementary and Alternative Medicine* (CAM), within a HSC degree.

Fiona's story: example of (expectant) recount genre	
Orientation *(orients the reader by introducing the author and what is to follow)*	I've been teaching English for 8 years now and have lived in lots of interesting places. I can't say I've always managed to learn the local language but I try . . .
Record of events *(events are retold in a chronological sequence)*	I first went to China and stayed there for three years and picked up enough language to survive on. Then I headed off to the other side of the world and spent two years in South America. After that I had 3 years in Spain and almost became fluent. I arrived in Moscow in February (−26 degrees) this year and was whisked off to my little (private) school. It was in a suburb of Moscow, ("little town" they told me, only 150, 000 inhabitants). I didn't have time for the official Russian lessons so I just learned the words for the important things—like food!
Reorientation *(a rounding off stage)*	I'm still learning Russian but it's a bit of an uphill battle . . .

Karalena's story: Example of (counterexpectant) exemplum genre	
Orientation *(orients the reader by introducing the author and what is to follow)*	The only experience I have ever had regarding CAM would be buying a bottle of aromatherapy massage oil to try and help relax my youngest child to encourage her to sleep all night IN HER OWN BED! (advice from morning show)
Incident *(a problematic event)*	however after nightly massages for 2 weeks she was still waking up, eventually i resulted back the old way, good old bribery no sleep no mcdonalds
Interpretation *(the significance of the events)*	and that was far more effective

As illustrated by the two sample stories, the recount and exemplum genres both have the same initial opening stage, the Orientation.[5] This stage functions to orient a reader/listener to what is to follow. The subsequent stages in each story genre differ, however, in line with the writers' different purposes. In the recount genre, the main body constitutes a factual retelling of events in chronological sequence (*for three years, then, after that, in February this year*). In an exemplum genre, on the other hand, the Incident stage deals with events that may cause problems for those involved. In Karalena's story the problem is her child not sleeping and the CAM therapies not working. The end stages for both genres are also different. The Reorientation in the recount rounds off the text by returning the reader to the point of departure (traveling and learning languages), whereas the Interpretation stage in the exemplum functions to give the events a significance that goes beyond the local and personal response (in this case the ineffectiveness of CAM).

We can set out the stages of the two genres as follows, using notation to show sequencing, recursion (where it occurs) and to differentiate stages that always occur and are core to a genre (i.e., obligatory) as opposed to those that are infrequent and therefore can be regarded as optional.

Recount: Orientation ˆ Record of Events ˆ (Reorientation)

Exemplum: Orientation ˆ Incident ˆ Interpretation

(Key: () = optional ˆ = followed by)

The system perspective on genres depicted in Figure 3.2 sets out a full set of choices in story genres. If the counterexpectant choice is made, a speaker or writer may show how events were resolved in some way (narrative genre) or, in line with their purpose for telling a story and the context in which they are telling it, they may work through the stages of an anecdote or observation genre. Thus, if they want to focus on an emotional reaction to events, they choose an anecdote, but if they wish to make a moral judgment, they choose an exemplum. Alternatively, if they wish to describe events set (rather than sequenced) in time and include some kind of personal response, then the genre would be an observation (see Martin & Rose, 2008, for further discussion). By mapping storytelling as a system of genres, just as in the case of clause-level structures, analysts can ask questions as to why one type of story was chosen or "emerged" rather than another, gaining insight into cultural and individual purposes and the contexts shaping these. Note that our use of the word "choice" is intended to convey that for all language users there are options, including at the level of text structure. Nevertheless, as previously commented on, people may not consciously make a choice and it is likely that genres emerge dynamically from a mix of bottom-up and top-down meaning-making activity.

3.2.2.2 Conceptual Genres

Within most, if not all, contemporary societies, another key activity besides storytelling is academic knowledge building, with much of this occurring within academic institutions. As specialists in particular fields of study, academics have different purposes for knowledge building. In the case of scientists, the purpose may be to explain natural phenomena; for historians, to debate different perspectives on the causes and consequences of prior events; and for architects, to create and specify designs. Thus, the systems of genres associated with any academic discipline or field of study vary, with explaining genres playing a key role in the sciences, arguing genres a central role in history, and design specification genres in architecture (and so on). In Chapter 2, we have already pointed out that Nesi and Gardner (2012) have identified 13 genre families of student writing across different fields of study.

Academic knowledge recontextualized for tertiary teaching and learning (as an aspect of the "pedagogic device" conceptualized by Bernstein and discussed in Chapter 2) may be exploited for different teaching-learning purposes. Aside from wider goals relating to the field of study and their underpinning rationales for knowledge building, academic departments design their curricula and assessment strategy in response to students' stage of learning (i.e., undergraduate or postgraduate, first year or third year). The shaping of knowledge may also be influenced by external stakeholders such as professional bodies (e.g., in medicine) and by various wider agendas such as those of employability, widening participation, and so on. Individual teachers' pedagogical approaches may also have an impact on how they recontextualize knowledge affecting, for example, the purposes for learning they prioritize in their assessment design.

To give an example of a *genre system* used for pedagogic purposes in a specific academic field of study, Figure 3.3 shows the system of genres that we mapped as part of our research into HSC as studied at the Open University in the United Kingdom. The genres shown in Figure 3.3 were seen by the department as important in developing HSC knowledge. This was corroborated in focus group discussions as well as evidenced by their use in students' textbooks and resources and in the design of assessment tasks. The figure demonstrates that importance is placed on students' capacity to classify and explain social phenomena as well as debate perspectives. The inclusion of *hortatory arguing genres* in which students not only analyze how the world *is* (*analytical arguing genres*) but make recommendations about how it *should be* shows that there is value placed on their capacity to propose practical action. Chapter 5 will elaborate further on these genres in relation to learning HSC knowledge.

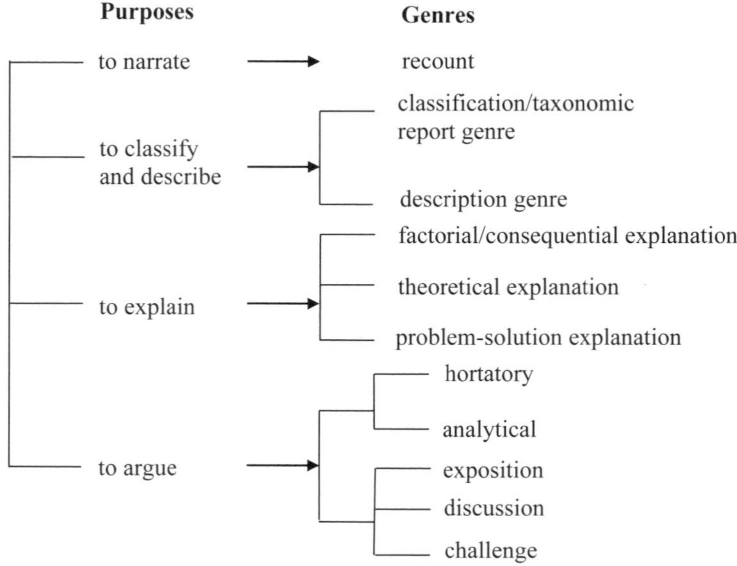

Figure 3.3 Key purposes and genres in introductory Health and Social Care: A system perspective.

3.2.3 Recap

In this section, we have provided an overview of a key theoretical principle underpinning SFL—the system-instance perspective—in order to emphasize that part of the meaning of a text or clause lies in what could have been chosen but was not. As the monograph progresses, we will keep returning to this notion in considering the pedagogic implications of text and language choices. It is interesting to speculate, for example, as to why Karalena (in Section 3.2.2.1 above) chose to construe her negative perspective on CAM through a story as opposed to argument genre (given that the context was an academic one).

In the following section, we develop further the SFL concept of genre, discussing in turn how the notions of genre stages and *phases*, genre families, and *macrogenres* provide tools for investigating the different ways in which students make meaning in their university learning.

3.3 Genre Theory and Analysis: Insights Into Learning

We would argue that, in large part, tertiary learning is constituted by students learning how to use language to achieve the academic and pedagogic purposes of a specific course within a particular field of study. Thus, introductory HSC study is largely constituted by students learning how to use language to achieve the purposes set out in Figure 3.3. This does not, of course, merely involve learning how to organize and stage texts (though this in itself may present considerable challenges to students). Rather, HSC study involves learning to marshal and manage a whole repertoire of language resources that construe the disciplinary concepts (the *ideational* meanings) that are the focal point for definition, classification, explanation, and debate and, in some cases, for professional application. Furthermore, it involves learning to use language to engage with a disciplinary community of academics and students and present knowledge and ideas that are interpersonally persuasive and textually coherent. Section 3.4 will deal with these latter aspects of meaning making in some detail. In the meantime, this section will continue to set out aspects of genre theory and analysis that we will draw on in later chapters. First, we discuss what have been identified as *elemental* genres and then consider the notion of genre families. We then look at stretches of meaning (referred to as phases) that occur within stages and consider how elemental genres can be incorporated into a text as embedded genres. We also consider how genres may combine together to form macrogenres. Finally, we consider the SFL perspective on genre in relation to higher education learning.

3.3.1 Elemental Genres

Genre theory within SFL originated in the 1980s in the context of conducting research into literacy and learning at the primary school level. It was found that children were given considerable practice in producing narratives but little opportunity to produce other kinds of texts with different purposes. SFL linguists therefore partnered with educators to map and make visible additional genres and ways of meaning making that students of primary-school age were expected to engage with but were rarely explicitly taught. The resultant set of genres is presented in Table 3.1.

Of particular importance to the classification of genres is the relationship between purpose and the lexicogrammatical configuration of a genre. Table 3.2 (pg. 52) compares two elemental genres to contrast key linguistic resources that express or realize the genres. In Section 3.4, we will discuss how other features of the context (beyond purpose) equally shape the linguistic resources used.

Where genre pedagogy is now implemented (across many schools within Australia, the United Kingdom, and elsewhere), the elemental genres tend to be taught and learned as clearly bounded prototypes but the ultimate aim is

Table 3.1 Elemental Genres—Purposes and Stages

Genre	Social purpose	Generic stages
personal recount	to retell a sequence of events in the writer/speaker's life	• Orientation • Record of events • (Reorientation)
narrative	to tell a story	• Orientation • Complication* • Evaluation* • Resolution
descriptive report	to describe specific things	• Orientation • Description
taxonomic report	to classify and describe phenomenon	• Identification of phenomenon and classification • Description of types or parts*
procedure	to give instructions	• Goal • Material • Steps*
explanation	to explain how something works	• Identification of phenomenon • Explanation sequence
exposition	to argue for a point of view	• Position • Arguments* • Reinforcement of position
discussion	to consider different perspectives on an issue	• Issue • Arguments for* • Arguments against* • (Position)

Key: ( ) = optional * = recursion

(or should be) to provide learners with powerful building-block genres that can be used and/or combined and/or adapted for individual purposes in infinitely variable ways. Of particular relevance for tertiary learning (and subsequent discussion in this book) are the ways in which teachers and students use the same elemental genre (such as the discussion genre) to make very different meanings in different fields of study and in relation to their audience and mode of delivery (as discussed in Section 3.4 below). Equally relevant is the way elemental genres develop into families of related or *agnate*

Table 3.2 Elemental Genres—Generic Stages and Lexicogrammar

Genre	Social purpose	Generic stages	Lexicogrammatical features
personal recount	to retell a sequence of events in the narrator's life	• Orientation • Record of events • (Reorientation)	— past tense — declarative mood — time Circumstances — personal pronoun *I*
discussion	to consider different perspectives on an issue	• Issue • Arguments for • Arguments against • (Position)	— present tense (and past where appropriate) — declarative mood (some use of interrogatives in spoken mode) — modality — nominal groups (often abstract)

genres, each with their specialized purposes. This is the focus of the next section.

3.3.2 Genre Families

In the 1990s, as SFL research into genres for learning progressed and a large-scale study of secondary school subject-specific literacy and learning was conducted (see Christie & Martin, 2005), it soon became apparent that for more advanced learning purposes teachers and learners need to go beyond elemental genres. In history, for example, rather than simply retell past events in an individual's life, secondary school students are expected to retell and evaluate generalized events (i.e., events occurring across groups of people and usually across long stretches of time). They are also expected to build in cause-and-effect relations between events. Recounts in history can therefore be more accurately described as a family of related recording genres with common goals and common language resources but with each member of the family having its own specific configuration of stages and patterns of grammar and lexis (*lexicogrammar*). Table 3.3 illustrates this point with reference to the recording genres in secondary school history (see Coffin, 2006, for discussion of other families of genre in school history).

3.3.3 Generic Stages, Phases, and Embedded Genres

3.3.3.1 Generic Stages

As discussed previously (and illustrated in Tables 3.1 and 3.2), the general steps that writers or speakers move through in order to achieve their specific

Table 3.3 The Recording Family of Genres

Genre	Social Purpose	Generic stages	Lexicogrammatical features
autobiographical recount	to retell the events of your own life	• Orientation • Record of events	— specific Participants — authorial "I" — language of time (e.g., *in 1957, at the age of 3, before long)*
biographical recount	to retell the events of a person's life	• Orientation • Record of Events • (Evaluation of Person)	— specific Participants — more specialized lexis — language of time
historical recount	to retell the events of peoples and nations in the past	• Background • Record of Events • (Deduction)	— generic Participants — specialized lexis — language of time
historical account	to account for why events happened in a particular sequence	• Background • Account of events • (Deduction)	— generic + abstract Particpants — specialized lexis — nominalization — language of time and cause-and-effect

purposes or goals can be identified linguistically as *generic (genre) stages*, that is, as core elements of text that serve specific functions and are constituted by particular configurations of grammatical and lexical choices. These steps are labeled according to their distinct function in achieving the overall purpose of the genre. Thus, within a discussion genre there are three main functional steps or stages: Issue, Arguments, and Position. Here are extracts from an instantiation of an argument genre (Figure 3.4) produced in a first-level HSC course in response to the assignment task/prompt reproduced below. The staging is shown in italics and there are annotations of key linguistic features in commented text.

How far was Lennox Castle Hospital an example of what Goffman calls a "total institution"?		
Seb's essay		
Issue *(a contestable proposition)*	The purpose of this essay is to assess the extent to which Lennox Castle Hospital can be considered an example of a "total institution". The hospital opened in 1936 and closed in 2002 and was in many ways typical of the large scale building complexes designed for the long term care of people with learning disabilities. But was it a total institution? ... In order to reach an overall judgement as to whether or not it can be described as a total institution I will critically analyse the available evidence on how it operated as an institution from the perspective of both residents and staff.	Modal finite chosen to show there are alternative ways of assessing the hospital. Interrogative choice used to show arguable aspect of proposition. Modal finite to show there are alternative ways of assessing the hospital Lexical choice to emphasize perspectival nature of the discussion
Argument 1	The first factor to be discussed is the notion of batch living. In essence, batch living is the opposite of individual living and is characterized by limited personal freedom – all choices as to how an individual lives his or her life are made by bureaucratic management structures. In relation to Lennox Castle, evidence of batch living is found in the design of identical and symmetrical buildings with residents living sixty to a villa (with, up until the 1980s, only two wards for sleeping) and staff eating together as a group of 600 people....	The key concept (batch living) is brought into relationship with the organization of the argument (first factor) defined through relational Processes Evidence of the abstract concept of batch living is provided through specific material details and concrete events
Position *(the overall stance/point of view)*	In sum, there is considerable evidence that the four factors associated with a total institution apply to Lennox Castle. ...	Absence of modality makes the proposition less arguable and more categorical The evidence is evaluated as *considerable*

Figure 3.4 Extracts from argument genre with key linguistic features.

3.3.3.2 Phases

While it is highly likely that the stages of a genre (such as those illustrated above) are instantiated in specific texts, there are smaller elements within any genre instantiation that are much less predictable and stable (i.e., they may or may not occur). These smaller substages or stretches of meaning, which can occur within any stage and often reoccur across a text, are referred to as *phases* by Martin and Rose (2007). Elsewhere they have been variously referred to as *text patterns* (Hoey, 1995) or *discourse phases* (Malcolm, 2010).

Some of the phases that we have found are common to texts produced by tertiary learners are: background; naming (e.g., *This is mise-en-scene*); defining concepts/terms, exemplifying concepts/terms, relating concepts, framing (classifying particular details by generalizing or abstracting), claim, and evidence/support.

The following extract, from a student named Seb's assignment, illustrates a defining phase:

> A total institution, according to the sociologist Goffman, is "a place of residence and work where a large number of like-situated individuals, cut off from the wider society for an appreciable period of time, together lead an enclosed, formally administered round of life" . . . .

3.3.3.2 Embedded Genres

In some cases, stages or phases may comprise elemental genres. That is, as students move into tertiary learning environments and the texts that they need to read and write inevitably lengthen and become more complex, elemental genres may be subsumed into a text and function at the level of phase. As such, they are referred to as *embedded genres* in that they have been *rankshifted* from operating at one level (whole text) to operating at another level (a component of a text). For example, a discussion genre is made up of the following stages:

> Issue ^ Argument* ^ Position

Within the Argument stages (typically comprising phases of claim and support/evidence), embedded recounts or explanations may function as support/evidence (see, e.g., Coffin, 2006; Woodward-Kron, 2005). When embedded as a stage or phase in a text, elemental genres are much more highly compressed than when functioning independently and are therefore sometimes referred to as mini or micro genres. The following extract from the earlier Wal-Mart discussion genre provides an illustration of an embedded factorial explanation that supports one of the writer's arguments. In this extract the writer argues that one of the benefits of an international takeover is cost reduction. She sets out three factors (in an embedded factorial explanation) explaining why this is the case.

Argument		Reduction in costs is another main reason for businesses to go multinational.
Embedded factorial explanation	*Factor 1*	By outsourcing their operations overseas businesses could be able to reduce their labour or transport costs.
	Factor 2	The avoidance of tariffs, when locating operations behind the "tariff walls," could contribute to businesses' competitive advantage over their rivals (Sloman et al., 1998, cited in Suneja, 2000).
	Factor 3	MNCs could also benefit from attitudes of host governments, when the country is trying to attract inward investments by "granting favourable tax differentials, depreciation allowances, and the provision of premises" (Sloman et al., 1998, cited in Suneja, 2000). For instance, the UK Government seeks to attract inward investment to depressed regions, where unemployment is high, e.g., South West (Suneja, 2000).

3.3.4 Macrogenres

Whereas early SFL genre analysis in primary and secondary school contexts tended to focus on single, clearly bounded genres, later research took an interest in accounting for how genres can combine to realize larger genres or, in Martin and Rose's (2008) terms, macrogenres. Unlike the case of embedding, however (where an elemental genre functions as a generic stage or phase and operates at a lower level, that is, is rankshifted), in a macrogenre, elemental genres combine on a more equal footing. Thus, if we return to the set of genres identified in HSC and set out in Figure 3.3, a macrogenre within that discipline area might typically comprise a classification report followed by a consequential explanation. The following assignment task, for example, prompts such a combination. While the first part calls for a classification of environments into enabling and disabling environments and a description of what each is (classification report), the second part asks for the kinds of alterations that can be made to such environments that have consequences for individuals' care and independence (consequential explanation).

> Explain what is meant by the term enabling and disabling environments. Give examples of how environments can be altered to give individuals receiving care more independence and choice.

More recently, the structuring or architecture of genres within genres (embedded genres) and genres combining with genres (macrogenres) has been extended by Humphreys (in her work on youth activist campaigns) to include *supra* and *mega* genres (see Humphreys, 2008). In particular, Humphreys considers the complex interactions of elemental genres within these larger genre structures or complexes. Blackwell (2011), in his research into university lectures, has also explored ways of extending SFL genre theory in order to account for the complexity and depth of structuring in university lectures and has also explored the potential for digression and nonlinear sequencing.

3.3.5 Genre and learning

In tertiary learning it is important to consider the degree of variation that occurs in students' instantiations of genres and in their combinations of these to form macrogenres. Thus, we would argue that it is important to teach or provide learners with prototypical genres in the foundational years of schooling and, as they move through secondary and tertiary education to continue to provide them with generalized, systematic guidelines as to how to create effective texts in line with disciplinary and teaching and learning purposes. However, it is also important to recognize that, particularly in tertiary learning, each student will create their own individual text and that teachers will often expect and allow for a certain amount of variation. The degree of variation may, however, vary with disciplines and departments as well as with individual teachers and depend on the genre in question.

There may also be variation in the kinds of genres students are expected to produce at different points in their study, with a tendency for increasing complexity as students move through their degree or move from undergraduate to postgraduate study. By complexity, we mean the way in which certain genres assume and subsume others. Argument genres, for example, often have embedded within them classification/taxonomic reports, recounts, and explanations, as mentioned earlier. Research reports and theses (usually undertaken in the final year of an undergraduate degree or at the postgraduate level) also require an assembly of genres in the form of a macrogenre. We refer to these kinds of increasing complexity in genre construction as *genre learning trajectories* (see Coffin, 2006, on this trajectory in the context of school history).

Fundamentally, genre learning trajectories reference the movement in complexity from interpreting the world in essentially descriptive terms (how the world is) or narrative terms (what happened) to recognizing the relativity of such interpretations. In other words, the genre learning trajectory is a shift from expressions of *categorical* meaning in reports, recounts, and explanations (i.e., meanings which are presented as nondebatable) toward *perspectival* meaning (i.e., meanings presented as points of view and hence debatable) in argument genres (as exemplified in Seb's discussion, excerpted above, as to whether Lennox Castle Hospital could be termed a "total institution"). Linguistically, argument and discussion genres typically comprise embedded reports, recounts, and/or explanations and thus assume capacity to construct these. By tracking the assignment tasks of students (in terms of genre complexity/difficulty) within and across each level of university, genre can therefore be used as a tool for mapping learning development.

3.4 Choices in Lexicogrammar: Social Context and the Concept of Register

Whereas genre is a way of theorizing the relationship between a writer or speaker's purposes and text structure, register serves to theorize the relationship between other aspects of context and lexicogrammar. In this section, we consider how register provides further insight into meaning making and reflect on its usefulness as an analytical and conceptual tool in relation to teaching and learning.

In Section 3.2 above we saw that, in response to the same assignment task, two students (Alena and Svetla) made different lexicogrammatical choices in their assignment introductions. We argued that different clusters of linguistic choices reveal a different orientation to meaning making (semantic orientation) that can be explained in part by differences in the way that teachers and students interpret and engage with their institutional and academic (i.e., social) context, in turn influenced by their experience of academic teaching or learning.

In SFL, three aspects of the social context are seen to have particular significance for the process of meaning making (see Figure 3.5):

(a) the subject matter or topic that is the focus of social activity;
(b) the social roles and relationships between the participants in the interaction; and
(c) the channel (e.g., computer mediated) and type of communication (e.g., print-based dialogue), including the degree of interactivity and spontaneity, and the role of language in relation to other semiotic resources.

Following SFL theory, the three aspects of social context (the contextual variables) are in part created through language and in part shape language use. We saw this earlier with the example of assessment feedback whereby different

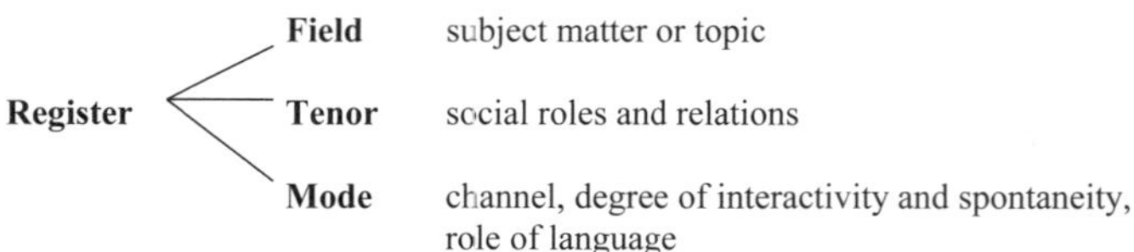

Figure 3.5 The register variables.

choices in language construe different constructions of teacher and student roles and different kinds of teacher-student relations:

Can you present your argument more clearly?

Next time present your argument more clearly.

Alternative expressions could suggest and create different relationships and types of communication. Thus, the feedback

Hey C, can u make yr arg. a bit clearer? I don't really get wot u r on about ☹

would construe a friendlier, peer-to-peer style of relationship and suggest a different channel and type of communication (possibly e-mail/text, more spontaneous, more interactive).

These brief examples provide evidence of how our social and, thus, teaching and learning contexts and realities are, in part, linguistically created. To understand in greater depth the relationship between contextual variables and language, we will examine in turn (in Sections 3.4.1–3.4.3) the three variables that collectively make up register, referred to as *field, tenor,* and *mode* as set out in Figure 3.5. It is important to emphasize here that field, tenor, and mode reference only those aspects of context that are of linguistic relevance. That is, register does not aim to comprehensively reference all material and nonmaterial details of a social situation. Rather, as a theoretical construct, it aims to identify only those aspects of a complex social reality that are intrinsically intertwined with the evolution of language and its meaning-making processes, or *metafunctions*. By using the term metafunction, SFL draws attention to the three overarching functions of language: the *ideational, interpersonal,* and *textual* metafunctions. These metafunctions, it posits, are integral to language and are aligned to the three register variables.

In sum, register serves as a kind of linguistic lens on social context.

3.4.1 Field—Making Meanings to Represent the World

Field refers to the intersection between the subject matter or topic of a social activity and ideational meaning making (or the ideational metafunction) as realized through particular linguistic systems and resources. It thus links to how we think about, and create links (logical or causal) between, people, places, and events, as well as abstract concepts; in other words, how we represent the world. In academic disciplines and tertiary learning contexts, language (and in some cases other semiotic resources) serves to specify the nature of the relationship of one entity to another within complex conceptual networks and discipline-based *taxonomies* (what we refer to in this monograph as *conceptual formations*).

3.4.1.1 Moving Between Contextualized and Decontextualized Meanings: Conceptual Formations, Taxonomies, and General-to-specific Language

In higher education, the abstract concepts and technical and specialized terms of different fields of study—the conceptual formations—play a core role in building, classifying, and framing academic knowledge. Using language to configure (or reconfigure) relationships between abstract general phenomena and concrete specific phenomena, as well as between abstract entities, is central to the learning and meaning-making processes that students are expected to engage with in tertiary study. As discussed in Chapter 2, the movement from contextualized knowledge and language to decontextualized knowledge and language is the means by which students learn to perceive and think about natural or social phenomena in radically new ways. Unsurprisingly, it is a shift that may be challenging to some students, destabilizing their existing semantic orientations. Recall James's words (the student voice introduced in Chapter 2):

> I prefer layman's terms. I don't agree with the, you know, using big massive jargon. You walk into someone and speak to them about personalization they ain't got a clue what you're talking about.

We glimpsed something of the linguistic process of students moving between more contextualized and more decontextualized discourse when we examined Svetla's assignment and saw how she brought into relationship the more abstract concept of a *large multinational corporation* with the more concrete example of *Wal-Mart*. Such a process of relating abstract entities to specific examples—the move from general to particular—is commonplace, but also central, in academic knowledge building. Svetla wrote:

> A multinational corporation (MNC) is a company that owns or controls subsidiaries in more than one country (Suneja, 2000). Wal-Mart, a US-based company and its largest retailer, is an example of a large MNC

with foreign subsidiaries in ten countries and a turnover of 2% of US GDP.

Further extracts from Svetla's assignment exemplify how, in general, many of the entities she discusses are abstract concepts that form part of business specific taxonomies. In the following extract, technical business terms are used to classify two types of buying overseas companies.

> One of the benefits of acquisitions is risk-spreading (Sloman et al., 1998, cited in Suneja, 2000). At the beginning of 1990s and throughout the decade the company was expanding into Mexico and Canada, mainly using combination of buy-outs and joint ventures.

Taxonomies and conceptual networks can be usefully mapped in the form of diagrams (though interestingly, in comparison with the sciences, this does not seem to be exploited in social science and arts textbooks or lectures as much as it could be). Figure 3.6 maps a "type of" relationship between *buy-outs* and *joint ventures* and the superordinate (*acquisition of assets*). It is a *classification taxonomy*.

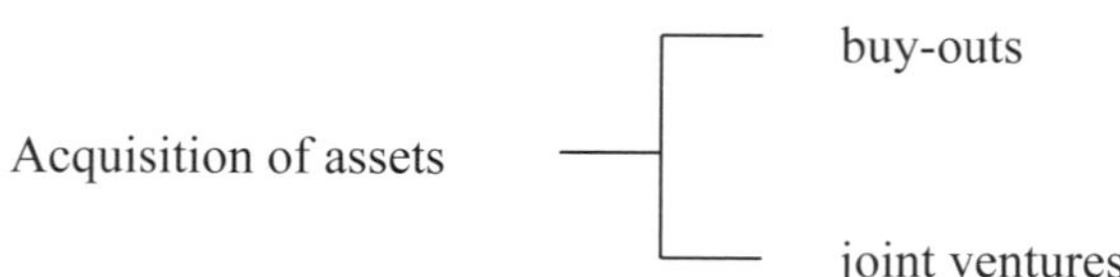

Figure 3.6 Classification taxonomy.

Figure 3.7 is a further example of how a taxonomy, this time from the discipline of Film Studies (overleaf/pg. 61), can be displayed in diagram form. This taxonomy shows a *compositional* relationship: costume, settings, and so on are all components of *mise-en-scene* (a term meaning "visual design of a film"). It is important to note that the terms used within the taxonomy (e.g., *costume*, *props*) are technical terms in that they are used differently in the context of film than in other contexts.

Whereas the term taxonomy refers to relationships between entities of the classification or compositional type, in this monograph we are using *conceptual formation* as an umbrella term to refer to all kinds of relationships that exist between entities and that form constellations of concepts (there is much overlap with Lemke's [1985, 1990] work on thematic formations and social action semiotics). As Chapter 4 will show, conceptual formations are constructed

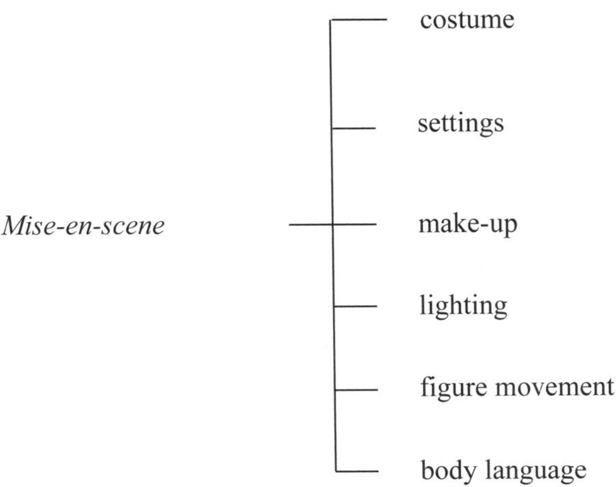

Figure 3.7 Composition taxonomy.

through continuous engagement with concepts and concept relations across multiple texts.

3.4.1.2 Key Resources for Building Ideational Meaning: Participants, Processes, and Circumstances

In order to identify and classify the language resources that have evolved for enabling us to build ideational meaning, SFL takes a functional, rather than structural, perspective and uses functional categories (e.g., Participant, Process) rather than traditional class ones (i.e., noun, verb, etc.). Furthermore, taking a system ("meaning as choice") perspective, it sets out the different options in relation to each language resource. (Note that the metaphor of resource is used in order to emphasize the meaning-making function of language.) We will look at these different options in the following subsection.

At the clause level, SFL categorizes the language resources for building field into three main elements: *Participants, Processes,* and *Circumstances*. Each of these offers a system of choices.

Participants

Participant is the general label referring to who or what is involved in the event or situation. Participant relates to the traditional grammatical terms of *subject* and *object,* though there is no neat overlap. Participants are underlined as follows:

> One of the benefits of acquisitions is risk-spreading (Sloman et al., 1998, cited in Suneja, 2000). At the beginning of 1990s and throughout the decade[6] the company was expanding into Mexico and Canada, mainly using a combination of buy-outs and joint ventures.

Participants can be distinguished as human or nonhuman, general or specific, abstract or concrete.

All the four Participants above are nonhuman and, aside from *the company*, are also general and abstract. The choice of abstract and general Participants is a feature of academic knowledge building and learning. That is, Participants are often encoded or *realized* by nominal (noun) groups which, as in the examples above, are frequently dense packages of information whereby the head noun, often an abstract concept (in this case *benefit*), is elaborated or modified through *pre* and *post modification*, itself often abstract. Thus *benefits* is premodified by the phrase *one of the* and postmodified by *of acquisitions*: *One of the benefits of acquisitions*.

Part of the abstraction of a nominal group such as *One of the benefits of acquisitions* is the fact that the head noun is often the result of packaging into noun form what would be more naturally or *congruently* expressed as a verb, as in *acquisitions can **benefit** companies*. This process of verbs (or indeed, adjectives or adverbs) being turned into nouns is referred to as *nominalization*. In this particular nominal group, the postmodification of benefits, *acquisitions*, is a further example of nominalization. More straightforwardly, Svetla could have chosen to write:

> When a multinational company buys another company this benefits the multinational because it spreads risk.

The question thus raised is *why* does Svetla, or indeed anyone involved in academic knowledge building, choose to compress and abstract meaning in this way? One response could be to mystify the ordinary person, to exclude them from the academic club. This has resonance with James's interpretation (the student introduced in Chapter 2 and mentioned in 3.4.1.1): "I prefer layman's terms. I don't agree with the, you know, using big massive jargon."

One of the functional motivations for packaging reality into abstract nominal groups, however, is so that, as things, they can more easily be brought into relationships with one another as part of a technical taxonomy or conceptual formation. As we have already discussed, these are fundamental to building theoretical knowledge (indeed, this chapter and monograph exemplify such a process!). Thus Svetla is able to bring in and relate *acquisitions* to the concept of risk (*risk-spreading*) and later to different types of acquisition (*joint ventures, buy-outs*).

Processes

The other main system for building ideational meanings at the clause level is that of Process. The Process is the action, event, or relationship presented in a clause and in this sense is the hub around which other information clusters. Typically, Processes are expressed by verbal groups. Processes vary in function. For example, they make it possible to identify and classify:

> A multinational corporation (MNC) <u>is</u> a company that owns or controls subsidiaries in more than one country

Equally, they can represent material activity:

> During that period Wal-Mart <u>acquired</u> foreign assets in Brazil

Table 3.4 sets out the main options in Processes. It also sets out the associated Participants. Thus, aside from choice of Participant as human or nonhuman, abstract or concrete, and general or specific, SFL conceptualization allows us to see with greater specificity the Participant roles that accompany Process choices.

Circumstances

The third clause-level resource for building ideational meaning is Circumstance. This resource provides additional information about a process or event, such as where, when, or why it occurred. Circumstances are more peripheral elements in the functional makeup of a clause in that they are often not essential to an understanding of what is occurring. In academic meaning making, however, they play an important role in the overall framing and/or specification of the event under discussion. As we have already seen in Alena's assignment, they may provide a temporal or spatial setting and are typically realized through prepositional phrases:

> <u>On 26 July 1999</u> Wal-Mart acquired a UK-based supermarket chain Asda
> (Circumstance of time)

> <u>In this assignment</u> I will critically look on the benefits and the costs of the
> (Circumstance of location)
> US-based multinational corporation

Table 3.4 Processes and Associated Central Participants

Processes	Main Participants	Example
Material (action, doing)	Actor Goal	**Wal-Mart** acquired **foreign assets.** (Actor) (Goal)
Mental (thinking, knowing, feeling, desiring)	Senser Phenomenon	**Wal-Mart** did not understand **local culture** (Senser) (Phenomenon)
Verbal	Sayer Receiver	**Sloman et al.** argue that an important benefit of (Sayer) expanding overseas . . .
Existential (there is, there are)	Existent	There is **no information in the case study** (Existent)
Relational (having, being)	Carrier Attribute Identified Identifier	In the U.K. **the workforce** is relatively **highly skilled** (Carrier) (Attribute) **The sequence after that** is **the sequence of the** (Identified) (Identifier) **manager and Cage's friend talking about his bad leg**

3.4.1.3 Recap

We use the word metafunction to refer to the ideational, interpersonal, and textual meanings. Figure 3.8 summarizes the register–metafunction–language connections from the perspective of field. By analyzing how different academic fields of study use language to make ideational meaning, we can make more visible the distinct ways in which academics theorize and in so doing create or discover new realities. Equally importantly, we can see how semantic variation in student cohorts may lead to students orienting in different ways to such representations. In our example texts from Business Studies, for example, we saw how Alena, in her introduction, used relational Processes to define and classify the entities (e.g., multinationals) under discussion and thus show she was engaging with the conceptual formation of the fields. Svetla oriented more to the concrete actions of what the company Wal-Mart *did.*

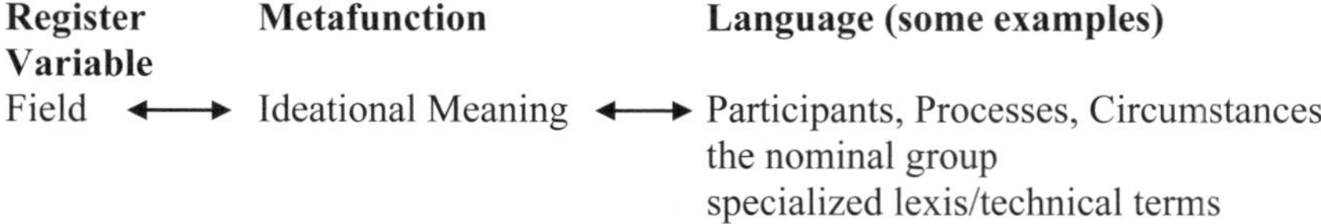

Figure 3.8 Field-ideational metafunction-language relationship.

3.4.2 Tenor—Making Meanings to Position Oneself and Interact With Others

Tenor references the point of connection between interactants' social roles and relationships and *interpersonal* meaning-making processes (the interpersonal metafunction), as realized through particular linguistic systems and resources. In higher education, students and teachers are constantly negotiating their positions, points of view, and relationships in both spoken contexts (e.g., seminars and tutorials) and written contexts (e.g., assignments and textbooks). Social media such as discussion forums are an increasingly common "third space" (i.e., somewhere between traditional spoken and written contexts) in which this occurs.

Interpersonal meanings and tenor both shape and are shaped by language choices. That is, language can be an index of how well a student and teacher know each other and how much contact they have (their material reality), but language can also function to create a sense of closer or more distanced relations that may have little bearing on the actual material reality. Thus, language may serve to delineate the roles and relative statuses of teacher/assessor and student/assessed and create a clear social hierarchy, or it may serve to blur the lines. The following two samples of teacher–student feedback illustrate this. In both cases, the students were learning at a distance and therefore the teacher's amount and frequency of contact was similar. However, one teacher's (Hussein) choice of language creates a friendly, peer-like relationship with his student, Sally, whereas the other teacher's (Alison) response is more formal and generates greater social distance.

One obvious difference between the two teachers' responses is their use of vocatives and sign-offs. Hussein's student is directly addressed by name while Alison's is not. Whereas Hussein's sign-off is the more informal *with best wishes*, Alison uses the more formal *regards*. Another difference is their use of more informal or formal lexis, for example, Hussein's choice of the colloquial phrasal verb *get in touch* compared to Alison's more formal choice of *contact me*. We shall explore other interpersonal language systems in the sections below.

Hussein's feedback

Your findings are very interesting indeed and you have made an excellent attempt to analyze these findings and integrate your references into your assignment which demonstrated both excellent understanding and use of course material.

Well done Sally—a lovely assignment! I look forward to your final assignment in a few weeks time but in the meantime please get in touch if you would like to discuss any aspect of this assignment.

with best wishes

Hussein

Alison's feedback

I decided to give you a grade 2 pass because you demonstrated good knowledge with some good research into your chosen community. The structure was good, clear and coherent with good use of course material and other sources of information to support your argument, also good use of appendices.

Overall this was a very good assignment. Please contact me for any further assistance. The next online tutorial will be around 24th July and the face to face is on the 17th Sept.

Regards Alison

3.4.2.1 Questions, Statements, and Commands

A fundamental language system for making interpersonal meaning is that of mood. The MOOD[7] system, which provides choices in declarative, interrogative, or imperative mood, makes it possible to ask questions, issue commands, or make statements. Significantly, we have already seen that mood choices are not necessarily in a one-to-one relationship with speech function. In our earlier example of assessment feedback (Section 3.2), three different mood choices all functioned to request a student to do something different in their next assignment and in this sense all three issued a command. However, whereas C is a straightforward, congruent expression (or realization) of a command (i.e., imperative mode) A and B are more indirect:

A. You need to present your argument more clearly.
B. Can you present your argument more clearly?
C. Next time present your argument more clearly.

In cases where there is no straightforward relationship between mood and speech function, the term "interpersonal metaphor" is used. Interpersonal metaphor is frequently used to play down and minimize social status differences, as exemplified in A and B above.

3.4.2.2 Positioning Oneself: Appraising Phenomena

In contemporary higher education contexts, the process of projecting one's role(s), status, and identity, particularly in written form, is complex. One complexity is that students may have frequent contact with their teachers and, in a context of increasing informalization in student–teacher relations, at least in the West, there may be few discernible signs of power or status difference in everyday oral interactions (such as seminars, chance encounters, etc.). However, in written assignments, the expectation remains that students will erase all signs of a familiar, known audience and, in some disciplines and/or departments, all signs of a subjective, personal self (by not using, for example, the personal pronoun *I*).

Another complexity is that although in reality students are less expert and have less status (for the most part) than their teachers, in their written assignments they are usually expected to adopt an authoritative position. At the same time, this position needs to be located in relation to views circulating within the wider academic community (both supporting and opposing views). Argumentation, whereby the teacher/assessor is persuaded to accept a student's line of reasoning and their appraisal of phenomena is critical, particularly in the arts and social sciences.

APPRAISAL[8] (Martin & White, 2005) is the main system of interpersonal language resources. It enables people to color ideational meanings; to align themselves with particular perspectives and values; and to engage in a process of negotiation in relation to these. APPRAISAL resources make it possible to open up propositions for debate and negotiation or, conversely, close debate down (using the resources of the *ENGAGEMENT* subsystem; see Figure 3.9). Compare the following two extracts, for example. The first (student) version is taken from a student's conclusion to the Business Studies assignment task discussed in Section 3.2:

> (student version) Asda Wal-Mart a MNC has positioned themselves in a very strong place and I can see their business to continue to grow they proven they can be adaptable, fast to react to economic changes and they understand the root of their business . . . .I only wish there were more companies that operated with these values.

(our rewritten version)

Asda Wal-Mart a MNC has positioned themselves in a very strong place and their business will continue to grow. They have proven they are adaptable, fast to react to economic changes and they understand the root of their business. More companies need to operate with these values.

The object of evaluation (Asda Wal-Mart) is appraised in the same way across the two versions: *very strong, adaptable, fast to react* (all positive *JUDGMENTS* within the *ATTITUDE* subsystem). There is a difference, nevertheless, in the way the JUDGMENTS in the first version are opened up to alternative positions (through the use of the modal *can*: *I* ***can*** *see their business to continue to grow, they* **can** *be adaptable*). Note, too, the highly subjective clause in the first version:

I only wish there were more companies that operated with these values.

This explicit subjective expression of irrealis (i.e., future oriented) AFFECT (*I only wish*) is absent in the rewritten version, contributing to an assumed alignment between writer and reader:

More companies need to operate with these values.

Figure 3.9 sets out the APPRAISAL systems showing how language users have choice in terms of how they appraise, grade, and give value to social experience. Thus, within the ATTITUDE subsystem, AFFECT comprises a set of language resources for appraising experience in affective terms, for indicating the emotional effect of an event. For example (AFFECT resources in bold):

Really **glad** to see someone making this point about the poverty problems in our own country.

I **look forward to** your final assignment.

The subsystem of JUDGMENT also encompasses meanings that serve to appraise human behavior, but unlike AFFECT, does this by reference to a set of institutionalized norms about how people should and should not behave. For example (JUDGMENT resource in bold):

. . . which demonstrated **excellent** understanding and use of course material.

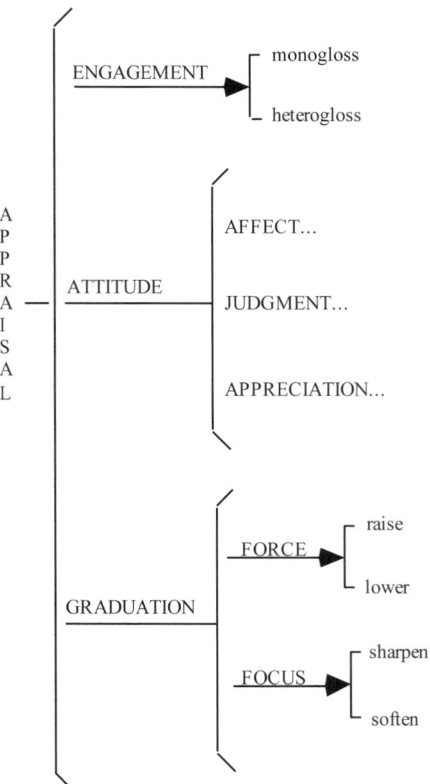

Figure 3.9 An outline of APPRAISAL resources in English (after Martin 2000).

The third subsystem of ATTITUDE, APPRECIATION, comprises language resources for valuing processes and products rather than behavior (APPRECIATION resources in bold):

The structure was **good**, **clear** and **coherent**.

GRADUATION comprises a set of resources for grading evaluations—"turning the volume up or down." These may be isolated "intensifiers" such as *very, really, slightly, a bit, somewhat, quite,* or may be fused into the experiential values of a word. For example:

Overall this was a **very** good assignment (GRADUATION: *FORCE*)

You made an **excellent** (=very good. GRADUATION: FORCE – *FUSED*) attempt

(note that there are two subsystems of GRADUATION but in this book we will only be focusing on FORCE)

Finally, ENGAGEMENT is a set of resources that enable a writer (or speaker) to either take up a position whereby their audience is construed as sharing the same, single worldview (MONOGLOSS) or, on the other hand, adopt a stance that explicitly acknowledges diversity with its implication for conflict and struggle among diverse voices (HETEROGLOSS). In terms of grammatical realization, the two systems, MONOGLOSS and HETEROGLOSS, draw on different resources. With reference to MONOGLOSS, the central grammatical structure that serves to background potential diversity of opinion is the positive declarative. For example:

> They have proven they are adaptable, fast to react to economic changes, and they understand the root of their business.

Such a structure encourages a reader to assume that the proposition is unproblematic and that it enjoys broad consensus. Thus, even though a writer's and reader's worldview may not be a shared one, the grammatical structure implicitly encourages alignment rather than directly opening up the proposition for negotiation.

The primary resource of HETEROGLOSS, *modality*, in contrast, signals that meaning is contingent and subject to negotiation (modality underlined in example):

> It seems to me that they have proven they are adaptable, fast to react to economic changes and they understand the root of their business.

Modality resources include *modal finites* (e.g., *can, may, might,* etc.), *modal adjuncts* (e.g., *possibly, probably*), and other phrases (e.g. *it seems, I think)* and serves to introduce explicit negotiability into a proposition. Hence, unlike the positive declarative, modalized propositions do not assume or simulate solidarity between writer and reader.

Another central resource for expressing HETEROGLOSS is the attribution of views and judgments to voices other than those of the writer, either by quoting or reporting (EXTRAVOCALIZE). This is central to academic knowledge building (see Coffin, 2010). For example, note the use of HETEROGLOSS in the following citations:

> CEO Andy Bond at the time admitted to the business becoming "drunk on its own success" (B200 TMA07, 2008, page 52). (EXTRAVOCALIZE: quoting)

> When domestic markets become saturated and sales growth slows, some companies look for new opportunities and new markets overseas (Sloman et al., 1998, cited in Suneja, 2000). (EXTRAVOCALIZE: reporting)

3.4.2.3 Recap

This section has provided an overview of the relationship between the contextual variable of tenor and the systems of language that are drawn on to make interpersonal meaning. This relationship is summarized in Figure 3.10. By analyzing the interpersonal dimension of academic meaning making, we can make more visible the ways in which academics and students develop and exchange points of view and perspectives on phenomena and position themselves in relation to each other and to alternative standpoints. The evaluative aspect of academic meaning making is often marginalized in subject teaching, where the focus is primarily ideational.

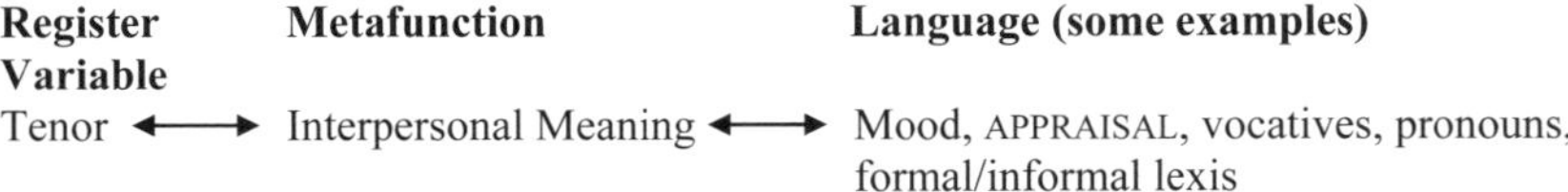

Figure 3.10 Tenor-interpersonal metafunction-language relationship.

3.4.3 Mode—Organizing Meanings: Previewing, Reviewing and Creating Cohesion

Mode refers to the point of connection between textual meaning making (the textual metafunction) and the channel and type of communication (i.e., how interactive and spontaneous it is, and the role of language in relation to other semiotic resources). For example, a spoken, casual face-to-face encounter usually correlates with high interactivity and spontaneity. Furthermore, the speaker and listener are close to each other and are often concerned with "here and now" situations. Gestures, facial expressions, and shared observations do a great amount of work in communicating meanings. In contrast, a formal academic writing situation usually correlates with less spontaneity and often limited (verbalized) interactivity (with usually just one set of final feedback comments from the teacher). In this situation there is usually time for planning and editing texts and for critically reflecting on information and ideas, and as a result, the language often shows high levels of compression and synthesis.

Mode refers to the way language shapes and organizes ideational and interpersonal meanings and at the same time itself is shaped by the channel of communication and degrees of interactivity and spontaneity. Key language systems and resources relating to mode are those of Theme, nominalization and cohesion.

3.4.3.1 The Mode Continuum

Many higher education teaching and learning situations sit somewhere between casual spoken encounters and formal academic reading and writing tasks, with seminars, lectures, online discussions, and email interaction falling at different points along what is often referred to as the mode continuum. Figure 3.11 illustrates this continuum. At one end language accompanies hands-on activity (language as action), whereas at the other end it is largely constitutive of the social activity (language as reflection). Between these two poles, moving from left to right, the different activities rely increasingly on language rather than physical action to make meaning and, in general, levels of spontaneity and the speed and frequency of interactivity diminish. In general, language as action correlates with contextualized language use while language as reflection correlates with decontextualized, abstract language use (as discussed in Chapter 2).

Language as ACTION **Spontaneous Speech**					Language as REFLECTION **Academic Writing**
e.g., language used by students during scientific experiment	face-to-face seminar discussion	email interaction	asynchronous online discussion forum	formal lecture	formal academic texts and assignment

Figure 3.11 The mode continuum in academic settings.

3.4.3.2 The Role of Language in Relation to Other Semiotic Resources

Mode is concerned with the role that language plays in a text and whether it does all the work or, alternatively, interacts with other semiotic resources (such as gestures, facial expressions, and visual images). Increasingly, in many higher education teaching and learning contexts, as we have mentioned elsewhere, a wide range of nonlinguistic meaning-making resources are being deployed; for example, diagrams, still and moving visuals, and various graphic resources including the use of color and font. As discussed in Chapter 1, multimodal meaning making is not a focus of this monograph. However, its role in learning contexts as students ever more integrate a range of visual and aural resources into their academic meaning making needs to be acknowledged (Coffin & Derewianka, 2008, Unsworth, 2011).

3.4.3.3 Organizing Meaning—Theme-New Patterns and Thematic Development

Theme refers to the initial elements in a text, section of text, or clause. These initial elements make it possible to set up and frame a text. In combination, patterns of Theme in a text, or its *thematic development*, contribute to the overall flow of meaning making.

MacroTheme

In Section 3.2 we saw how Alena and Svetla used the opening paragraph of their written assignment (a discussion genre) to set out their overall aim (also reproduced below): to critically discuss the costs and benefits of Asda's merger with Wal-Mart. Svetla also previewed other elements she would cover in her assignment, including (a) a history of Wal-Mart and its expansion into other countries and (b) the reasons for becoming a multinational company. Alena, on the other hand, used her introduction to set out and define a key category for her discussion, *multinational corporation,* as well as to give a very brief overview of Wal-Mart and Asda, the entities her assignment would focus on as requested by the assessment task, which read:

> Wal-Mart is a U.S.-based multinational corporation. Critically discuss the likely costs and benefits of its takeover of Asda, a UK-based company.
>
> **Svetla's introduction**
>
> In this assignment I will critically look on the benefits and the costs of the US-based multinational corporation which overtook a UK-based company. At the beginning I will discuss a history of the Wal-Mart, US company and it's expand into the other countries as well as why companies and businesses which go multinational.
>
> **Alena's introduction**
>
> A multinational corporation (MNC) is a company that owns or controls subsidiaries in more than one country (Suneja, 2000). Wal-Mart, a US-based company and its largest retailer, is an example of a large MNC with foreign subsidiaries in ten countries and a turnover of 2% of US GDP. On 26 July 1999 Wal-Mart acquired a UK-based supermarket chain Asda, with its 229 stores located mainly in the south of England. The following essay represents a critical discussion of the likely costs and benefits of the merger.

In written academic texts at the *language as reflection* (literate) end of the mode continuum, opening sections potentially play an important role in providing the overarching, higher order message of the text. In SFL these are referred to as *macroThemes*. By highlighting the key ideas, areas, or arguments that the writer or speaker will go on to elaborate, they assist the writer in organizing the hierarchy of concepts they will use in their assignment and equally assist the reader in making sense of the ensuing text. From the perspective of a student writer, constructing a macroTheme can help them to focus on the direction of what will follow and thus develop their textual meaning making (i.e., the shaping of ideational and interpersonal meanings). Of course, it may be the case that the student uses a macroTheme to initially predict what she or he will write, but then refines it in a later draft once the meanings in the ensuing text have settled.

HyperTheme

At the level of paragraph or text section, writers may make use of the initial sentence to scaffold their meaning making in a similar way to the initial paragraph. This initial element at paragraph or section level, where it occurs, is referred to as *hyperTheme*. Like macroThemes, hyperThemes provide an orientation as to what is to come and thus contribute to developing the writer–reader relationship: they establish expectations about how the text or paragraph will unfold.

Thus in the following paragraph (from the Business Studies assignment) the underlined hyperTheme functions to introduce the benefits of Wal-Mart's take-over of Asda. The student thus links back to the assignment task as well as previewing the precise benefits they will elaborate on, namely, balance of payments, employment, and taxation.

> <u>To the UK government and economy, benefits are represented in employment rate, the balance of payments and taxation.</u> Wal-Mart directly invested in the UK to support Asda Wal-Mart became the second biggest supermarket in the UK by 2005. Its operation brought a direct flow of capital into the UK. After Wal-Mart entered into the UK, the organisation employed staff with the new stores opening. It reduced unemployment rate in the UK, the host government got benefit from Asda Wal-Mart's growth. As the one of the biggest supermarket chain in the UK, Asda paid corporation tax to Inland Revenue in a high level each year, so the host state got large benefit from Asda's contribution.

Clause-level Theme

At the clause level, Theme can similarly be used to organize meaning. As with choices in macro and hyperThemes, the meanings we choose to highlight at the start of a clause are generally purposeful and functional. While in theory it is possible to almost randomly rearrange the chunks of meaning that make up an English clause (i.e., the Processes, Participants, and Circumstances) and still end up with something that makes some kind of sense, the coherence may be badly affected. In SFL, Theme is the technical term for the first element or departure point at the level of clause. Theme is formally defined as stretching as far as, and including, the first ideational element in a clause (i.e., the first Participant, Process, or Circumstance). For example, returning to Alena's and Svetla's introductions, which we have annotated to show clause-level Themes, we can see how they make different choices regarding the elements they foreground: their clause Themes. As discussed earlier, these choices underlie the two students' different orientations to meaning making (with Alena focusing primarily on abstract and business concepts and Svetla focusing initially on the academic writing task, as illustrated below, and subsequently on material entities).

Alena's introduction

A multinational corporation (MNC) is a company that owns or controls
(Theme = Abstract non human Participant)
subsidiaries in more than one country (Suneja, 2000).

Wal-Mart, a US-based company and its largest retailer, is an example of a
(Theme = Non human Participant)
large MNC with foreign subsidiaries in ten countries and a turnover of 2% of US GDP.

Svetla's introduction

In this assignment I will critically look on the benefits and the costs of the US- based
(Theme = Circumstance)
multinational corporation which overtook a UK-based company.

At the beginning I will discuss a history of the Wal-Mart, US company and it's expand
(Theme = Circumstance)
into the other countries as well as why companies and businesses which go multinational.

Clause-level New

In SFL, the concept of *New* complements that of Theme.[9] In effect, from clause to paragraph/section to whole text it answers the question, what is the news? Thus, taking one of the examples above, the New information (presented in italics) is as follows:

A multinational corporation (MNC) *is a company that owns or controls subsidiaries*
(Theme) *(New)*
in more than one country.

Wal-Mart, a US-based company and its largest retailer, *is an example of a large MNC*
(Theme) *(New)*
with foreign subsidiaries in ten countries and a turnover of 2% of US GDP

Although in this case Alena chose not to, a writer may pick up the New in one clause and use as a Theme in the next in order to aid cohesion between the meanings he/she is making and communicating. The following rewrite illustrates this:

> A multinational corporation (MNC) is a company that owns or controls subsidiaries in more than one country (Suneja, 2000). → *An example of a large MNC with foreign subsidiaries in ten countries* and a turnover of 2% of US GDP is Wal-Mart, a US-based company and its largest retailer.

Patterns of Theme and New are deployed to cohesively weave sentences together across a whole text.

HyperNew

Just as hyper- and macroTheme function to preview the forward direction of a text, *hyperNew* functions to review a section of a text and in so doing drive forward the main arguments or points of the text, as illustrated in the underlined clause below:

> To the UK government and economy, benefits are represented in employment rate, the balance of payments and taxation. Wal-Mart directly invested in the UK to support Asda Wal-Mart became the second biggest supermarket in the UK by 2005. Its operation brought a direct flow of capital into the UK. After Wal-Mart entered into the UK, the organisation employed staff with the new stores opening. It reduced

> unemployment rate in the UK, the host government got benefit from Asda Wal-Mart's growth. As the one of the biggest supermarket chain in the UK, Asda paid corporation tax to Inland Revenue in a high level each year, so the host state got large benefit from Asda's contribution.

MacroNew

Like hyperNew, *macroNew* also functions to review and gather up the main points but at the level of whole text. This is exemplified in the following assignment conclusion (the position stage of a discussion genre).

> In conclusion, the above analysis of the likely costs and benefits of the acquisition of Asda, a UK-based company, by Wal-Mart, a US-based multinational corporation, has revealed that the merger was quite beneficial for both parties. Given similar marketing techniques of the two companies, cultural and lingual similarities, it can be assumed that the takeover was a successful and smooth process in comparison with Wal-Mart's expansion into other countries. Some benefits for the host economy, like stimulation of local competition and creation of new jobs, were revealed.

In summary the combination of macro-, hyper-, and clause-level Theme and New serve as the infrastructure for the overall message or argument of a text. Figure 3.12 gives a schematic overview of the first and final section of an assignment responding to the assignment task discussed in this section. It shows how the macroTheme foreshadows the meanings picked up in hyperThemes 1 and 2; in other words, how they connect to the benefits part of the issue under discussion. HyperNews 1 and 2, on the other hand, pick up and reinforce the main point of the preceding paragraph. In turn they are gathered together in the macroNew.

3.4.3.4 Cohesion

In order to ensure meanings flow, the English language has developed a set of *lexical* and *grammatical cohesion* resources. These serve to link concepts and ideas (e.g., as part of a taxonomy or conceptual formation) as well as to track ideas.

Lexical cohesion

Both sense relations (such as those of similarity of meaning, or *synonymy,* and oppositeness of meaning, or *antonymy*) and *lexical repetition* bind texts together. Whereas lexical repetition is simply a matter of words repeating

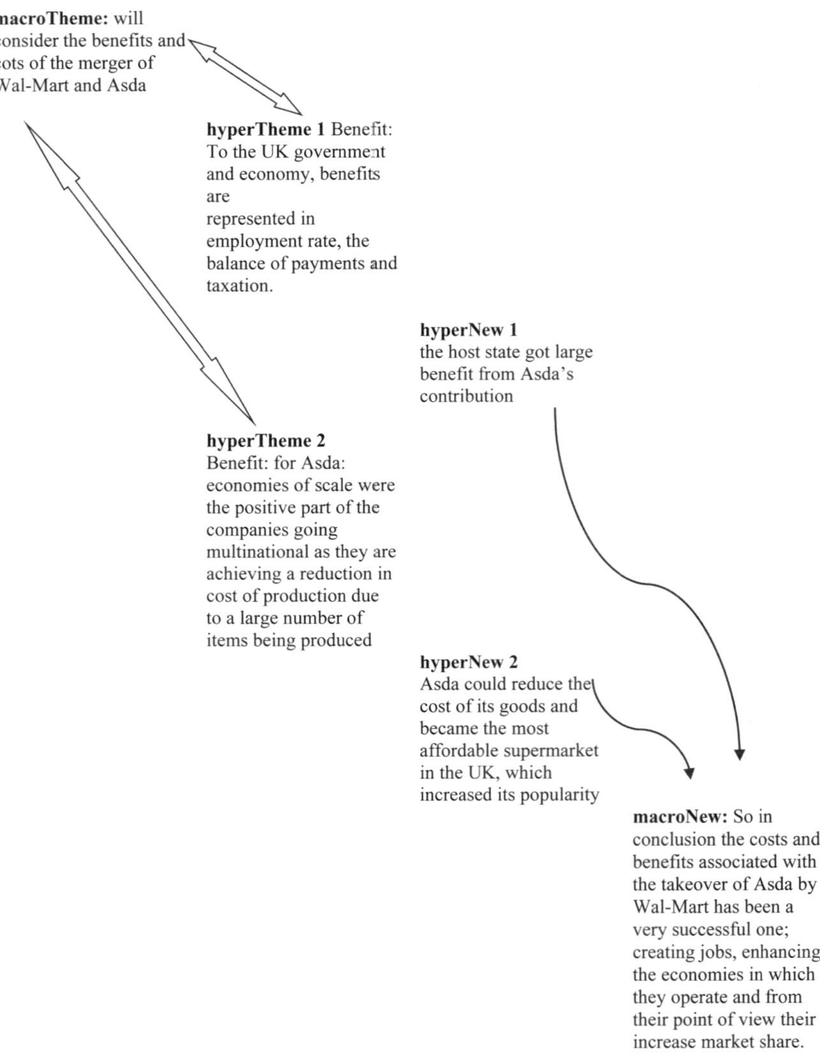

Figure 3.12 A skeletal overview of Theme-New structuring of discussion.

previous ones (though the repeated lexical item may be morphologically different, e.g., *acquire* rather than *acquisition*), the main types of sense relations referred to in this book are those of *meronymy*, which underpins compositional taxonomies, and *hyponomy*, which underpins classification taxonomies. *Collocation*, which is achieved through the association of lexical items that regularly co-occur, is also referred to. These different kinds of sense relations all contribute to the formation of conceptual formations (see Section 3.4.1.1).

Figure 3.13 shows the relation between subclass and class referred to as hyponymy, with *co-hyponymy* referring to the relation between the members of the same class. Figure 3.14 shows the relation between parts and whole referred to as meronymy, with *co-meronymy* referring to the relation between the different parts.

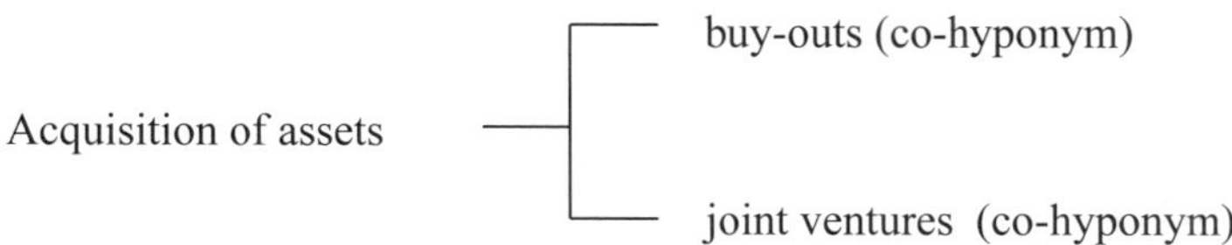

Figure 3.13 Hyponymy sense relations (class and subclass).

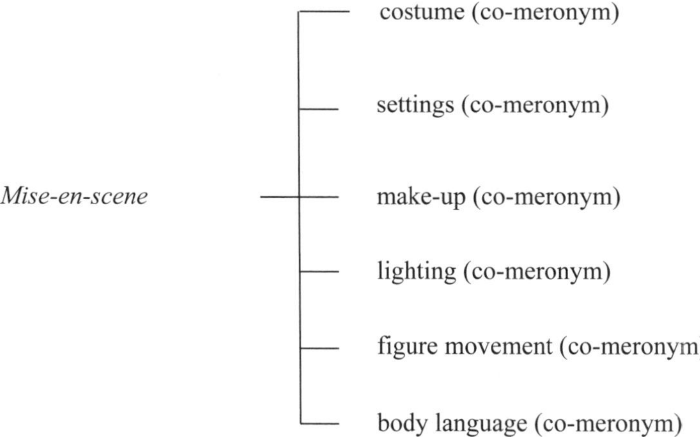

Figure 3.14 Meronymy sense relations (part-whole).

Grammatical cohesion: Reference

Reference words function to track elements across a text. Thus, the use of the reference word *this* in the second sentence below distills the sense of the previously stated problem of language barriers for multinationals and relates it to further problems concerning expansion into the developing world:

> The most common problems which facing multinational corporations are barriers regarding language. *This* can be a big problem if the company is expanding into the developing part of the world.

Table 3.5 Nominalization

Meaning	Congruent form	Nominalized form
event/process	verb, e.g., *to benefit, pay, contribute, grow*	*the benefit, payment, contribution, growth*
quality of object or event	adjective, e.g., *critical, similar*	*the critique, similarity*
	adverb, e.g., *critically, similarly*	
logical connector	conjunction, e.g., *because*	*cause, reason*
	connective, e.g., *therefore*	*consequence, result*

When reference words are used ambiguously or imprecisely, they may create or reflect ambiguity or imprecision in how ideas are being developed. For example, in the following text it is not clear what *this* (italicized in the text) is referring to:

> Such are the Wal-Mart publicized "Morning Cheer" that requires all staff members to greet in the morning. Although this practice worked in other countries, in Germany it was opposed by the working staff and development managers showing a blind eye for the requirement to learn the German language and *this* had communication problems and incurred costs with putting efforts in training and developing issues with local unions and consumer voices.

3.4.3.5 The Nominal Group and Nominalization

A key resource for packaging meaning is the *nominal group*. Elsewhere we have already noted that in academic meaning making, nominal groups that realize Participants are often both densely packed and abstract (i.e., the head noun, often an abstract concept, is elaborated or modified through pre- and postmodification, itself often abstract). Furthermore, there is a tendency to represent events, qualities of objects and events, and logical connections not in their most "natural" or congruent form as verbs, adjectives, adverbs, and conjunctions but as nouns, a process referred to as *nominalization*. Table 3.5 illustrates the shift from congruent to nominalized forms, taking examples from the text extracts in this chapter.

There are a number of functional reasons why nominalization is common in academic meaning making. It allows the formation of technical terms such as *buy-outs, joint ventures, figure movement, batch living*. It also allows the development of abstract concepts and properties such as *cultural and linguistic similarities, factors, limited personal freedom*. Many areas of academic knowledge deal not with "real" tangible objects but with abstract concepts, properties, and theories. Another reason is that nominalization allows us to bring together one complex thing with another as illustrated here:

global expanding	leads to	longer and more complex lines of communication
nominalization	verb	nominalization
Actor	Process	Goal
Inward investment	stimulates	economic activity and job creation
nominalization	verb	nominalization
Actor	Process	Goal

Nominalization also allows for the measurement, comparison, classification, evaluation, and ordering of events in that English has more resources for building up the representation of a thing (a noun) than it does for other grammatical phenomena such as verbs or adjectives.

Finally, nominalization allows us to organize texts in terms of abstract ideas, reasons, causes, and so on, the type of decontextualized language that, we argue in this monograph, defines so much of academic meaning making and that presents students with more complex forms of communication than they may be familiar with. Thus, the lexicogrammatical pattern that characterizes macro- and hyperThemes and, to some degree, clause-level Themes is the use of dense and often abstract nominal groups (as underlined in the example below):

> To the UK government and economy, benefits are represented in employment rate, the balance of payments and taxation.

3.4.3.6 Recap

This section has provided an overview of the relationship between the contextual variable of mode and language resources that are available for making textual meaning. This relationship is summarized in Figure 3.15. By analyzing textual meaning making we can bring to the fore some of the main linguistic resources

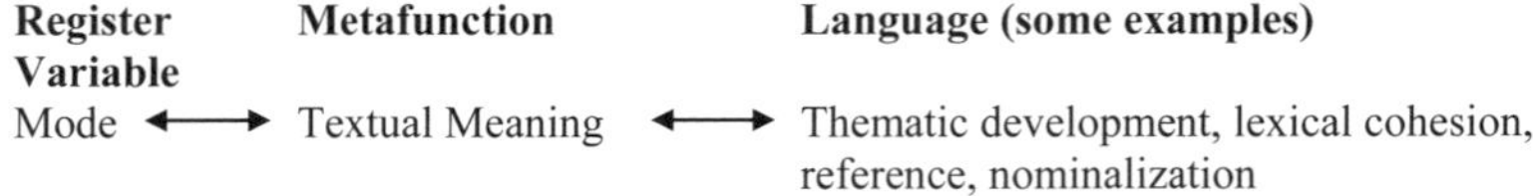

Figure 3.15 Mode-textual metafunction-language relationship.

that work to organize texts and make them cohesive. How they do this will depend on how spontaneous or edited a text is, among other contextual factors.

Language, learning, and semantic orientation

The main focus of this chapter has been to consider the overall architecture of SFL and provide an overview of its analytical tools. We have also tried to foreground their relevance to research into, and understanding of, teaching and learning as essentially a language-based phenomenon. We have shown that a key tenet of SFL is to theorize language as a meaning-making resource and, as such, at the heart of all learning. Thus, it links, in a systematic manner, specific language systems and resources with three overarching types of meaning making (ideational, interpersonal, and textual) that are in a bidirectional relationship with aspects of the social context (the subject matter, social relations, and channel of communication, as theorized in the concept of register) and overall goal or purpose of an interaction (as theorized in the concept of genre).

This conceptualization of language and learning stands in contrast not only to cognitive approaches to learning and development, where language is often peripheral, but also to formal approaches to language and learning, where the center of interest is the accurate control of syntagmatic structure. This is not to argue that form is unimportant and that syntactic errors should not be identified and dealt with. Certainly in many of the extracts from students' work that we have explored in this chapter, it is clear that some students are still developing control over the formal rules of English. Inevitably, therefore, there will be errors of form that may impede clear communication and that may need ironing out. In Svetla's introduction, for example, there are errors in the use of prepositions, articles, and the formation of nouns.

Nevertheless, our central proposition in this monograph is that ideational, interpersonal, and textual meaning making also is in a state of development and that to support and facilitate language development from this perspective is integral to supporting students' academic learning. This is because the world of learning is a sociosemiotic world, largely construed through language.

From a pedagogic perspective, although we have not focused specifically on the kinds of teaching and learning interventions that SFL insights might lead to, we would like to make the following proposals at this stage:

- From the point of view of SFL genre theory, genres are configurations of meaning and are directly associated with the development of subject knowledge. Their identification and linguistic description makes it possible to explicitly teach students how to configure meanings that fulfill disciplinary purposes.
- From the point of view of the SFL construct of register, context, meaning, and language choices are co-constitutive. Heightened awareness of this relationship alongside developing the analytical tools to make it explicit makes it possible for teachers and students to semiotically mediate the world of learning with greater (meta) awareness.
- Through developing awareness of the linguistic systems central to academic meaning making such as those outlined in this chapter (the reservoir) and the resources that students have available (their repertoires), teachers can become more aware of students' semantic orientations. Understanding students' semantic orientations may help to explain why, in relation to their academic and disciplinary context, some students' texts may be less high-scoring than others. This may be a first step in supporting students to develop a wider range of linguistic/meaning-making choices from which they can select.

In Chapters 4–6, the analytical tools and the insights their use generates will be further elaborated. In Chapter 4, we will use the notion of genre and the ideational and textual metafunctions to look at how students learn the field and the language of the field in Film Studies. In Chapter 5, the field of study changes to HSC. In that chapter, our focus is the use of genre to track the learning trajectory of students and to consider the role of semantic orientation in moving back and forth from more contextualized to more decontextualized meaning making.

Chapter 6 uses the construct of register to look more closely at textual, interpersonal, and ideational meaning making in the context of online teaching and learning. In particular, it considers how, in that environment, both visible and invisible semiotic mediation can support students in developing their meaning-making repertoires within a field of study.

Notes

1 Participant and Theme are systemic functional labels for clause elements that focus on how such elements work to make meaning in the clause. These will be discussed further in Section 3.4.1.
2 Note that where there are discipline-specific references within sample student texts we do not provide full reference details.
3 Please note that all student texts that we draw on throughout the book are presented exactly as written by the student including any errors of grammar, vocabulary, or referencing.
4 SFL distinguishes different types of verbs or Processes. These will be discussed further in Section 3.4.1.2.
5 Following SFL conventions, functional labels have initial capitals. This includes clause-level functional labels such as Process, Actor, or Circumstance as well as functional labels for genre stages such as Orientation, Position, and so forth.
6 *At the beginning of 1990s* and *throughout the decade* are analyzed as Circumstances in SFL. Rather than being entities directly involved in the event they are functioning to give additional background information (in this case temporal information).
7 The use of small caps for system terms follows SFL conventions.
8 Small caps are used for APPRAISAL and its sub-systems to distinguish a technical from a non-technical use of the terms.
9 The presentation of Theme and New here is somewhat of a simplification of the two systems in SFL, Theme-Rheme and Given-New.

CHAPTER 4
"This Is Description, Not Film Analysis": Semiotically Mediating Genre, Conceptual Formations, and Text Development

4.1 Introduction

This chapter looks at how students learn the language of Film Studies, learn Film Studies through language, and learn about Film Studies language. Film as an object of study brings nonacademic and academic knowledge and discourses into relationship and highlights the tensions entailed in negotiating from one to the other. In some ways, this offers a microcosm of the transition entailed in the move from nonacademic contextualized knowledge—in this case, film as an experience of entertainment—to academic decontextualized knowledge—in this case, film as an object of study—and so constitutes a case study of the role of language in learning across the higher education curriculum. Adopting a LASS approach to the learning of Film Studies, or any other academic subject, involves paying attention to how language is used in the making of meanings in these academic contexts.

Imagine a well-resourced, high-tech lecture theater in a new[1] British university. A Film Studies teacher has just completed a lecture on film genres and the role of *mise-en-scene* in classic Hollywood cinema. The students have returned from their break carrying sweets, chips, and soft drinks. There is a sense of expectation as the lights in the theater dim, the mournful notes of a country and western guitar sound out, and the screen where the teacher's slides had been projected now shows the actor Nicholas Cage climbing out of a beat-up Cadillac on a North American desert highway. It is the start of *Red Rock West* and the students are about to begin analyzing the film for how visuals are used in the narrative of this country noir genre.

At least they are if they can resist the urge to suspend their disbelief in response to the power of the film narrative, the visual devices they are being asked to analyze, and the hypnotic effects of a darkened room and a flickering screen. After a lifetime of induction into the world of cinema—particularly of the Hollywood variety—they know what is expected of them as cinema-goers.

Language Learning 64:Suppl. 1, June 2014, pp. 85–145

DOI: 10.1111/lang.12040

What they are less familiar with is what is expected of them as film analysts. This is an early film viewing in their Film Studies course and for many the tension between the two roles is still acute. Over the coming two semesters, they are likely to develop the film analyst role to the point where some of them will complain that their enjoyment of a Friday night at the cinema has been irreparably damaged. Others will develop into articulate and well-informed participants in Film Studies seminars and in postcinema pub discussions. Still others will have been watching with more practical purposes, motivated by the ambition to produce their own films and eager to understand the tricks of the trade.

Students' engagement with the film will depend in part on their use of language, how they interpret the words of the characters in the film, and how they respond to the film. However, Film Studies is also a multimodal context in which nonlinguistic modalities, including auditory ones (such as music) and visual ones (such as lighting) play a key role in both the objects of study and students' responses to these objects of study.

The phenomenon of multiple modalities is mirrored in the phenomenon of multiple discourses. In a Film Studies course, students' familiar meaning-making processes and associated ways of talking about film viewing are challenged by new ways of looking at film and new ways of talking about film viewing that are presented in the course. The reorientation of familiar meaning-making processes that the course will encourage is signaled by its name, which is *Ways of Seeing*. Students who enroll may or may not be prepared for the challenge to their familiar ways of seeing that the course will offer. Equally, they may or may not be aware of the role that unfamiliar discourses will play in challenging their ways of communicating about film. Finally, they may or may not be prepared to find that, among the semiotic resources that they are expected to use for communicating in a Film Studies course, written language plays a central role.

They are not alone in any misapprehension they demonstrate here. As a subject in the Media Studies curriculum, Film Studies shares in the obloquy suffered by Media Studies at the hands of many critics (often from outside the university) who regard it as lacking in academic credibility and depth and inappropriate for university education (for an illustration of such criticism, see Frean, 2008). In practice, Film Studies, along with many subjects in the Media Studies curriculum, collocates discourses ranging from those of the most arcane academic scholarship to those of the most mundane of everyday conversation. In Hasan's terms, it confronts the contextualized with the decontextualized (Hasan, 2009; and see Section 2.3.1 in Chapter 2). As mentioned above, it does this across an array of modalities. The result is an area of study that has an enormous diversity of genres and registers. This is the environment into which students in *Ways of Seeing* are entering. Their encounters with the academic reading material of the course and their engagement with the academic assignments that they do in the course often reveal the tensions inherent in working across the range of modalities, genres, and registers that constitute Film Studies, particularly for those students whose own backgrounds and ambitions may be more aligned with the film industry than with the academy.

For Film Studies and Media Studies teachers, the challenges presented by the study of film and media for their students can be revealed in students' written assignments. At the university where the research on which this chapter is based was carried out, external examiners of students' final-year assignments commented on how standards of writing called for attention. As is often the case in commentaries on students' writing, it was unclear whether these were references to students' understanding of Film Studies subject matter or simply to ungainly or careless writing styles. Such separation between academic content and use of language in writing about that content was referred to in Chapters 1 and 2 and was contested from a LASS perspective.

This chapter is based on a LASS action research project with first-year film students implemented by one of the authors in collaboration with a Film Studies teacher who wanted to support students to write meaningfully about the subject matter he was teaching. He had previously suggested to students that they should attend one of the university's general writing classes. However, neither they nor he had found these writing classes relevant to their needs. In this action research project, therefore, a language specialist and a subject specialist set out to embed language development within the Film Studies curriculum. Into the first-year course, *Ways of Seeing*, we embedded a language development strand called *Ways of Writing*. The *Ways of Writing* approach was based on SFL analysis of many examples of Film Studies assignments from previous years and ongoing dialogue with students and their teacher during the 2 years of the action research project.[2] Through close integration of the two strands and the team teaching approach we adopted, the first-year students in the course came to regard writing as integral to Film Studies. The project is an example of the kind of collaboration between research and pedagogy on which we think a LASS approach depends.

4.2 The Context of a University Film Studies Course

The film-viewing scenario presented above offers a glimpse of the context in a university Film Studies course. This context can be elaborated using the three dimensions of register that SFL adopts in the analysis of context: what is going on (field), who is involved (tenor), and how language is being used (mode) (see Chapter 3, Section 3.4). These categories are not being used here in a formal linguistic analysis of register but as a frame for organizing impressions and insights gathered from immersion in the Film Studies department during the action research period.

4.2.1 Field: What Is Going On?

The field of Film Studies is a dynamic one, located within the larger field of Media Studies. Media Studies has developed from the combination of several foundational disciplines but has also sought to maintain a critical, continuously emergent and sometimes nondisciplinary character. Tensions among the components of the field of Media Studies are best represented by "theory–practice divide." In Film Studies, this comes from the attempt to bring together what some say are the incompatible activities of critical theorizing about the medium of film, on the one hand, and the practical production of film and related visual artifacts on the other (Elliot, 1997, 2000). This theory–practice divide is conflated with another divide—particularly pertinent in new universities—between the academically oriented study of film and vocationally oriented training in film production.

4.2.2 Mode: What Role Is Language Playing?

The divides in the field of activity are reflected in the different roles language plays in construing Film Studies knowledge: on the one hand, the style of communication is abstract, nominalized, and dense, realized by the written texts of various schools of critical theory; on the other hand it is concrete, verbal, and dynamic, realized by the oral and practically oriented texts of film production and consumption. Mode is further characterized by interaction between language and other semiotic resources, particularly visual and musical ones (*multimodality*).

4.2.3 Tenor: Who Is Involved?

The tenor of relations between students and teachers in Film Studies courses at a new university is influenced by the object of study (often popular culture) and the diverse educational experiences and aspirations of the participants (ranging from traditionally academic to contemporarily vocational). Students are, to some extent, positioned as equals by teachers. Their personal experience of contemporary popular culture and their creative agency is acknowledged. Nonacademic knowledge and the values and relationships of everyday life as represented in film, television, radio, music, and other media can be seen as more privileged in this environment than in some other university courses. This encourages more vernacular forms of address. Both students and staff may have entered higher education from nontraditional backgrounds: vocationally oriented further education programs or access courses in the case of some students; art school, media industry, or further education in the case of some staff. For some, these experiences serve to reduce distance in relationships and contribute to a tenor of solidarity. On the other hand, students are also positioned as apprentices from the media practice perspective and as novice academics from the theoretical perspective. In this respect, there is a tendency toward relations of greater distance and less solidarity.

4.3 Writing Film Analysis on a Film Studies Course

Most of the writing that students were required to do in the *Ways of Seeing* course was referred to as essay writing by the department. Essay prompts were designed to encourage students to apply the Film Studies concepts that had been introduced in the course in analysis of particular films or types of film. In these essays, they demonstrated both their grasp of the conceptual formations that constituted *Ways of Seeing*'s representation of the world of Film Studies and also their ability to use these formations to analyze film.

Although most of these students were entering the world of Film Studies for the first time, the film analysis procedures that they were called on to carry out in these assignments bore a strong resemblance to the procedures that the Film Studies scholar Bordwell (1989) describes professional academic film critics doing. In Bernstein's terms (1996; and see Chapter 2, Section 2.5.1), this amounts to a clear illustration of the recontextualization for pedagogic purposes of a professional academic procedure in an educational context. Bordwell proposes that through the application of conceptual frameworks in the analysis of a film, an analyst (whom he refers to as a "critic" in the quotation below) generates a new representation of the film, which he refers to as "the model film." He suggests that the model film can be constructed either inductively, working upward from cues in the actual film that the analyst interprets through conceptual frameworks that relate to the cues, or deductively, working downwards from a preselected conceptual framework that the analyst uses the film to illustrate.

> One critic may start with concrete textual cues and then cast about for schemata, heuristics and semantic fields that seem appropriate; another critic may start by presupposing certain semantic fields and then, finding

> some cues that fit, call upon schemata and heuristics that will extend the interpretation. **In any event, conceptual structures of the sort I have laid out would seem to be central to the process . . . [of] production of the critic's model film.** (Bordwell, 1989, p. 202, emphasis added)

It could be argued that such a procedure is central to the whole of higher education, in which commonsense (or contextualized) knowledge is confronted and challenged by and transformed into uncommonsense (or decontextualized) knowledge. The translation of the familiar and everyday experience of films into conceptually reframed model films represents in microcosm the academic activity that is repeated throughout higher education. By engaging directly with students in this procedure, the *Ways of Seeing* and *Ways of Writing* course was designed to lay a foundation for students' writing—and learning—throughout their Media Studies degree.

In order to illustrate the film analysis procedure outlined above, an example will be presented in the following section. It was written by students after the film viewing described in the introductory scenario of this chapter. This assignment was set very early in the *Ways of Writing* strand in order to bring writing into focus through a process of metasemiotic mediation. This involved evaluating each student's text using an SFL-based evaluation instrument. (See Appendix 4.5 and Bonanno & Jones, 2007). The evaluation was used as the basis of a one-to-one discussion with students about their ways of making meaning in writing, with a particular emphasis on the nature of the text produced.

For reasons that will be explained below, the genre for the assignment task is referred to as a *taxonomic film analysis*. Because this models film analysis in a particularly clear way, it is seen as a key genre in Film Studies. In this assignment, the conceptual framework used to construct the model film is based on the key concept of *mise-en-scene.*[3] *Mise-en-scene* is a technical Film Studies term that refers to the role of visuals in the design of a film. A taxonomic film analysis based on the concept of *mise-en-scene* has the capacity to transform a student's perception of film, laying the foundation for film to become an object of study as opposed to an experience of entertainment. In this sense, *mise-en-scene* can be regarded as a *threshold concept* (Meyer & Land, 2005). According to Meyer and Land, comprehending a threshold concept is a transformative experience; once a threshold concept is grasped, understanding of the object of study can never be the same again. For this reason, threshold concepts are also regarded as troublesome. Often during the *Ways of Seeing* course, students would comment on how their sense of enjoyment of an evening at the cinema had been disturbed by Film Studies concepts. Film viewing was ceasing to be a familiar experience of immersion in a narrative flow and the interactions of film characters; instead, the constructedness of film had entered into the experience and Hollywood's veil of illusion was being lifted. More broadly, deconstruction of the ways in which meanings were made in film provided a glimpse into the constructedness of meaning throughout the entire social world.

In the next section, two students' engagements with the threshold concept of *mise-en-scene* through the genre of taxonomic film analysis are examined from a LASS perspective.

4.4 Taxonomic Film Analysis

The assignment students were asked to write after the film viewing described earlier prompted a taxonomic film analysis. The assignment was:

> In what ways does *mise-en-scene* work to construct meaning in film noir, with particular reference to the first 15 minutes of *Red Rock West*?

Bearing in mind the two approaches to model film production that Bordwell (1989) refers to, students could handle this assignment in one of two ways. They could approach the analysis inductively, concentrating on how the meaning of *Red Rock West* unfolded in the first 15 minutes, mapping observations about the *mise-en-scene* onto the narrative development of the film, starting with the concrete textual clues, to use Bordwell's words. Alternatively, they could approach the analysis deductively, taking the *mise-en-scene* conceptual framework to the film and looking for illustrations of the framework in the film. Whichever approach students adopted to carry out the analysis in the first place—and it would also be quite possible to blend both of them—they would subsequently have to decide which of these approaches, or another one, should be used to structure their writing of the analysis.

In order to illustrate some of what is entailed in writing this assignment, texts by two students (Tyrrell and Everton, pseudonyms) will be examined in this chapter (texts are presented in full in Appendices 4.1 and 4.2). Tyrrell is an Afro-Caribbean British female of around 18–20 years old who had come to university studies from further education college, where she had studied a Film Studies vocational qualification and two A-Levels. Everton is an Afro-Caribbean British male of around 18–20 years old, who had also come through a further education college pathway, where he had focused exclusively on vocational Film Studies and other subjects. We will carry out an analysis of each student's text to demonstrate how the meaning-making of a text can be described from an SFL perspective. Before that, it might be helpful if readers would read through the texts in Appendices 4.1 and 4.2 in order to get an initial sense of their content, style, and structure. For ease of reference, paragraphs are labeled with a letter and sentences with a number.[4]

From a quick reading of Tyrrell's assignment, the taxonomic structure of the text is very clear. Each paragraph deals with a different element from the *mise-en-scene* taxonomy (see Chapter 3, Figure 3.7). Such taxonomic structuring is missing from Everton's text. The contrast between these two assignments is more than just a difference of style and approach. For the Film Studies teacher, Everton's text was not doing the kind of work that he expected. His comment was, "this is description, not analysis." It is worth recognizing that this is a comment on Everton's film analysis rather than on his writing in a narrow sense. It would be possible to adopt a narrow approach and draw Everton's attention to some formal features of sentence level vocabulary and grammar that could be developed. However, the real issue for the Film Studies teacher was the cognitive work the text represented. The teacher's concerns were functional, not formal.

As we have proposed (see Chapter 1, Section 1.3), a LASS approach to teaching and learning does not make a distinction between form and function. Form at the sentence, paragraph, and text levels is important, but not for its own sake. The significance of form lies in its functional value. From an analysis of a large number of film students' assignment texts, there was little evidence of students who "couldn't write" in a formal sense. What was more evident was that there were students who couldn't write *appropriately*, that is, they were not "doing the work" of Film Studies in their assignments. Sometimes, the challenges of doing Film Studies work through the written mode was manifested in accumulations of formal errors that created incoherence in the text. However, it was not difficult to assume that the roots of such incoherence lay in the unfamiliarity of the cognitive work of Film Studies, the extraordinariness of the discourses that students were encountering, and the challenges of composing extended pieces of writing in unfamiliar genres and registers.

In order to understand the ways in which a LASS approach to teaching and learning can contribute in this context, and outline the relationship between the cognitive work of Film Studies and the formal and functional linguistic features of students' assignments, we will start by examining the staging of these two examples of students' film analysis.

4.4.1 Stages in Two Students' Taxonomic Film Analyses

The taxonomic film analysis genre is a macrogenre (see Chapter 3, Section 3.3.4) consisting of a classification report and a theoretical explanation. On the basis of a close reading of the content of each text, and using the paragraphing to help, the staging of the two students' texts can be represented as follows:

Text 1 (Tyrrell)

Orientation to task (analysis using a taxonomy of analytical elements) ^ Orientation to taxonomy ^ Orientation to "theory" (i.e., "*mise-en-scene* makes meaning") ^ Orientation to phenomenon (film) ^ Application of taxonomy and theory to phenomenon ^ Reprise of main aspects of application of taxonomy and theory

Text 2 (Everton)

Orientation to task (analysis using a taxonomy) ^ Orientation to phenomenon (film) ^ Orientation to "theory" (i.e., "*mise-en-scene* makes meaning") ^ Recount of film story-line ^ Evaluation of some uses of taxonomic elements

The key difference between the two texts is in the application of the *mise-en-scene* taxonomy and the associated theory. Despite proposing that it is his intention to use the *mise-en-scene* taxonomy to demonstrate it makes meaning, Everton makes only passing references to one of the elements, the shot, in the main part of the assignment. He comes back to the concept of *mise-en-scene* in his concluding paragraph, but apart from this being late in the analysis, it is an evaluative reference and not an analytical application of the elements of *mise-en-scene* to the film.

Central to Tyrrell's text is the *mise-en-scene* taxonomy. Central to Everton's text is the recount of the film. The recount does not function as the model film referred to by Bordwell. To become a model film, the actual film has to be processed through the "schemata, heuristics, and semantic fields" of the *mise-en-scene* taxonomy. Tyrrell is just beginning to move in that direction. She is not yet being asked to fully analyze a film; she is being asked to demonstrate her knowledge of some tools that she will go on to use in film analysis once she has developed familiarity with their use. Everton, in the Film Studies teacher's view, has hardly begun the journey toward analysis. This is not exclusively because he has produced a recount. As Bordwell proposes, it is possible to analyze film on the basis of a recount. But doing so requires the analyst to conceptually frame the recount using the *mise-en-scene* elements taxonomy and to apply the theory, *mise-en-scene works to construct meaning* in their representation of the model film. Not doing this means the recount remains unanalyzed. This was what the teacher's comment was referring to.

Taxonomic film analysis was not a genre introduced in Chapter 3. As mentioned above, it is a macrogenre consisting of a classification report and a theoretical explanation. Theoretical explanation is a frequently occurring key genre in the development of decontextualized meanings in university study across many subjects and situations. We have referred to it in this particular situation as taxonomic film analysis in order to acknowledge one of its key purposes in Film Studies, which is to analyze film. There are other uses of theoretical explanation both in Film Studies itself and across other subject areas where the term "taxonomic film analysis" is not appropriate. One of these will be discussed in the next chapter.

4.4.2 MacroTheme and HyperTheme: Thematic Development in Tyrell's Text

To understand more fully the contrast between the kind of work that is being done by these two students in their different texts, we will start by looking more closely at the thematic development of Tyrell's text at macro- and hyper-Theme levels (see Chapter 3, Section 3.4.3.3). Genre staging is scaffolded by the thematic development of a text at all levels, including also clause-level Theme. MacroTheme and, to a certain extent, hyperTheme are features of text which are closer to the awareness of a reader who is not particularly aware of more specialized linguistic features. It is quite common for subject teachers to comment on the effectiveness of a students' "introduction" (i.e., the macroTheme in SFL genre theory). Subject teachers may comment on "the topic sentence" of paragraphs (i.e., the hyperTheme in SFL genre theory), and writing specialists frequently do. Using SFL to explain the relationship between text structure and text function, this taxonomic film analysis genre provides a powerful illustration of how macroTheme (introduction) and hyperTheme (topic sentence) are more than simply stylistic devices to make a text easier for a reader to read; it demonstrates very clearly how macroTheme and hyperTheme scaffold the cognitive work of film analysis.

Figure 4.1 presents the macroTheme, the hyperThemes, and the macroNew (conclusion) from Tyrrell's text. The bolded words are technical terms. These terms have been semiotically mediated and adopted by Tyrrell from the input texts that she has engaged with. The primary text was the lecture on *Genre and mise-en-scene* that the Film Studies teacher delivered before the film viewing. Secondary texts included sections of a number of Film Studies textbooks from the course bibliography. The class had also been given an academic journal article dealing with key motifs from the film noir genre. Tyrrell has constructed a conceptual formation based on the concepts of *mise-en-scene* and film noir

In what ways does *mise-en-scene* work to construct meaning in film noir, with particular reference to the first fifteen minutes of Red Rock West?[1]

Lighting, the shot, setting, location, props and costume are some key **elements of mise-en-scene**. When effectively presented within **the context of the genre**, in this case **film noir**, each of the aforementioned elements of *mise-en-scene* can work to construct **meaning** for the audience. There are various **cinematic codes** (discussed in this essay) within the genre of film noir that **audiences** can instantly recognise and identify. However, this would not be possible without the significant contribution that *mise-en-scene* makes to aid **the narrative of the film** by constructing meaning in **the visuals**.

Costume and props play an essential role in creating **verisimilitude** and conveying different **meanings** within the context of the film's genre, in particular "country noir"....

"Films are also dependent on **props** as a device for conveying **meaning**. In a familiar sense props are **definers of genre**" (Rowe, 1997, p. 101)....

Orr makes an interesting observation on comparing the appearance of the car (as **a prop**) to the temperament of its owner. ....

The setting and location of Red Rock West differs from that of the traditional big city metropolitan settings of **film noir** of the 1940s and 50s. ....

The various **ways in which actors and locations are lit and shot** can instantly convey **meanings** by creating atmosphere and influencing the way a character is perceived. ....

Significantly **the lighting in the *mise-en-scene* of the bar** creates an atmosphere of duplicity. ....

After having meticulously studied **the various ways in which mise-en-scene works to construct meaning in Red Rock West.** It can be deduced that **the very concept of mise en-scene** withholds **a significant amount of importance in clearly constructing and conveying meanings to the audience visually**.

[1] *Bold: Key concept terms*
Underlining: Words representing the central proposition "mise-en-scene makes meaning"

Figure 4.1 Tyrrell's text: macroTheme, hyperThemes, macroNew, the theory, and technical terms.

that she both uses and develops in her writing of the assignment text. The central process from the title, *mise-en-scene constructs meaning,* which is in fact the theory that the assignment sets out to test or demonstrate, is reiterated in various wordings throughout the text and has been underlined wherever it occurs.

The technical terms Tyrell uses constitute part of the ideational resources she has for representing the world as a configuration of decontextualized meanings. They are grouped and listed below.

Elements of mise-en-scene	Meaning	Genre	Film viewers
the visuals	meaning	the context of the genre	audiences
elements of *mise-en-scene*	cinematic codes	film noir	
	the narrative of the film	"country noir"	
lighting	verisimilitude		
the shot	definers of genre		
setting	an atmosphere of duplicity		
location			
props			
costume			

The key decontextualizing device is the threshold proposition *mise-en-scene works to construct meaning.* Variations of this proposition occur prosodically (in a wavelike and accumulative pattern) throughout the assignment:

> ***Mise-en-scene* works to construct meaning**
> *mise-en-scene* works to construct meaning
>
> constructing and conveying meanings to the audience visually
>
> creating verisimilitude and conveying different meanings
>
> a device for conveying meaning
>
> can instantly convey meanings by creating
>
> creates an atmosphere of
>
> *mise-en-scene* works to construct meaning
>
> clearly constructing and conveying meanings to the audience

4.5 Conceptual Formations

What we have done in this analysis so far is to focus on an aspect of the textual meaning (thematic development) combined with an aspect of the ideational meaning (technical terminology). This technical terminology is only meaningful when it is brought into configurations of meaning prompted by the assignment title to constitute a taxonomic film analysis. The purpose of the *Ways of Seeing* course is to enable students to build a conceptual formation of this area of Film Studies. As introduced in Chapter 3, a conceptual formation is a constellation of concepts and concept relationships that constitute an area of knowledge (see Lemke, 1985, 1990, on *thematic formations* for the origins of this analysis). A conceptual formation is a more abstract representation of the field that a text is engaged with than is actually represented by the text itself. A conceptual formation is constructed through continuous engagement with concepts and concept relations across multiple texts. It is an intertextual product.

A conceptual formation is also a socially constructed configuration of knowledge. An individual's semiotic mediation of a conceptual formation is likely to be partial, personal, and communal. Each individual, in their engagement with a formation, will interpret, appropriate, and adapt the concepts and their relations in ways that reflect the individual's previous experience, current knowledge, and future goals. In educational environments, a teacher's conceptual formation is highly influential in relation to the students and to some extent constitutes the complete conceptual formation as far as students are concerned. How far individual students are able or willing to make the teacher's conceptual formation their own is one of the things that assignments are designed to test as well as enable.

So, for our purposes, a conceptual formation is being regarded as an idealization of the ideational field that Tyrrell and Everton are engaging with through their writing of a taxonomic film analysis. In order to illustrate what a conceptual formation might look like, in the following sections we will build up a representation of the formation around the proposition *mise-en-scene works to construct meaning*. This representation is derived from the film teacher's lectures on the subject, the literature he advised the students to read, and a large number of students' taxonomic film analysis assignments. After developing the representation of the formation, we will then return to examine further Tyrrell's use of Theme to scaffold her reconstruction of the conceptual formation as a taxonomic film analysis text.

4.5.1 Taxonomic Representation of the Experience of Film

A central conceptual relationship in the conceptual formation is the taxonomy of elements of *mise-en-scene*. *Elements of mise-en-scene* is a taxonomic grouping made up of six elements. It is a compositional taxonomy, which breaks an entity (*mise-en-scene*) down into its parts (or *elements*); as introduced in Chapter 3,

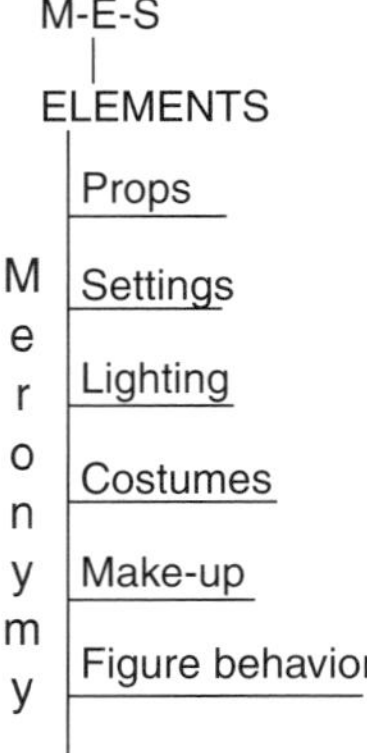

Figure 4.2 Conceptual formation: MES elements taxonomy.
Note: The continuing line below "figure behavior" indicates that the list of elements of *mise-en-scene* represented here is not exhaustive. This convention is used in a number of other places in the conceptual formation figures.

this constructs a sense relationship of meronymy (Chapter 3, Figure 3.14). Each element of the compositional taxonomy constitutes a category for *mise-en-scene* analysis (see Figure 4.2).

The French term *mise-en-scene* is a technical term in its own right. To use it a student needs to have some sense of the definition of the term, and all the assignments analyzed attempted to define it. The process of *naming* (an entity with a technical term) and *making the name technical* (by defining it) is central to taxonomic film analysis and many other configurations of decontextualized meaning.

Less obviously, all the subcategories of *mise-en-scene* are also technical terms. They are used with a particular range of meanings within the context of a specialized field of activity that may be different from the range of meanings they have in nontechnical everyday contexts. An illustration of this is the term *lighting,* a relatively familiar term from everyday conversation, but among its technical attributes in a Film Studies context, it can be further taxonomized as shown in Figure 4.3.

Making terms technical and discovering new taxonomies for familiar everyday words is part of the process whereby students' experience of the world is transformed. Working with the *mise-en-scene* taxonomy in order to partition representations of experience constitutes the beginnings of a move from commonsense to uncommonsense representations of that experience, from contextualized to decontextualized meanings.

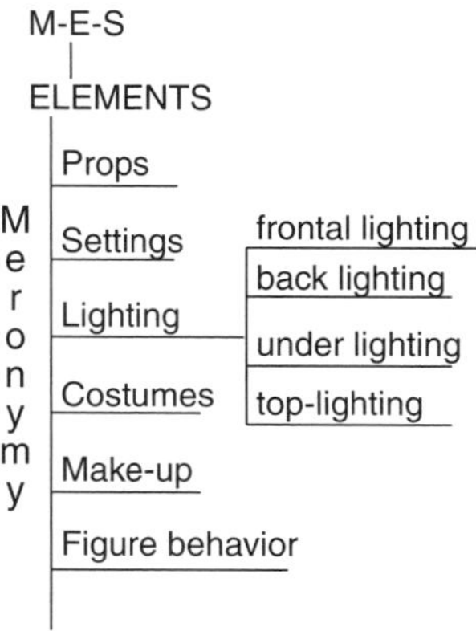

Figure 4.3 Conceptual formation: Taxonomy of lighting.

4.5.2 General-to-Particular Representation of Experience

As well as partitioning experience into elements, a taxonomic pattern is inherently also a more general to more particular pattern. *Elements of mise-en-scene* stands in a general relationship to the more particular elements of *mise-en-scene* like *lighting*. Very often there is a parallel pattern of more abstract (decontextualized) to more concrete (contextualized). For example, *elements* is more abstract than *props*. Awareness of how to manipulate and exploit such general-to-particular and abstract-to-concrete relations is what students are developing as they develop their skills of film analysis. Bordwell's notion of the model film depends on a movement between the more specific and concrete "textual cues" and the more general and abstract "schemata, heuristics, and semantic fields."

4.5.3 Making the Term *meaning* Technical

Applying the taxonomy of *mise-en-scene* elements to a film involves a certain amount of decontextualized meaning making in which concrete elements of the film (such as *a hat*) are reclassified as an element of *mise-en-scene* (such as *a prop*). However, the most decontextualizing activity in taxonomic film analysis is to apply what could be referred to as "the theory" that *mise-en-scene works to construct meaning.* In this theory, the term *meaning* might seem to be a familiar and everyday word. However, in applying the theory in Film Studies, students are extending the conceptual formations of the word *meaning* beyond its everyday use. In this way, the term *meaning* is made technical. Making a term technical often involves providing a technical definition for a term. In many of the students' *mise-en-scene* analyses, the term *mise-en-scene* was defined

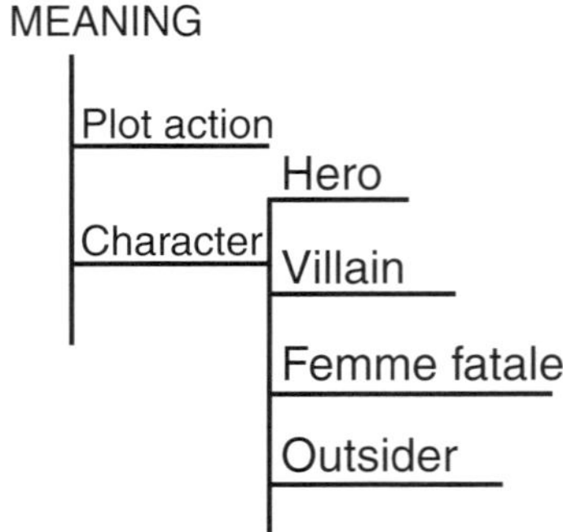

Figure 4.4 Conceptual formation: Taxonomy of meanings: Character.

and its technical meaning established. However, in the case of *meaning,* the term is made technical not through an explicit definition but by being used in technical ways. As students apply the theory of *mise-en-scene constructs meaning* in taxonomic analysis, students will begin to develop taxonomies of *meaning* which are less obvious than the *mise-en-scene* elements one. These are institutional interpretations of meaning. An example is the taxonomy of meanings that cluster around certain kinds of props (such as white hats = good, black hats = bad) and the types of character (hero, villain, femme fatale, etc.) that are developed around such props. One of these taxonomies of institutional meanings is illustrated in Figure 4.4.

Not all *meaning* terms lend themselves to being so evidently taxonomized. Much more common are conceptual formations where terms are not taxonomized but are related through collocation. For example the term *verisimilitude* collocates with the terms *meaning* and *mise-en-scene*. Verisimilitude is a technical term that refers to the ways in which a film satisfies audience expectations of how the world is represented within a particular genre of film. Verisimilitude does not have the same meaning as other apparently similar words like *realism*, *realistic,* or "convincing sense of reality." It is not realistic, for example, for people to sing their interactions with each other, but such behavior may have verisimilitude in a film musical. *Realism* is an area of film study scholarship in its own right which this assignment is not engaging with. To begin to collocate *verisimilitude* rather than *realism* with *meaning* and *mise-en-scene* is part of the purpose of the assignment as shown in Figure 4.5, where the term *realism* is crossed through to indicate it does not belong in this part of the conceptual formation.

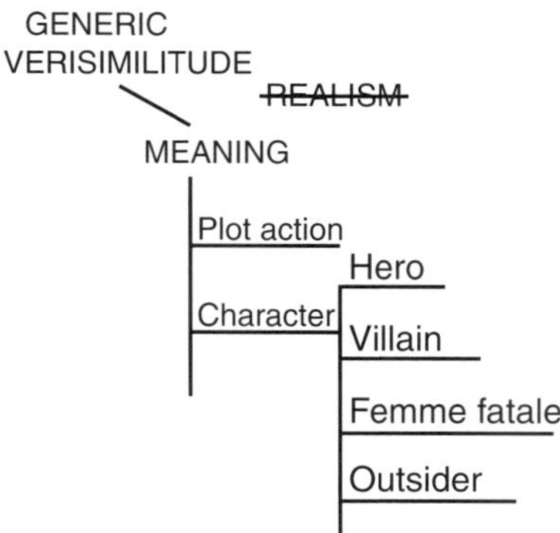

Figure 4.5 Conceptual formation: Generic verisimilitude as a collocate of meaning.

4.5.4 Theoretical Explanation in the Development of Uncommonsense Knowledge About Film

The proposition *mise-en-scene constructs meaning* brings into relationship the technical term *mise-en-scene* and the technical term *meaning*. This proposition is the theory that students are asked to develop and demonstrate their understanding of. Treating the words *mise-en-scene, construct,* and *meaning* as *colligates*, that is, as syntagmatically related in a clause, locates this text in uncommonsense, decontextualized discourse. The abstract term *meaning* is common in both everyday and Film Studies contexts. In everyday contexts, it appears in such clauses as: *Do you get my meaning?* and *I don't see the meaning of that.* However, it is much less commonly colligated with *constructs* as it is in the clause, *mise-en-scene constructs meaning.* Outside Film Studies, *meaning* is a thing that is likely to be transmitted (*get)* or perceived *(see, understand),* while within Film Studies, *meaning* is a thing that is frequently constructed *(created, made, established)*. The everyday thing, *meaning*, is more likely to be a Participant in a Process where another Participant is human; for example, *Do* ***you*** *get my meaning?* This is not so in Film Studies; in the proposition *mise-en-scene constructs meaning, meaning* is a Goal in a material Process where the actor is an abstract term standing for inanimate objects such as props or lighting (see Figure 4.6). In the extracts from Tyrrell's text there are eight realizations of this proposition.

Applying the theory *mise-en-scene constructs meaning* to their explanation of film as a phenomenon makes *mise-en-scene* a threshold concept with the power to transform students' perception of film irrevocably.

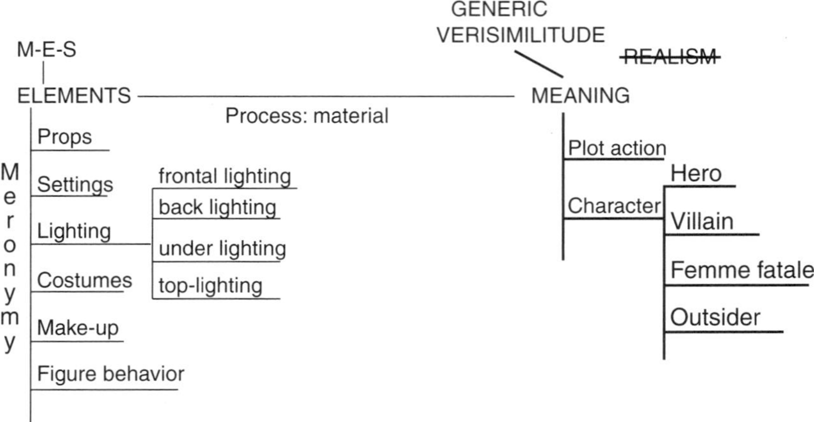

Figure 4.6 The conceptual relationship between elements and meaning is represented by the material Process *construct*.

4.5.5 The Broader Conceptual Formation

Another partial representation of the conceptual formation of *mise-en-scene constructs meaning* brings into focus several other key concepts and concept relations that have a bearing on the work that Everton and Tyrrell are doing in their film analysis assignment. The *Ways of Seeing* course focuses on the making of meaning in *Hollywood films* of the *classic narrative* variety, as opposed to European cinema, or Hollywood films that are not of this type. In such Hollywood films, the concept of *film genre* is significant in the analysis processes and the teacher is interested to see if students engage with this area of the formation. Figure 4.7 represents this broader conceptual formation where the concepts *genre, classic narrative*, and *Hollywood cinema* have been added.

4.5.6 Applying Conceptual Formations to a Particular Film

This whole network of concepts—and many more that are not represented here and that the students will develop an understanding of during the course—is brought to bear on particular films that they watch in the film-viewing sessions of the course (see Figure 4.8).

Conceptual formation is therefore the term used here to represent the "schemata, heuristics, and semantic fields" that Bordwell refers to as the basis of the "model film" that is created by a film analyst (see Section 4.3 above). Each student will develop their own conceptual formation, more or less similar

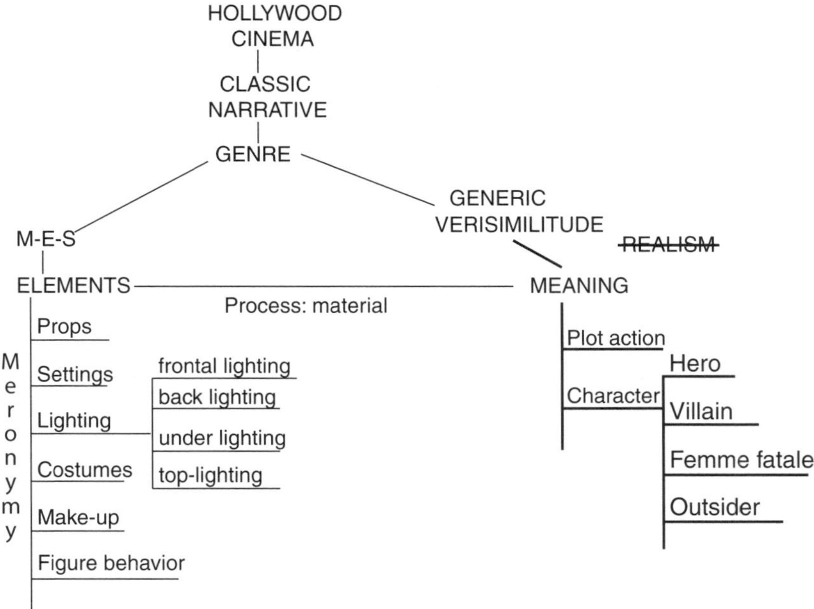

Figure 4.7 Conceptual formation: Related concepts of genre, classic narrative, Hollywood cinema.

to the one that the teacher presents during the lectures, which the students will supplement from their own reading and experience. Students' assignments are attempts to draw on and at the same time extend these formations. It is this process that constitutes the work of a Film Studies assignment. In this case, the work is achieved by configuring meanings into a taxonomic film analysis.

A key textual feature that scaffolds this Film Studies work is thematic development of the text. In the next section, we will look again at how the macroTheme and hyperThemes of Tyrrell's text scaffold her conceptual formation into a taxonomic film analysis, and at the same time shift the focus down into her engagement with this particular film, *Red Rock West,* at the clause level.

4.6 MacroTheme, HyperTheme, and Theoretical Explanation

4.6.1 MacroTheme, HyperTheme, and Theoretical Explanation in Tyrrell's Text

As already illustrated, in the macroTheme of her text, Tyrrell uses technical concepts from the field to frame the analysis. These include the *mise-en-scene*

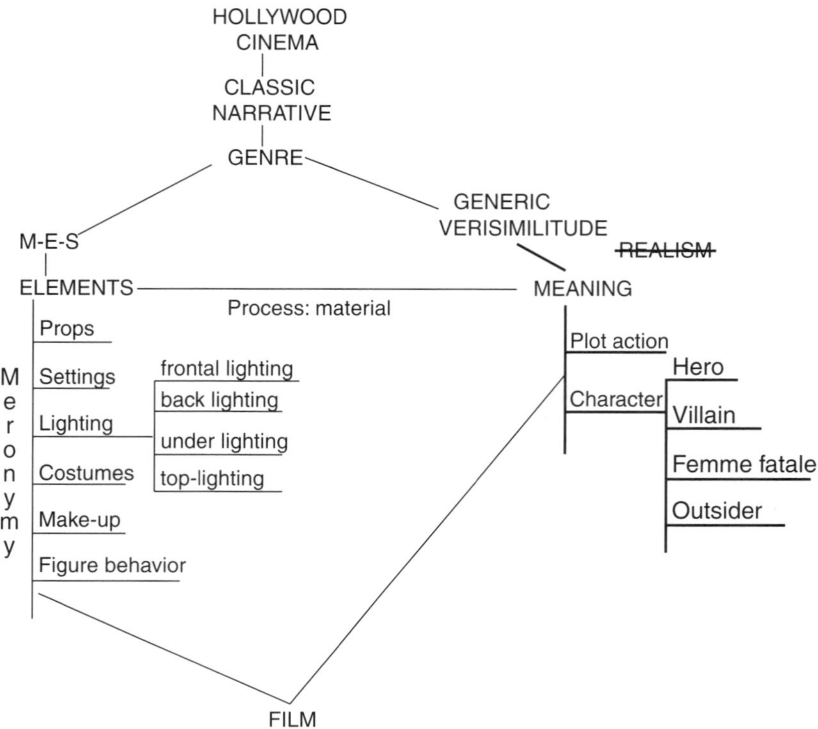

Figure 4.8 Conceptual formation of *mise-en-scene constructs meaning* applied to a particular film.

taxonomy; the conceptual relation that constitutes the central proposition of the assignment, *mise-en-scene constructs meaning;* and a number of other Film Studies concepts that belong to the conceptual formation presented by the teacher. Tyrrell builds each subsequent paragraph of the text around one element from the *mise-en-scene* taxonomy and a repetition of the threshold proposition *mise-en-scene constructs meaning.* The taxonomy of *mise-en-scene* elements is used as a set of technical categories that organize the analysis. The text moves from high-level generalizations about meaning in the macroTheme to generalizations at a lower, more specific level in the hyperThemes. Within each paragraph there is a pattern that is repeated: in the hyperTheme, the central conceptual formation, *mise-en-scene constructs meaning,* is contextualized for one element of the *mise-en-scene* taxonomy and then exemplified in a more contextualized way through a description or recount of film material in

Stages and phases	MacroTheme	
Presenting taxonomy (*mise-en-scene elements*)	A1 (**Lighting, the shot**), setting, location, props and costume are some key elements of *mise-en-scene*.	The key concepts which paragraph F will be about
Presenting theory (*mise-en-scene-makes-meaning*)	A2 When effectively presented within the context of the genre,in this case film noir,each of (the aforementioned elements of *mise-en-scene* can work to construct meaning for the audience.)	representation of the theory at a general level
	A3 There are various cinematic codes (discussed in this essay) within the genre of film noir that audiences can instantly recognise and identify.	
	A4 However this would not be possible without the significant contribution that *mise-en-scene* makes to aid the narrative of the film by constructing meaning in the visuals.	
HyperTheme Identifying particular elements (*lighting and shot*) Presenting theory (*element-makes-meaning*) at general level	F1 The various ways in which actors and locations are (**lit and shot**)within *mise-en-scene* can instantly convey meanings and messages to the audience by creating an atmosphere and allowing the audience to read into certain characters just by the way their images are presented.	These particular elements are specifically located in the theory, *mise-en-scene* constructs meaning, in the hyperTheme
Describing phenomenon (a particular scene from film) with focus on particular manifestation of the element	F2 The interior of Wayne's bar only seems to be (**illuminated by a single source of dull and opaque light, possibly a key light coming from the exterior through the front door and windows.**)	The element, lighting, is represented by an explicit example from the material film
Applying *element-makes-meaning theory* to this particular manifestation of the element	F3 This chiaroscuro (creates the appearance of a dim, murky and seedy atmosphere in the bar) creating low-key lighting on the character's faces.	The theory, *mise-en-scene* constructs meaning, is demonstrated by a specific example of *mise-en-scene* and meaning from the film
Making generalization about element-makes-meaning theory in context of this film genre	F4 (This type of lighting is appropriate for the film noir context of the narrative.)	The significance of genre in the conceptual formation and in the assignment title is emphasized

Figure 4.9 Matching the generalizations of the macroTheme to a more contextualized hyperTheme and exemplifying from a particular film.

the rest of the paragraph. Particular meanings from the film that illustrate the general category of meaning that has been attributed to the element in the hyperTheme are identified and commented on. This movement from the more decontextualized to the more contextualized (referred to as a *matching pattern* by Hoey, 1995) is repeated prosodically throughout the text. An example is given in Figure 4.9 relating the generalizations of paragraph A, the macroTheme, to paragraph F, which is about the particular element, *lighting,* in this particular film, *Red Rock West*.

In what ways does *mise-en-scene* work to construct meaning in film noir, with particular reference to the first fifteen minutes of Red Rock West?[1]

Introduction

In this diagnosis I will be answering the question, "In what ways does ***mise-en-scene* work to construct meaning in film noir**, with particular reference to the first fifteen minutes of **Red Rock West**?". *Mise-en-scene* originates from the theatre, it is also used for films. *Mise-en-scene* is everything that is visible within the frame. The main elements of *mise-en-scene* are the **settings, costumes and make-up, lighting, and figure movement and body language.**

Red Rock West was directed by John Dahl. **Red Rock West** is a **modern day film noir, Neo-noir or country noir**, and this film as demonstrates. John Dahl uses Lara Flynn Boyle as the **femme fatale, a lot of good looking Wyoming atmosphere**, and **a twist filled plot** which starts when an innocent penniless drifter (Nicholas Cage) walks into a bar and is mistaken as a killer....

I will be studying and discussing the first fifteen minutes of the film, **Red Rock West**. The film starts off with **an establishing shot** of a road which disappears into the distance, I think **this shot** was used to give you the idea that it's the middle of nowhere. The **next shot** you see the main character, Nicholas Cage, immuring from a bad nights sleep, he was sleeping in his car. He then starts preparing himself for the long day ahead. He puts on his jeans then starts doing one handed press ups, this could be done for a couple of reasons.

He wants to stay fit

or

This shows how he prepares himself for the day ahead (like inTaxi Driver)

My opinion is option two.

Conclusion

I think that the **mise-en-scene** was used very well in "Red Rock West". The **zooming in and shading** kind set the mood for the film but also the characters emotions. Mise- en-scene to me is important to all films but referring it to **film noir** mise-en-scene is important. **Film noir** is a complex **genre** it has many **elements** which splits it up from all the other types of genre, it's a mystery with twists and turns the subjects covered are money, love, betrayal, murder. In the reading given to the class by John Orr "The road to nowhere", he describes **film noir** as a deadly triangle: love, passion, money. He also goes on to says,"The thing I like the most about the old film noir was that in the beginning you're left in mystery until the end. I also like the **low key-lighting** I think that it **sets the mood and adds to the suspense**.

---

[1] *Bold: Key concept terms*

Underlining: Words representing the central proposition, mise-en-scene makes meaning

Figure 4.10 Everton's text: macroTheme, hyperThemes, macroNew, the theory, and technical terms.

4.6.2 MacroTheme, HyperTheme, and Theoretical Explanation in Everton's Text

Everton did not establish the conceptually framed paragraphs that Tyrrell did—although his paragraphs are units of meaning that perform purposes. The schematic version of Everton's assignment in Figure 4.10 is presented differently than that of Tyrrell's assignment in Figure 4.1. As with Tyrrell's text, the macroTheme and macroNew paragraphs are presented in full. However, as there were only two other paragraphs in Everton's text, in addition to the hyperThemes, several subsequent sentences of these paragraphs are presented. In the same way that they were for Tyrrell's text, the key concepts from the teacher's conceptual formation are in bold and the *mise-en-scene constructs meaning* proposition is underlined.

Figure 4.10 shows that the macroTheme appears to set up the *mise-en-scene* taxonomy as the conceptual framework for the analysis. However, subsequent paragraphs do not create the matching pattern identified in Everton's text, nor is the threshold proposition *mise-en-scene constructs meaning* used after it is referred to in a repetition of the title in the macroTheme.

Although there is evidence that Everton is drawing from the *mise-en-scene* taxonomy, there is far less use of concept terms and the threshold proposition *mise-en-scene makes meaning* than in Tyrrell's text. The Themes of many sentences in the analysis indicate that the text is about the film actors, the filmmaker or the student himself. This pattern is replicated at the macro- and hyperTheme levels. The absence of the *mise-en-scene* taxonomy and the *mise-en-scene constructs meaning* theory means that the events and situations in the film are not decontextualized. The text stays close to a filmgoer's experience. This is particularly pronounced in the affective response and emotive evaluation of the second paragraph where terms such as *a lot of good looking Wyoming atmosphere* and *a twist filled plot* come from the conceptual formations of popular film review. A central motivation for Everton in studying Media Studies was to develop the skills of media production and in this text he situates himself more as a director of the narrative than as an analyst applying the *mise-en-scene* taxonomy. At this stage in his learning, taxonomic film analysis was both mystifying and incongruent with his goals. During interviews, Everton expressed similar concerns about the negative impact of academic discourse on his learning to those expressed by James in Chapter 2.

4.7 The Language of Film Analysis—Representing Film

In order to construct their different model films, Tyrrell and Everton reveal different semantic orientations (see Chapter 2, Section 2.2) and associated linguistic resources. Tyrrell uses abstract concepts to fragment the storyline of the film into illustrative extracts that exemplify the proposition *mise-en-scene makes meaning*. In effect, she turns the film into an object of study. To do this she has to use language in ways that would be unusual outside the context of Film Studies writing. Everton's representation of the film reproduces the dominant feature of a classic Hollywood film, which is its storyline. Narrative is more common in everyday communication than analysis (see, e.g., Bruner, 1990, pp. 45, 80; Martin & Rose, 2008, p. 49) so the language of Everton's text is more congruent with everyday speech. These differing representations of film are generated in language choices at the word, clause, and sentence levels. This section will examine the language of four representative sentences from each student's text in order to illustrate how word choice and arrangement determine whether an assignment is an analysis or a description of a film. See Chapter 3, Section 3.4.1.2 for the terms and concepts of this ideational analysis.

The first set of sentences are taken from Everton's text and they illustrate the four main Process types for construing field.

Sentence 1
Material

Cage	growls and stops	at the closest gas station
Actor	material Process	Circumstance:Location

In Everton's text there is a high incidence of material Process clauses like this, in which characters from the film are in the functional role of Actor in the clause. In some clauses, the camera, the filmmaker, or Everton himself is the active Participant. As these Participants are concrete and animate rather than abstract, the text builds a particularly "material," as opposed to abstract, model of the film being analyzed.

Sentence 2
Relational

The sequence after that	is	(the sequence) of the manager and Cage's friend talking about his bad leg
Identified	identifying relational Process	Identifier

In this relational clause, the thematic Participant is a material element of the film (a film *sequence*). The Identifier that follows the Process (*is*) provides details of the film sequence, which is thus functionally in the Identified role. As with the first type of clause, the focus is on material aspects of the film. In Everton's text, relational clauses of this type are less common than material doing clauses, but when they do occur they tend toward more material meanings, attributing material Identifiers to material Identifieds.

Sentence 3
Verbal

He	tells	Cage	there are lots of jobs there
Sayer	verbal Process	Receiver	Verbiage

The main clause in sentence three is a verbal clause. Most film narrative is carried by interactions between people who say things to each other. This clause presents such an interaction between one of the other characters and Nicholas Cage, with the other character in the Participant role of the Sayer. As with the previous clause examples, this clause focuses on particular (as opposed to general) and material (as opposed to abstract) aspects of the film.

Sentence 4
Mental

You	're just seeing	the silhouettes of the characters
Senser	mental Process	Phenomenon

Film analysis itself can be seen as an exercise in perception—seeing and thinking about film in various ways—and at the same time, perception is a central theme of film analysis—how characters in films see and think about each other, how audiences see and think about film, and so on. Learning to take up a position from which perception is managed is therefore an important part of analyzing a film. By choosing the Participant, *You,* to occupy the Senser role in this mental clause of perception, Everton identifies himself and his reader with an embodied and unified audience perception of the film, which is a commonsense, rather than analytical, position to occupy.

The following sentences illustrate the same Process types in Tyrrell's text.

Sentence 1
Material

Each of the aforementioned elements of *mise-en-scene*	can work to construct	meaning
Actor	material Process	Goal

As with the material clause examined in Everton's text, the verb group is made up of the material Processes (*work to construct*). However, in Tyrrell's text, the Participant in the Actor role is not animate, nor concrete; it is a generalization *(each of the aforementioned elements of mise-en-scene)*. The Participant that the Actor is *working to construct* is even less concrete; it is the abstraction *meaning*. In fact, the material Processes, *work to construct,* are metaphorically shifted from a physical realm to a symbolic one. For language users experienced at this kind of film analysis, such metaphorical usage of a material Process will not seem unfamiliar. But, generalized Participants doing material Processes to produce abstractions is a less familiar usage for students new to film analysis. For this reason, *mise-en-scene* is identified here as a threshold concept and this sentence as a threshold proposition in this film analysis. To identify *mise-en-scene* as a threshold concept means that as students start to build the field of film analysis around the proposition *mise-en-scene constructs meaning*, it can lead to a change in their understanding of film. The suspension of disbelief that characterizes much of the film viewer's experience may be disrupted and the film itself may come into focus as an object of study. However, there may be much learning still to do, both of this "troublesome" threshold concept itself and of the language involved in using it in film analysis.

Sentence 2
Relational

Lighting, the shot, setting, location, props	are	some key elements of *mise-en-scene*
Identified	relational Process	Identifier

In this clause, the Process "to be" *(are)* is used to set up a technical taxonomy. The taxonomy itself is of generalities and is a step away from the material details of the film. This technical taxonomy works together with the abstractions in Sentence 1 to organize conceptualizations of the film around the key concept of *mise-en-scene.* Students who write this kind of clause are relating the material substance of the film to meanings that the film can be seen to be making. These are disciplinary meanings (for example, that "chiaroscuro lighting is used to create murky and seedy atmosphere in film noir"). In effect, they are distancing themselves from the film as a personally experienced narrative and objectifying the film in terms of general and abstract categories (or following Halliday and Martin—see, e.g., Halliday & Martin, 1993—"thingifying" the film). Importantly, they are objectifying or thingifying the abstraction, *meaning,* and by so doing, opening up possibilities for a range of disciplinary meanings to be considered. Students who can create and implement such a taxonomy and work with it in this way are engaging in a central act of film analysis (cf. Bordwell, 1989, on applying conceptual schemata to film narrative). This clause type is thus central to the process of taxonomic film analysis that students are being asked to perform for this assignment.

Sentence 3
Verbal

In his chapter, The Road to Nowhere,	John Orr also	discusses	the role money plays as a visual device and cinematic code in film noir
Circumstance:Location	Sayer	verbal Process	Verbiage

In the world of Film Studies, it is not only film characters who speak; critics, academics, and other voices can also be heard. Marshaling these voices is another way that students turn film into an object of study. To experienced academics, this is obvious. To new Film Studies students, it is something they are learning to do. In this example of a verbal clause, Tyrrell has exploited an academic Sayer to introduce new concepts, *visual device, cinematic code,* and so on, which can be used to frame the film as an object of study. Learning to apply these concepts in her analysis has already begun through what might be called Tyrrell's "ventriloquation" (Bakhtin, 1982) of the words of an experienced film analyst.

Sentence 4
Mental

Audiences	expect to see	characters in contemporary American West settings to wear denim
Senser	mental Process	Phenomenon

In this mental Process, presumptions are made about what audiences *expect to see.* As with Everton's use of the pronoun, *You,* the use of the term *audiences* in the Participant role might be regarded as representing perception as unified and universal. However, there is a significantly different reality represented by using the noun, *audience,* rather than the pronoun, *You.* The reader and the writer are no longer identified with the audience, which has become objectified and also begun to fragment (it no longer necessarily contains *you* or *I*). This objectification is valued in the field since it means that the perception is not necessarily the analyst's personal opinion; rather, it can be imported into the analysis from outside, from "authorized" analytical perspectives. The fragmentation opens the way to diverse points of view even though there is no mention of them here. A student may not be aware of all this potentiality as they select the term *audience* rather than *you,* but it is likely that making this choice is a small part of the transformative process that the application of *mise-en-scene* in film analysis can entail.

Tyrrell and Everton are building their representations of film differently. The evidence for this lies in their writing: they are using language differently at the word, clause, sentence, paragraph, and text levels. The difference, of course, is not simply one of language. They are using language differently because they are doing different things: they are analyzing differently. The abstract Participants, metaphorical Processes, taxonomies, technical terms, and ventriloquation that Tyrrell uses are linguistic resources for doing film analysis and can only really be understood within that context. The material Actors and Processes of Everton's assignment are not recognized by the Film Studies teacher as film analysis.

4.8 Mediating Film Analysis Using a LASS Approach

The goal of the preceding SFL analysis has been to demonstrate the close relationship between a student's use of language and the purposes of their writing and learning within a particular disciplinary context. A LASS approach to teaching and learning proposes that learning Film Studies is actually learning how to speak and listen to and, particularly, read and write the language of Film Studies in order to pursue Film Studies purposes.

In responding to Everton's use of language, there are aspects that could be addressed in the terms on which he has based his text: some changes to subject–verb agreement, punctuation, and sentence structuring would improve the quality of the narrative-based analysis he has written. But this would not address the evaluation expressed by the film teacher of this assignment: that it is not analysis. This can only be addressed by reference to the *meanings* Everton is making; in other words, to his engagement with the conceptual formation of the field and social purposes of the text he has written. Supporting this work may seem more like the job of the film teacher than a language teacher. But from a LASS perspective students are always making meanings in context, and as those meanings are made in language, a linguistically responsive pedagogy is needed to support students.

What is at stake when someone writes are their meaning-making practices. In these students' cases, these include their semantic orientation to what an assignment task like this entails, their linguistic experience of enacting writing like a taxonomic film analysis, their motivations for being on the course, and their career goals. It might seem that a language specialist's involvement in this context would be with the language system, but the language system is an empty formality when detached from the social action and conceptual formations of the field of Film Studies.

The analysis shows that to write a taxonomic film analysis text, a film student needs the linguistic resources that enable them to:

1. name and make technical (by defining and exemplifying) a range of field-specific terminology, and use such terminology in clauses that relate the terms to each other in field-appropriate ways;
2. apply a material taxonomy (of *mise-en-scene* elements) to a particular film in ways which begin to demonstrate the technical meanings of everyday terms like *lighting*;
3. deploy the decontextualizing, abstracting, and transforming power of the proposition *mise-en-scene constructs meaning*;
4. demonstrate the abstract and decontextualized value of the term *meaning* applied in the analysis of a particular film sequence and the constellation of possible readings that can be made according to criteria from the conceptual formation of concepts constituting this area of Film Studies;
5. construct a "model film" (Bordwell, 1989), or "thingify" (Halliday & Martin, 1993) a film, through application of the various schemata offered by the conceptual formation;
6. elide the film-viewer and film maker from the making of meaning;
7. manage the movement up and down between decontextualized high-level abstractions and generalizations and low-level contextualized details and particulars;
8. convert a film narrative into a conceptually framed film analysis;
9. organize a text by patterns of lexis and grammar at the text, paragraph, and sentence level, including at the macroTheme, hyperTheme, and clause-Theme levels and within paragraphs at general and particular levels.

Teaching and learning this language of Film Studies would be difficult outside a Film Studies classroom, but it does not follow that simply by immersion in such language inside the Film Studies classroom students will acquire it, as witnessed by the external examiners' comments on the quality of third year film students' writing. This is why the *Ways of Writing* course was embedded in the *Ways of Seeing* course rather than taking place separately. In the Film Studies classroom the functional value of assignment features like introduction, paragraph topic sentence, general-to-particular, and concrete-to-abstract can be related directly to the transformational concept of *mise-en-scene* and the transformational proposition *elements of mise-en-scene construct meaning,* or to any other Film Studies conceptual formation that is studied.

In order to engage film students in this level of awareness of the role of language in learning, it was necessary to adopt an approach that resonated with their primary motive for being in the Media Studies Department, which was to work with media products and processes. The metasemiotic approach we adopted presented film analysis as a process that was achieved through language and modeled assignment writing as a meaningful production process, comparable with the production of other media products. This permitted us to address explicitly with students the reading and writing demands of the *Ways of Seeing* course. Through this approach, students who would not necessarily have shown interest in the texts they had to read and write developed skills in metasemiotic mediation and an equivalent interest in written texts to the one they acquired in film.

4.8.1 Syllabus and Metalanguage

To give an indication of how a LASS based approach to teaching and learning can be implemented, some illustrations from the *Ways of Writing* strand of the *Ways of Seeing* course are presented in this part of the chapter. These illustrations are followed by an evaluation of the impact of the approach.

The first illustration is the parallel outline syllabus of the *Ways of Seeing* and *Ways of Writing* strands for the first semester of the course (see Table 4.1). Although it will not be obvious from this brief outline, the *Ways of Writing* part of each session links directly to texts and Film Studies concepts that had been introduced in the *Ways of Seeing* part of the session. Wherever possible, Film Studies terminology and concepts were transferred from the *Ways of Seeing* curriculum and used in metasemiotic mediation of written text, even where their application to writing was a matter of analogy rather than of genuine transfer; for example, referring to hyperThemes as "establishing shots" or cohesion as "continuity editing" (see further examples in Table 4.2).

This syllabus was mediated through an approach based on the Sydney *genre teaching and learning cycle* (see, e.g., Humphrey & Macnaught, 2011;

Table 4.1 Parallel Film Studies and literacy syllabus

Wk	Ways of Seeing	Ways of Writing
1	*Mise-en-scene*/Genre Film screening: *Red Rock West*	**Why don't they all write the same** Genre = Context+Form; *Contrastive analysis of film "review" and Film "Studies" texts*
2	*Mise-en-scene*/Genre Film screening: *Mildred Pierce*	**Orientation to the assignment prompt** The opening scene of a taxonomic film analysis: *Contrastive analysis of 10 introductions* **Take-home diagnostic taxonomic film analysis assignment**
3	Sound/Position Film screening: *Raging Bull*	**Orientation to the assignment prompt** Work done in macroTheme, setting the scene for a taxonomic film analysis: establishing a conceptual framework
4	Sound as signifier/Hierarchies of sound (below the dialogue) Film screening: *A Man Escaped*	**Ways of reading—the dialogic way** Active reading by interrogating a text Exploiting text patterns, paragraph structure, establishing shots *Joint reading/note-taking activity*
5	Classical editing/Context Film screening: *The Silence of the Lambs*	**The whole assignment text** Feedback on diagnostic writing task *Discussion of extracts and reformulations from student assignments*
6	Classical Editing/Continuity Film screening: *Don't Look Now*	**Notemaking as production: making choices** Using general-particular patterns in text for note-making *Joint reading/note-making*
7	Classical Narrative Film screening: *Patriot Games*	**Continuity devices in writing: reader and writer responsibility** *Formative take-home assignment on Continuity Editing (another taxonomic analysis)*

(*Continued*)

Table 4.1 Continued

Wk	Ways of Seeing	Ways of Writing
8	New Hollywood and narrative Film screening: *Taxi Driver*	**Writing assignments like a reader** Readerly and writerly text *Joint construction of assignment 2, Continuity Editing*
9	New Hollywood and narrative Film screening: *Pulp Fiction*	**A taxonomic film analysis is not a narrative** Student views on a good analysis *Discussion using three examples of Continuity Editing assignment*
10	Classical Narrative and authorship 2 Film screening: extracts	**Modeling final assignment text** *Students discuss and propose conceptual frameworks in response to four final assignment prompts*

Table 4.2 Parallel Film Studies terms and literacy concepts

Film Studies terms		Literacy concepts
Mainstream Hollywood	-	Dominant Textual Conventions
Cinema audience	-	Audience (particularly the course teacher)
Film Themes	-	Conceptual Framework of Written Text
Opening Scene	-	MacroTheme
Scene	-	Paragraph
Establishing Shot	-	HyperTheme
Point of View Shot	-	Writer Position
Continuity Editing	-	Cohesion/Coherence
Art Cinema Film	-	Artful Manipulation of Genre Norms/Knowledge
Auteur	-	"Writerly" Text (i.e., not working for the reader)
Marks of Production	-	Author-in-the-Text
Film	-	Writing as Product (Text)
Filmmaking	-	Writing as Process (Text Construction)
Key Concepts	-	Abstractions/Generalizations

also see Chapter 7, Section 7.5.1) in which illustrative texts are deconstructed from a context, genre staging, language and learning perspective, and students are supported in creating their own texts on the basis of the insights obtained. The emphasis throughout the first semester was on the textual form of

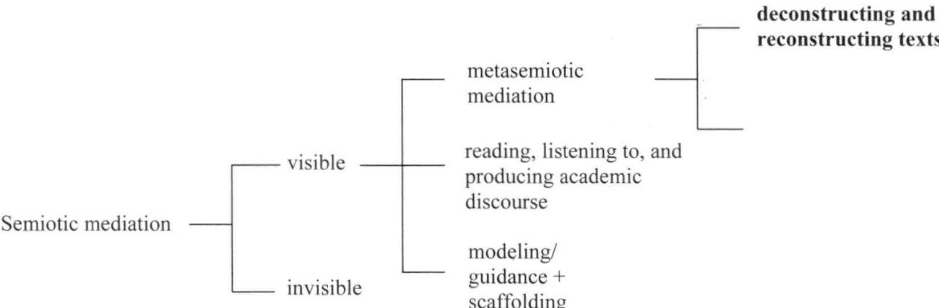

Figure 4.11 Deconstructing and reconstructing genres as a form of metasemiotic mediation.

university Film Studies discourse. This was represented as dominant, different from everyday discourse, and reflective of the work that constitutes university-level education. Figure 4.11 extends the semiotic mediation options first introduced in Figure 2.5 in Chapter 2 with the metasemiotic activity referred to above: deconstructing and reconstructing genres. (The metasemiotic activity of deconstructing and reconstructing genres will be elaborated in Chapter 7, Section 7.5.1.)

Film Studies terms that students were learning were used in metasemiotic mediation of written text in the *Ways of Writing* strand, including *genre, text, context, verisimilitude, narrative form, meaning,* and *meaning making*. Other Film Studies terms were used as synonyms, or metaphorical equivalents, of language and literacy terms and are presented in Table 4.2.

In debates about genre pedagogy there is often concern about the quantity and complexity of terminology required to carry out metasemiotic mediation. The strategy adopted in this course was to exploit metasemiotic terms that were already familiar and salient for students (see Chapter 7 for more discussion about this).

4.8.2 Illustrative Materials

Appendices 4.3–4.5 present three sets of materials from the *Ways of Writing* strand that illustrate the semiotic and metasemiotic mediation of the syllabus.

Appendix 4.3 introduces the notions of genre and register and exploits the notions of field, tenor, and mode (without actually using those terms).

Appendix 4.4 emphasizes the function of the macroTheme in setting up the conceptual framework of the analysis by presenting a variety of assignment introductions for students to evaluate.

Table 4.3 Comparative data on some features of the language of Everton's first and final taxonomic film analyses

	First Text	Final Text
Total Sentence Themes	**52**	**64**
Theme participants:		
Film character	47%	1.5%
Mise-en-scene	7%	20%
Elements	0%	53%
Clause Types		
Material	45%	40%
Relational	25%	40%
HyperThemes		
Mise-en-scene elements construct meaning pattern	0	6
Paragraphs		
Units of ideas?	Not in main body	Yes
Movement from general to particular (Matching patterns)	No	Yes

Appendix 4.5 is the adapted version of the Sydney University diagnostic tool, Measuring the Academic Skills of University Students (Bonanno & Jones, 2007), which we used to metasemiotically mediate feedback on a diagnostic writing activity in the second week of the course. Everton's and Tyrrell's texts were written in that diagnostic activity.

4.8.3 Impact of the *Ways of Writing* LASS-based Pedagogy

Everton's view was that there was too much writing in the *Ways of Seeing/Ways of Writing* Film Studies course. He was oriented to making films and his use of language reflected this, as demonstrated in his first film analysis. However, he appeared to develop his writing skills through the course and, with them, new knowledge about film. Ten weeks after writing the assignment that was analyzed here he wrote a similar but longer *mise-en-scene* taxonomic film analysis. This time his text was judged to be analysis and not description by his teacher, and Everton commented on how much he enjoyed doing *mise-en-scene* analyses. Over the semester, he had participated in 12 weeks of the writing development strand, *Ways of Writing*.

Table 4.3 presents comparative data on some features of the language of his first and final taxonomic film analyses.

The Theme analysis of these sentences show that more than half of the sentences in Everton's final *mise-en-scene* analysis were about elements of *mise-en-scene*. Almost no sentences were about film characters. In other words, his viewing of the film was no longer determined by the narrative of the film text. The more abstract concept of *mise-en-scene* constituted the Theme of one fifth of all the sentences in his final text reflecting the fact that the transformative proposition *mise-en-scene constructs meaning* had become central to his analysis. The more abstract nature of his analysis is further achieved by an increase in relational clauses from 25% to 40% in which the Identified and Identifier or Carrier and Attribute frame the narrative material Processes with technical or abstract film analysis concepts. Reflecting this sentence level shift from material description to abstract analysis, the overall design of his text was strongly aligned with the macroTheme and hyperTheme patterns demonstrated above in Tyrrell's text.

However, it has to be acknowledged that Everton did not attribute his much more successful end-of-course assignment to the learning he had experienced during the *Ways of Writing* strand. It is possible that he was right in this evaluation of his situation. Perhaps it was through his immersion in the dialogue around film and his continuous exposure to film analysis concepts in the lectures during the semester that he built his understanding of the film analysis process. But it is also quite likely that the metasemiotic mediation of the design of film analysis texts, the use of Film Studies concepts in writing, and the dialogue about the particularities of film analysis language that he experienced in the *Ways of Writing* course contributed to the acquisition of Film Studies knowledge and Film Studies language that he demonstrated in his end of course assignment.

Whether or not Everton was right in his evaluation of the writing course, in their end-of-term evaluations of the course, the majority of students acknowledged the impact of the *Ways of Writing* strand on their writing behavior. The same change observed in Everton's writing was evident across the entire cohort. From the beginning to the end of the course, there was a marked increase in the use of Film Studies conceptual formations and the features of taxonomic film analysis genre. It was also possible to compare this class with the preceding year's *Ways of Seeing* class (referred to as Year 1 in Table 4.4), which had not received the *Ways of Writing* input. The table shows that the number of students awarded B grades by their teacher for their *Ways of Seeing* assignments in Year 2 (the *Ways of Writing* year) went up to 32% from only 5% in Year 1; the number of students scoring C grades went down proportionately, with 63% scoring C grades in Year 1 compared to only 47% in Year 2. As with any educational intervention there are many variables that could be responsible for

Table 4.4 Comparison of end of course assessment scores in the year before the WOW/WOS project (Year 1) and after the first year of the WOW/WOS project (Year 2)

Assignment grades (awarded by subject teacher)	Year 1 (before WOW)%	Year 2 (after WOW) %
A	0	0
B	5	32
C	63	47
D	21	15
EFG	11	6

(Number of students per year = 70)

the improvement in *Ways of Seeing* grades in Year 2. However, a potentially significant variable was the increased time and attention that was invested in metasemiotic mediation of reading and writing in *Ways of Seeing* in Year 2.

A comparison of the linguistic features of assignments across the two years showed that it was not only grades that had changed. There was also a noticeable difference in the extent to which students in each year used the technical conceptual formations of Film Studies, their design of the taxonomic film analysis genre, and, as with Everton's second assignment discussed above, the incidence of relational clauses and sentence Themes that were conceptual rather than animate or concrete. Particularly noticeable was the increase in the incidence of the transformational proposition *elements of mise-en-scene construct meaning*. Table 4.5 provides statistics from a comparison of the macroThemes of the six top-scoring assignments from each of the years, showing which terms were named.

Table 4.5 shows top scoring students in Year 2 (the *Ways of Writing/Ways of Seeing* year) using the words *meaning* and *verisimilitude* in the macroTheme of their analyses significantly more than top scoring students in Year 1 (the year before the intervention).

Table 4.6 shows how many students named and also defined (made technical) a technical term in their macroTheme, indicating that they recognized the role of the term in their conceptual formation. The first number indicates how many assignment texts named the concept, the second number indicates whether it was defined, described, or explained, that is, made technical. Of eight key terms used across the top scoring assignments in Year 2, five were defined or explained (i.e., made technical): *mainstream cinema, meaning, genre, verisimilitude,* and *narrative.* Among these terms, the most striking is *mainstream cinema*. Five out of six texts used and defined this term in the

Table 4.5 Occurrence of named technical terms in the macroTheme of 6 top-scoring assignments from Year 1 and Year 2

Concept[a]	Year 1	Year 2
Elements	26	14
Meaning	6	21
Genre	1	3
Verisimilitude	1	7
*Realism	*3	0
Mainstream	4	6
Narrative	3	6

[a]Each named term was counted once only for each text, regardless of the number of times the same term occurred. *Meaning* was expressed by the word *meaning* itself and a number of field-specific technical terms such as *coherence, codes,* and *suspension of disbelief. Verisimilitude* appears more times than the total number of texts because one writer distinguished three kinds of verisimilitude. *Realism* is asterisked because of its inappropriateness to the field of this assignment task.

Table 4.6 The occurrence of concept terms made technical in the macroThemes of Year 1 and Year 2 top-scoring taxonomic film analyses

	Year 1		Year 2	
Concept	Named	Made Technical	Named	Made Technical
Mise-en-scene	6	4	6	5
Elements	6	0	6	0
Meaning	2	0	4	2
Genre	1	0	3	1
Verisimilitude	0	0	3	1
Realism*	4	1	-	-
Mainstream	4	1	5	5
Combination	2	0	2	0
Narrative	0	0	5	1
Total No. of Concepts made technical		6		15

**Realism* does not belong in this conceptual formation.

macroTheme, most of them explicitly proposing that its definition was a prerequisite to applying the *mise-en-scene* taxonomy in a film reading. This contrasts with the Year 1 texts, four of which named *mainstream cinema* but only one of which defined it or located it in a taxonomy of cinema types.

The comparison across these two student cohorts shows the Year 2 students developing precision and systematicity in their analysis of film through the medium of writing. For students coming into the university from backgrounds where such analytical writing, and its associated thinking, was not common, and where film was primarily an object of entertainment or a creative industry that they hoped to enter, such writing (and its associated reading) might seem of questionable relevance. The purpose of the LASS-based writing course, embedded in the Film Studies course, was to open up for consideration by the student group the nature and value of this kind of academic writing about film. An indication of the appeal of this approach was provided the year after the action research project was ended and the following year's students did not receive the *Ways of Writing* input. Second-year students who had experienced the LASS-based program set up a support group for students in the subsequent year, in which they metasemiotically mediated the insights into writing they had gained during the action research period.

4.9 Conclusion

The emphasis throughout this chapter has been on the use of language in the context of Film Studies revealed through a LASS-based action research approach. It has demonstrated the metasemiotic awareness that the initial and ongoing research informed and how this awareness was used in metasemiotically mediating student development of the taxonomic film analysis genre. Central to the metasemiotic mediation was the classification of Film Studies knowledge represented by the conceptual formations presented by the Film Studies teacher and the reading material he asked students to study. His own semiotic mediation of students' engagement with these texts, which constituted his framing of the learning experience provided by the *Ways of Seeing* course, was reinforced by the metasemiotic mediation provided by the framing of the *Ways of Writing* strand in that course.

How relevant are the findings of this action research project for students and teachers in other areas of the university curriculum? How transferable are the meaning-making skills and knowledge that have been uncovered here in the Film Studies curriculum? It seems likely that, if the object of study was not film but was some other phenomenon, then the linguistic resources that have been related to film analysis here could be employed in the study of that phenomenon. The conceptual formations would be different, and this would affect how the taxonomic analysis was realized. But in order to turn a phenomenon into an object of study and to establish distance from that object, that is, to make decontextualized meanings, it is likely that the set of demands placed on students' linguistic resources would be very similar. For this reason, it should be possible to recontextualize insights from this context in other contexts. However, the recontextualization must be carried out sensitively and cautiously if it is not to amount to the imposition of ways of doing, being, saying, and perceiving that are specifically appropriate to Film Studies. In the next chapter, we will show how insights into taxonomic analysis and theoretical explanation are relevant to the development of knowledge in a Health and Social Care course.

Notes

1 In the United Kingdom, a large number of former polytechnics and education colleges were granted university status in 1992. These were subsequently referred to as "new," or sometimes, "modern," universities.

2 The research entailed both text and context analysis. Texts were analyzed across two years of the *Ways of Seeing* course. First, in preparation for the *Ways of Writing* teaching intervention, 100 essays from the previous year's students, representing four different genres, were analyzed to different levels of detail. During and after the year of the *Ways of Writing* intervention, a similar number of student texts were analyzed, most of which were examples of the taxonomic film analysis genre reported on in this chapter. In order to gain further understanding of the context, the language specialist attended all the *Ways of Seeing* lectures and seminars throughout the year, engaged in ongoing dialogue with the Film Studies teacher, and carried out between two and four hours of interview with each of 20 students. Every week, the language specialist delivered a one-hour *Ways of Writing* session in a slot between the Film Studies lecture and a film viewing. Because both the Film Studies teacher and language specialist were keen to represent academic writing as integral to Film Studies itself, the language specialist's role became blurred with the film teacher's role, and to some extent the film teacher and the students regarded the language specialist as a participant in the teaching and learning of Film Studies, as indeed he was. This blurring provided more access to students' experiences of learning Film Studies and the film teacher's role in this than nonparticipant observation would have. For more information about the research behind this chapter please see Donohue (2012).

3 Following the convention in Film Studies, the French term, *mise-en-scene,* is italicized.

4 Please note that all student texts that we draw on throughout the book are presented exactly as written by the student, including any errors of grammar, vocabulary or referencing.

Appendix 4.1

Tyrrell's Taxonomic Film Analysis Text
Note: Paragraphs are indicated with letters and sentences with numbers.

***Assignment*: In what ways does *mise-en-scene* work to construct meaning in film noir, with particular reference to the first 15 minutes of *Red Rock West*?**

"*mise-en-scene* is inescapably visual and a vital element of style, and of meaning" (Bill Nichols, *Movies & methods*, University of California Press, 1976)

A1 Lighting, the shot, setting, location, props and costume are some key elements of mise-en-scene.
A2 When effectively presented within the context of the genre, in this case film noir, each of the aforementioned elements of *mise-en-scene* can work to construct meaning for the audience.
A3 There are various cinematic codes (discussed in this essay) within the genre of film noir that audiences can instantly recognize and identify.
A4 However this would not be possible without the significant contribution that *mise-en-scene* makes to aid the narrative of the film by constructing meaning in the visuals.

B1 Costume and props play an essential role in creating verisimilitude and conveying different meanings within the context of a film's genre, in particular "country noir."
B2 Costume worn by Wayne and Michael contributes significantly to the generic verisimilitude of the film.
B3 Audiences expect to see characters in contemporary American West settings to wear denim, cowboy boots and cowboy style shirts.
B4 Their costumes also visually convey meanings to the audience about their respective characters.
B5 The protagonist is dressed in light serene colors, stone washed denim and a white cowboy style shirt, giving the audience an indication that this is possibly a good character.
B6 Whilst Wayne is attired in dark somber colors, black trousers and waistcoat with a navy blue shirt conveying to the audience that this is a dark and sinister character.

C1 "Films are also dependent on 'props' as a device for conveying meaning. In a familiar sense props are definers of genre," An Introduction to Film Studies, "Film Form and Narrative" Allan Rowe, Routledge, p. 101.

C2 The prop element of *mise-en-scene* in Red Rock West distinctively works to construct meaning for the audience.
C3 When we see a substantial amount of dollar bills in Wayne's office it immediately becomes a visual device conveying meanings connected with crime and misconduct.
C4 It is a widely recognized and accepted presentation of money in film noir thus aiding generic verisimilitude.
C5 The money effectively aids the narrative as we soon discover that the cash being offered to the protagonist is directly connected with murder.
C6 In his article entitled "The Road to Nowhere" John Orr also discusses the role money plays as a visual device and cinematic code in film noir,
C7 "money is variously expressed through kidnapping and ransom, drugs, cars (and) gambling.
C8 Whatever it is, the stash of stolen bills in the black suitcase bypasses the anonymous world of plastic and the invisibility of credit.
C9 It is there for all to see" (Orr, 1998, p. 210).

D1 Orr makes an interesting observation comparing the appearance of the car (as a prop) to the temperament of its owner
D2 "The noir automobile is the flash used car which has seen better days-the white finned Cadillacs favored by Dahl.
D3 The car's transient identity matches its owner's.
D4 It is traded in, its number-plates changed and it never musters respectability." p216
D5 Orr sums up the meaning conveyed by the car as part of the film's mise-en-scene succinctly in a key sentence.
D6 "The car's transient identity matches its owners"
D7 This statement is decidedly true with regards to the protagonist's character as he himself is a drifter moving aimlessly from one town to another in search of work.

E1 The setting and location of Red Rock West differs from that of the traditional big city metropolitan settings of film noir of the 1940s and 50s.
E2 Orr tries to set up a new category of film noir by describing films similar to Red Rock West like "After Dark, My Sweet," "Kill Me Again" and "The Last Seduction" as "reworking(s) of the 1970s road movie" and "the new hybrid of country noir."
E3 This new genre that Orr has created takes conventions from film noir and the road movie.

E4 The settings and locations in Red Rock West correspond with this notion of "country noir" the opening scenes instantly present images of small town western America, the dusty opening road and the desert landscapes.
E5 The interior of Wayne's bar/saloon works effectively in *mise-en-scene* for its narrative context, the audience identifies the interior and exterior of the bar with that of one that could in found in contemporary small town western America.

F1 The various ways in which actors and locations are lit and shot within *mise-en-scene* can instantly convey meanings and messages to the audience by creating an atmosphere and allowing the audience to read into certain characters just by the way their images are presented.
F2 The interior of Wayne's bar only seems to be illuminated by a single source of dull and opaque light, possibly a key light coming from the exterior through the front door and windows.
F3 This chiaroscuro creates the appearance of a dim, murky and seedy atmosphere in the bar creating low-key lighting on the character's faces.
F4 This type of lighting is appropriate for the film noir context of the narrative.

G1 Throughout interaction in the bar between Wayne and the protagonist both of them are illuminated with low key lighting both characters faces appear to be half lit, with one side completely in shade and the other in sharp contrast lit.
G2 The bar scene is the first time we see Wayne so the way in which he is lit and shot creates an image of his character for the audience.
G3 He constantly appears in medium close up shots, the harsh low key lighting on him makes his clothes appear completely black giving the audience an impression that he is a sinister and unsavory character.
G4 This image of Wayne's character is continued in his office where he is framed in a lot of choker shots creating a dramatic emphasis illustrating his disturbing character and intentions.

H1 Significantly the lighting in the mise en sene of the bar presents the viewer with a meaning as to why both characters are lit in such a way.
H2 This presents the audience with the duplicity of both characters.
H3 The lighting symbolizes that both characters are literally in the shade about each other's ulterior motives.
H4 This notion is continued in another shot when the protagonist is walking from the bar into the office.

H5 The rest of the bar is illuminated whilst his image is completely black causing him to appear in complete silhouette exemplifying the fact that he is completely in the dark about what is happening.

I1 The outset of Red Rock West is shot with a wide angle lens giving deep perspective shots of the open road that appears to be vast and incessant.
I2 A shot of the protagonist standing next to his car framed in sharp focus whilst the depth of field is created with a deep perspective shot of the road ahead of him symbolizes his constant journey through life as a drifter travelling on the perpetual open road.

J1 After having meticulously studied the various ways in which *mise-en-scene* works to construct meaning in Red Rock West.
J2 It can be deduced that the very concept of mise en-scene withholds a significant amount of importance in clearly constructing and conveying meanings to the audience visually.

Appendix 4.2

Everton's Taxonomic Film Analysis Text
***Assignment*: In what ways does *mise-en-scene* work to construct meaning in film noir with particular reference to the first 15 minutes of *Red Rock West*?**

Introduction
A1 In this diagnosis I will be answering the question, "In what ways does mise-en-scene work to construct meaning in film noir, with particular reference to the first fifteen minutes of Red Rock West?."
A2 *Mise-en-scene* originates from the theater, it is also used for films.
A3 *Mise-en-scene* is everything that is visible within the frame.
A4 The main elements of *mise-en-scene* are the settings, costumes and make-up, lighting, and figure movement and body language.

B1 Red Rock West was directed by John Dahl.
B2 Red Rock West is a modem day film noir, Neo-noir or country noir, and this film as demonstrates.
B3 John Dahl uses Lara Flynn Boyle as the femme fatale, a lot of good looking Wyoming atmosphere, and a twist filled plot which starts when an innocent penniless drifter (Nicholas Cage) walks into a bar and is mistaken as a killer.
B4 J.T. Walsh wants him to murder his wife, while the seductive Boyle would like it the other way around – and that's all before the real killer (Dennis Hopper) arrives in town.

B5 John Dahl mixes black comedy into the noir sensibility here, and the actors (especially Nicholas Cage and Dennis Hopper, who were spot on) run with the idea.

C1 I will be studying and discussing the first fifteen minutes of the film Red Rock West.
C2 The film starts off with an establishing shot of a road which disappears into the distance, I think this shot was used to give you the idea that it's the middle of nowhere.
C3 The next shot you see the main character, Nicholas Cage, immuring from a bad nights sleep, he was sleeping in his car.
C4 He then starts preparing himself for the long day ahead.
C5 He puts on his jeans then starts doing one handed press ups, this could be done for a couple of reasons.
C6 1) He wants to stay fit
or
C7 2) This shows how he prepares himself for the day ahead (like in Taxi Driver)
C8 My opinion is option two.
C9 The fact that his home is a beaten up rusty Cadillacs and he has a damage leg also he has no money, life can't be that good for him.
C10 After the press ups he shaves then puts on a white cow boy looking shirt and looks at himself in a mirror and say, "Nice to meet you . . . ."
C11 The next shot is the white Cadillacs from a distance driving into an oil field.
C12 Nicholas Cage's character meets with someone he seems to know and walk into an office.
C13 In the office he is told to complete an application form.
C14 The sequence after that is of the manager and Cage's friend talking about his bad leg.
C15 It is at this point that the mise-en-scene is used very well, the camera is focused at the window of the office and you're just seeing the silhouettes of the characters.
C16 Then the camera slowly moves down and focuses on Cage who hears the whole conversation and then starts walking away.
C17 He gets into his car thanks his friend for the help, while his friend apologies.
C18 As Cage is driving down the road he starts punching the ceiling of the car this is a medium long shot from inside the car.
C19 Their is a close up of the fuel gauge.
C20 Cage growls and stops at the closest gas station.

C21 Cage is outside his car.
C22 He looks into his wallet to see only five dollars then starts calling for some service.
C23 He walks inside the gas station calling still.
C24 As he turns round to walk out he sees some money stashed under the counter, again this is when *mise-en-scene* is at it's very best.
C25 Nicholas Cage's face is very shady on one side of his face as he stares at the money.
C26 The camera slowly zooms in onto his face and you are lead to believe that he is fighting his conscience.
C27 He shrugs it off and begins to walk away.
C28 As he walks away an old man walks in, (he works there) and works out what just happens.
C29 He starts talking to Cage then tells him about Red Rock West.
C30 He tell Cage that there are a lot of jobs there.
C31 (Next Shot) As the white Cadillacs drives past we are shown the location we have just arrived in due to the town sign, which to me has two meanings:
C32 1. Just an ordinary town show
C33 2. The sign represents no escape
C34 We are show a man working in a bar cleaning glasses.
C35 There is a Close up of his face as he looks outside.
C36 He notices the Texas number plate on a white Cadlilacs.
C37 Cage walks into the bar and orders a coffee.
C38 The bar tender starts asking questions then tells him to come round the back.
C39 As Cage sits and listens to what the bar tender say.
C40 One side of his face is hidden with in the shades the bar tender face looks very shady.
C41 As the bar tender tells Cage what he has to the shade on the side of his face slow dimmers.

Conclusions
D1 I think that the *mise-en-scene* was used very well in "Red Rock West."
D2 The zooming in and shading kind set the mood for the film but also the characters emotions.
D3 Mise- en-scene to me is important to all films but referring it to film noir *mise-en-scene* is important.
D4 Film noir is a complex genre it has many elements which splits it up from all the other types of genre, it's a mystery with twists and turns the subjects covered are money, love, betrayal, murder.

D5 In the reading given to the class by John Orr "The road to nowhere," he describes film noir as a deadly triangle:

love

passion money

D6 He also goes on to says,
D7 "The thing I like the most about the old film noir was that in the beginning you're left in mystery until the end"
D8 I also like the low key-lighting I think that it sets the mood and adds to the suspense.

Appendix 4.3

Teaching Materials From Session 1 of the *Ways of Writing* Course
This first set of materials introduces the notions of genre and register and exploits the notions of field, tenor and mode (without actually using these terms)

WHY DON'T THEY ALL WRITE THE SAME?

This activity starts looking at how writing is different. That is, writing is not one thing. It is different things in different situations. There are different *genres* of writing. In the activity, there are three pieces of writing which seem more or less the same. The activity explores how they are different.

The real purpose for doing this is to lead into thinking about how writing for Ways of Seeing is different from (and the same as) other writing you may have done.

There are three pieces of writing (i.e. *texts*). For each one you are going to consider three questions:

1 Why is this being written about?
2 How is this being written about?
3 What other ways of writing about it are there?

Question 1 deals with *purpose* and *context*
Question 2 deals with *stages, language* and *interpersonal relations*
Question 3 compares the three texts

TEXT 1 from *100 Best Films of the Century*, by Barry Norman

1 Why is this being written about?
Purpose and *context*

Look at the list of some possible purposes Barry Norman may have had and tick any that you think may be appropriate.
Add any purpose that you think is not on the list.

1. It is a way for Barry Norman to make some money
2. Barry Norman wants to share his pleasure in the film with as many people as possible
3. Barry Norman wants to boost his reputation as the people's film critic
4. It accompanies a television series
5. Barry Norman wants to make a contribution to Media Studies
6. ________________________

2 How is this being written about?
Stages (i.e. the procedure the writer has gone through)

Below is a list of steps that Barry Norman has taken to construct the text. They are not in the order that he took them. Using 1 to indicate the first step, 2 to indicate the second . . . and so on, put the steps into the right sequence.

He writes:

___________Reasons for the film's popularity
___________A classic moment to capture the character of the film
___________A background to the film's production
___________An explanation of its exceptional success

Draw a line in the text to show where each stage begins and ends

Barry Norman has included two visuals. Do any of the reasons below explain why.

He includes visuals

___________To fill up empty space
___________To evoke key moments from the film
___________To back up some of the claims he makes in the text

2 How is this being written about?
Language

The language Barry Norman chooses to write tells us a lot about what's going on in this text. There are two aspects of the language that are important: *the subject* and the *relationship* between Barry Norman and his readers.

The subject
Below is a list of expressions that clearly belong to a text about film (and not one about banana importation, for example). Find the expressions and underline them in the text and then add more expressions to the list that obviously signal this is a text about film.

run-of-the-mill, top-of-the-bill program filler
a plot
Warner Brothers
George Raft
faultless supporting cast
the sparkling dialogue
the chemistry that crackled
the perfect romantic film
a story of star-crossed lovers
in the end

2 How is this being written about?
Language

The relationship between Barry Norman and his readers.

Below is a list of expressions Barry Norman uses. Below that is a table with a number of words to describe *the kind of person* Barry Norman thinks he is and *the kind of relationship* he has with his readers. Judging from the expressions tick the boxes that best describe Norman and his relationship with the readers. Find at least one more expression in the text that you think fits in with these expressions and add it to the list.

the world knows and loves
we love it for a variety of reasons

the chemistry that crackled between Bogart and Bergman

a friend	a student	a media analyst	an authority on films	a man in a pub	informed member of the cinema audience
uncertain	confident	friendly	critical	knowledge-able	entertaining

3 What other ways of writing about it are there?
This question focuses on the differences between texts.

Go back to the list of purposes in question 1.
Are any of these purposes appropriate to a university assignment?

Go back to the subject expressions in question 2.
Tick any of these expressions which are appropriate to a university assignment and cross any which are not
Why do you think so?

Go back to the relationship expressions in question 2.
Do they signal the relationship between a student and a teacher?
Why/why not?

TEXT 2 from *The Oxford Guide to Film Studies (an academic Film Studies text)*

1 Why is this being written about?
Purpose and *context*

In this case there are two "writers": the editors of *The Oxford Guide to Film Studies* who chose this extract from a text to include in their Guide; and the author of the original text from which this extract has been taken, Rick Altman.

Look at the list of some possible purposes the editors may have had and tick any that you think may be appropriate.
Add any purpose that you think is not on the list.

1. They want to create the impression the Guide is very intellectual
2. They want to provide a variety of viewpoints on film criticism
3. Rick Altman is a very important writer and the editors want to look important
4. They want to include some entertainment in their Guide
5. ____________________________________

Look at the list of some possible purposes Rick Altman may have had in writing the original text and tick any that you think may be appropriate. Add any purpose that you think is not on the list.

1. He wrote it as a university assignment
2. It is the text of a speech he gave at a film award ceremony
3. He wanted to engage in a written debate about the true nature of Hollywood
4. He wanted to make a name for himself
5. He wanted to make an old film sound very interesting
6. He wanted to contribute to the understanding of Hollywood within Media Studies
7. ____________________________________
8. ____________________________________

2 How is this being written about?
Stages (i.e. the procedure the writer has gone through)

Below is a list of steps that Rick Altman has taken to construct the text. They are not in the order that he took them. Using 1 to indicate the first step, 2 to indicate the second . . . and so on, put the steps into the right sequence.

He writes . . .

_____ A basic statement of the theme of his argument
_____ An example of a film to illustrate his theme
_____ Support for his theme (*character psychology/cause-effect*)
_____ Support for his theme (*evidence of symbolism in character, setting, etc.*)
_____ Support for his theme (*universal and mythic qualities*)
_____ Support for his theme (*tension and the film's conclusion*)
_____ Repetition of the theme and conclusion

Draw a line in the text to show where each stage begins and ends

Rick Altman has included no visuals. Why not?

2 How is this being written about?
Language

The subject – academic language
Again the text is full of expressions that clearly belong to a text about *film*. However, there are also other expressions which could appear in other academic texts about other subjects (*society*, for example, or *literature*).

The first list below consists of expressions which are closely linked to Film Studies, many of which are *technical* words from the field. The second list consists of expressions which are linked to Film Studies but are also *more general academic* words. Find the expressions and underline them in the text and then add more expressions to each of the lists. (Don't worry too much about where each expression belongs, they are not clean-cut distinctions)

Closely linked to Film Studies
linear narrative stretches from
atmosphere provides melodramatic backdrop
character psychology
advance the film
minimally motivated
plot-unifying Macguffin
embodiment of audience desires
melodramatic framework
psychological progression
heighten the air of impending doom

More general academic words
operates as
presupposes
owes its longevity to
express the changing state of their emotions
apocalyptic intensity
stereotypically

2 How is this being written about?
Language

Relationship: Who is involved? What sort of person is the writer? What sort of person is the reader?
The following activities look at some expressions which answer these questions

Paragraph 1

Who is Rick Altman talking to in the expressions listed below – especially who is *we*? Underline the expressions in paragraph 1. Tick the box(es) with the most likely audience for Rick Altman's text.

his friends	cinema audiences	newspaper film critics	media analysts	film producers

was seen as
study after study attempted to
we now have reached the point where we acknowledge
maybe the classical text is not as unitary as was once thought

Paragraph 8

Who is Rick Altman *talking to* in these expressions? Underline the expressions in paragraph 8. Tick the box(es)

his friends	cinema audiences	newspaper film critics	media analysts	film producers

Why does Casablanca continue to enchant audiences around the world?
Because of its . . . Yes, without a doubt.
Because of the film's melodramatic underpinnings? Yes again

Who is Rick Altman *talking about* in these expressions? Underline the expressions in the text. Then answer the questions by ticking the boxes below

The film's suspense and expectation are carefully used to focus our attention on the future. As we dutifully fill all the plot's little gaps, we settle comfortably into the spectator position allotted to us.

Who *uses suspense and expectation*?

his friends	cinema audiences	newspaper film critics	media analysts	film producers

Who is *we*?

his friends	cinema audiences	newspaper film critics	media analysts	film producers

What sort of person is Rick Altman, judging from the expressions below? Underline the expressions. Then tick the most appropriate boxes

a friend	a student	a teacher	an authority on films	a man in a pub	a person in the cinema
uncertain	confident	critical	humorous	knowledge-able	other

Paragraph 2
Take the case of...
Casablanca does not owe its longevity to this familiar story line
If Casablanca continues to enjoy success, it is not so much because ... but because...
The secret of this film lies in...
... that capture our more immediate attention

Paragraph 6
We should not conclude, though...

3 What other ways of writing about it are there?
This question focuses on the differences between texts

Go back to the list of purposes in question 1.
Are any of these purposes appropriate to a university assignment?

Go back to the list of steps in question 2.
Tick any of these steps which are appropriate to a university assignment

Language – subject

This is to compare the subject language of Barry Norman and Rick Altman.

Paragraph 6 in Rick Altman deals with the ending of the film. Find the section where Barry Norman deals with the same thing.

The section in Barry Norman begins with the words:

----

and ends with the words:

Barry Norman's expressions	Rick Altman's
they did not go off together in the end	psychology and time
they sacrificed love for duty and so ensured their love would last for ever	
If Bogart and Bergman had gone off together in the end it would not hold its special place in the memory	

Language – relations

Barry Norman evaluates the film in these words:

It's the perfect romantic film . . . it holds a special place in our memories

Rick Altman asks

Why does Casablanca continue to enchant audiences around the world?

Who is Barry Norman identifying with? Write B in the appropriate box below

Who is Rick Altman identifying with? Write R in the appropriate box below.

a person in the cinema	cinema audiences	newspaper film critics	media analysts	film producers

Appendix 4.4

Teaching Materials from Session 2 of the *Ways of Writing* Course

The materials for the second session, *Orientation to Question,* emphasized the function of the macroTheme in setting up the conceptual framework of the analysis, by presenting a variety of assignment introductions for students to evaluate. A selection of the 10 macroThemes is presented.

ORIENTATION TO QUESTION

The opening paragraph acts as a frame for the assignment. It sets the scene for everything that follows. For that reason, it often operates at a high level of abstraction in order to allow plenty of space for the action. But at the same time it orients to the question, picking up themes that are crucial to the discussion that follows.

Read through the following opening paragraphs. They are the first paragraph from 10 assignments answering the question:

In what ways does *mise-en-scene* work to construct meaning in mainstream cinema?

For each example decide how many of the comments listed below apply. Tick the box with the appropriate number for each relevant comment. There will normally be more than one for each paragraph. When you have finished look at the follow up task on the last page.

COMMENTS

This opening paragraph . . .

1 orients to *genre*

2 orients to *narrative*

3 orients to *context*

4 orients to *audience-character relationships*

5 orients to the *elements* of *mise-en-scene*

6 orients to *editing*

7 orients to *construction of meaning*

8 orients to assignment procedure

9 defines *mise-en-scene*

10 quotes at length from an authority

11 repeats the question

1
Films create an impression of reality but, in fact, an audience is looking at a construction. Possibly the most obvious elements that construct meaning in a film are the plot, the character, the dialogue and the acting. However, meaning depends on a context: the meaning of the words "I love you" between two lovers in a romantic setting is different to their meaning between two strangers in a deserted and dark back alley. *Mise-en-scene* plays a large part in creating the context for the action of a film and so makes an important contribution to the construction of meaning. In particular, it signals what genre the film is.

1	2	3	4	5	6	7	8	9	10	11

2
In order to answer this essay question I have researched into the various ways that *mise-en-scene* constructs meaning in mainstream cinema. I have presented and defined the main aspects of *mise-en-scene* and backed up each statement with various examples from films and quotes from books. I have drawn particular attention to two mainstream films that I believe contain good examples of mise-en-scene; "All the President's Men" (1976) and "The Postman Always Rings Twice" (1981)

1	2	3	4	5	6	7	8	9	10	11

3
"Mise-en-scene. French term – literally, the placing of a scene – for the act of staging or directing a play or a film. Derived from the terminology of the theatre, the term has acquired in recent years an additional meaning in its application to the cinema. Andre Bazin, and subsequently other theoreticians and critics have used it to describe a style of film directing basically distinct from that known as Montage. Whereas montage derives its meaning from the relationship between one frame to the next through editing, *mise-en-scene* emphasizes the content of the individual frame" **(pp. 813–814, The International Film Encyclopaedia by Ephraim Katz)**

1	2	3	4	5	6	7	8	9	10	11

4
Mainstream cinema as we have come to regard it is the classical Hollywood cinema. It has become the dominant form of the film in the Western world and is based upon a narrative structure of beginning, middle and end. In the beginning there is an orientation, followed by a disruption to the situation generating a conflict consisting of a main plot and subplots and minor characters leading to a resolution at the end. This narrative form has become dominant for a number of reasons, including economic, cultural and psychological ones.

1	2	3	4	5	6	7	8	9	10	11

8
To answer the question 'In what ways does *mise-en-scene* work to construct meaning in mainstream cinema?' we must first be able to understand what *mise-en-scene* actually is. *Mise-en-scene* is a term that originated in the theatre and has been adapted to film; it refers to everything that is visible within the frame. Some of the key elements of *mise-en-scene* are the setting, costume and make-up, lighting, and figure movement and body language. These elements all work together to create the right image and atmosphere for the scene.

1	2	3	4	5	6	7	8	9	10	11

9
Blade Runner is a good example of a film with mise-en-scene. In <u>Blade Runner</u> Los Angeles is very dark and dismal. Skyscrapers are densely packed together towering into the sky, the sky is full of smoke and there is fire and small explosions. All through the film it is constantly raining in Los Angeles. There are very strong shadows, because of the neon lights, and the streets look very seedy. The people fit in to this situation. When Pris is first seen in the rain she has frizzy bleached hair, wearing a studded dog collar and her stockings are held up by garters but when Deckard finds Pris her costume changes and she looks more like a grotesque clown. Because she reveals this ugly side Deckard is justified in shooting her. It is also noticeable that Leon and Roy Batty both wear long black coats, not white coats. Finally, "Zhora is a pleasure goddess.

When she dons cyberpunk garb, she becomes a hard-edged animalistic beast woman" (pp. 5 of 10 Francesca Myman).

1	2	3	4	5	6	7	8	9	10	11	12

Paragraph 9 has a number of problems. A major one is that it is made up of a large amount of detailed information but does not clarify how this relates to the question. It is purely *descriptive*.

In order to relate to the question and provide a frame of reference for the assignment that follows, this paragraph could indicate the *abstractions* that are illustrated by the details.

The list below lists a number of abstractions relevant to the question. Tick those abstractions that are illustrated (although not specifically mentioned) by the details in the opening paragraph 9.

mise-en-scene	
location	
genre	
make up	
sets	
verisimilitude	
costume	
mainstream cinema	
lighting	
body language	
film noir	
the shot	
story	
dialogue	
figure movement	
meaning	
visuals	
acting	

There are probably three opening paragraphs which create a good frame for the discussion which follows in the rest of the assignment. The other paragraphs are far less successful.

Identify the three paragraphs you think are the most successful. Write the numbers below and next to each one write one or two sentences about the reason for your choice.

Imagine you were writing the introduction to the assignment title given on the first page. You are going to use *Blade Runner* and one other film (of your choice) to illustrate your answer. Sketch out a rough outline for an opening paragraph.

Read back over your opening paragraph. Which of the list of abstractions below have you used? Are there others not on the list which you have included? Add them at the bottom of the list.

mise-en-scene	
location	
genre	
make up	
sets	
verisimilitude	
costume	
mainstream cinema	
lighting	
body language	
film noir	
the shot	
story	
dialogue	
figure movement	
meaning	
visuals	
acting	

On the basis of your review of your opening paragraph, write a second draft making any changes you believe could improve it.

Appendix 4.5

Diagnostic Assessment Sheets (Literacy Raters)

This is the evaluation rubric used to metasemiotically mediate a "diagnostic" taxonomic film analysis that students wrote between session 1 and session 2 of the WOW strand.

COURSE ___________________ NAME ___________________

KEY TO RATING
4 = good/minor problems/mainly accurate/largely appropriate
3 = reasonable/minor problems/some inaccuracies/some inappropriacies
2 = only fair/some problems/often inaccurate/often inappropriate
1 = poor/major problems/inaccurate/inappropriate

CRITERIA				
A. Use of source material – is information taken from the lectures, the reading and the film correct and appropriate for the task?	4	3	2	1
1. relevant information from reading is employed 2. irrelevant information from reading is avoided 3. film material is interpreted correctly 4. film material is transferred correctly 5. written and film information is integrated with the text 6. text is free from plagiarism 7. bibliography constructed correctly				
B. Structure and development of text – is the structure and development of the answer clear and appropriate to the question and its context?	4	3	2	1
1. text structure (genre) is appropriate to the task 2. introduction sets the theme 3. beginnings of paragraphs and sentences orientate to theme 4. critical evaluation of evidence 5. use of evidence consistent with the theme 6. statement of conclusion follows from argument/interpretation & relates to theme				
C. Control of academic writing style – does the grammar conform to appropriate patterns of written academic English	4	3	2	1
1. appropriate use of abstract words				

(*Continued*)

CRITERIA				
2. appropriate combinations of words 3. appropriate relationship with reader 4. control of continuity devices in text 5. control of categories 6. appropriate choice of vocabulary 7. appropriate evaluation language				
D. Grammatical correctness	4	3	2	1
1. clause structure follows recognisable & appropriate patterns of English 2. correct subject verb agreement 3. consistent and appropriate tense choice, correctly formed 4. correct singular plural noun agreement				

[Adapted from materials created by the MASUS Project, University of Sydney (Bonanno & Jones, 2007)]

CHAPTER 5
"48 Marks Knocked Off for Academic Writing or Lack of Really Annoyed Me": Genre, Conceptual Formations, and Semantic Variation

5.1 Introduction

> I've never done academic study, academic writing, and I have had run-ins with my tutor, on the basis of my last assignment, my last essay, I thought I'd put together a balanced argument. I had—fifty two was the score—which is a pass I know, it's over forty. But forty eight marks knocked off for academic writing, or lack of, really annoyed me.
>
> That was annoying because he put on the feedback—and his feedback is good—but it was very much along the lines of oh you know "Your feedback: you've got lots of information in here, you've put lots of information together but you haven't done this, you haven't done that."
>
> . . . I worry that there is someone sitting there with certain notes, certain guidance, and that if you put anything extra in they either wouldn't know or would not know how to mark it.
>
> – James, Health and Social Care student

James, who was first introduced in Chapter 2, is a Health and Social Care (HSC) professional coming to terms with the academic expectations of a foundation-level HSC course at a distance university. As the HSC profession expands, more and more HSC professionals like him from increasingly diverse educational backgrounds are entering Higher Education in pursuit of academic qualifications that will further their careers. University Health and Social Care departments respond by constructing courses that will enable these professionals to engage with study in ways that are meaningful and relevant to their professional interests as well as being grounded in academic knowledge and practices. At the university in which James is studying, the Introduction to Health and Social Care course has been carefully designed to support students'

Language Learning 64:Suppl. 1, June 2014, pp. 147–204

DOI: 10.1111/lang.12041

entry into the academic study of HSC. Very good accounts of the approach adopted by the department have been published by Northedge (2003a, 2003b), in which he outlines the ways in which the curriculum and pedagogic strategy of the department responds to the enormous size of the student body (6,000 students recruited every year onto the introductory course alone) and the enormously diverse range of backgrounds of the students (who include senior HSC managers, social care assistants, and informal caregivers) in the course.

By means of a judicious blending of discourses from everyday, professional, and academic contexts, the course engages students in knowledge building and debate about the field of HSC from an academic perspective (Northedge, 2003a, pp. 23–24). In effect, the course supports "legitimate peripheral participation" (Lave & Wenger, 1991; Wenger, 1998) by students in the discourse communities that constitute academic HSC. Northedge proposes that students "internalize [academic discourse] . . . primarily through participation rather than from explicit explanation" (Northedge, 2003b, p. 174). However, alongside their participation, the course does provide students with explicit study skill development based on Northedge's study skills book (Northedge, 2005), and, in combination with extensive guidance provided with each assignment, this constitutes a form of metasemiotic mediation for students as they make their way through their study.

Given the course's intention to develop students' engagement with the reading and writing of academic HSC discourses, teachers on the course are particularly concerned with how to support this engagement through assignment preparation and feedback. In order to enhance the writing support provision already in place, the department approached one of us for help with developing resources that could support student writing "at sentence level." The following two extracts from different students' assignments on the course provide examples of the kind of writing that prompted the department's concern. The first extract is from Nimet, a student who emigrated from Turkey to England 2 years before the extract was written. She was working as a HSC residential worker. She recognizes that her knowledge of English is being put under great strain by her study of the HSC course but she is determined to continue her study and welcomed the opportunity to participate in this research project. The other extract is from Zuna, who was introduced in Chapter 2.[1]

Extract A (from Nimet's assignment text)

Shameem Nawaz (Resource 13, p. 65 to p. 70) about black and minority ethnic for disabled children short break care shows us important for a disabled child to have an ethnically matched placement as they are not aware of cultural differences and short break doesn't involved children living away from home for long period of time. However its kind of important children with sensory impairments as they sense of smell, sight touch, sound and language. Being unfamiliar cultural environment make them uncomfortable and bestressing.

Extract B (from Zuna's assignment text)
In practice, the idea of exclusion is mainly used in three contexts. The first is financial: exclusion is identified with poverty, and its effect on a person's ability to participate in normal activities. The second is exclusion from the labor market: exclusion is strongly identified with long-term unemployment though there is some research evidence to question whether long term unemployed people are really excluded. Third, there is exclusion in its social sense, which identifies exclusion partly with alienation from social networks, and partly with the circumstances in Thornhill community for example, advocacy for socially excluded people is also poor in this community.

HSC teachers have to decide whether and how to respond to such writing; whether to intervene at the level of ideas, reading comprehension, writing purpose, sentence construction, paragraph organization, or elsewhere. In our collaborations with the HSC department, after some initial unsuccessful attempts to develop resources that focused on sentence-level issues, it became clear to us that a more holistic approach was needed. In response, we carried out a LASS investigation of the situation using SFL genre theory. As in the action research project discussed in the last chapter, LASS provided a research framework as well as a pedagogic approach. Chapter 7 will describe further how a LASS approach depends on an integration of research and pedagogy in what can be seen as continuing action research.

In this case, we were bringing a LASS approach to a subject course in which accessibility and embedded study skills were already well developed. By treating language as a meaning-making resource and paying attention simultaneously to the structural, functional, and contextual dimensions of language in meaning making, SFL genre theory took us beyond the sentence level we initially focused on. It took us to the texts that the sentences came from, the assignment tasks students were responding to, and the reading material and subject matter of the course they were engaging with. As we will show in this chapter, the kinds of sentence level issues exemplified in the two student paragraphs above emerge at the interface of all these contexts of language use.

The research for this application of a LASS approach foregrounds the student experience of writing one of the HSC assignments in order to provide more insight into the proposal that students approach assignment tasks with diverse predispositions toward using language in certain ways and toward making meanings in certain ways. In the research we were particularly interested in students' explanations of the ways their texts were designed. We also wanted to find out how appropriate, accessible, and useable they found our genre analyses. We carried out discussions with students that we called *mediated text analysis* for reasons that will be explained in the chapter. From these discussions we observed differences in how students interpreted their contexts of study and differences in their linguistic repertoires for responding to these contexts. We propose that these differences are evidence of semantic variation, as it is called in SFL theorizing (see Chapter 2, Section 2.3). Such semantic variation is traced back to previous experience of language use and the predispositions toward types of language use and meaning making that this experience establishes. We also propose that mediated text analysis discussions provide another example of metasemiotic mediation (see Chapter 4, Figure 4.11)

To provide some background for these proposals, we will return to the discussion of semiotic mediation that we began in Chapter 2. As we proposed in Chapter 2, following Hasan (2005), students and teachers are both engaged in semiotic mediation in learning and teaching situations. Semiotic mediation is both an internal and an external process. Internal (i.e., intramental) processes of language use create the understanding that occurs through semiotic mediation: language mediates meanings to the mind. External (i.e., intermental) processes constitute the scaffolding of that understanding: language users interact in semiotic exchange. External semiotic mediation processes can be either invisible—as they predominantly are in the everyday interactions of family, community, and professional life—or visible, as they are, primarily, in education, and in some contexts of everyday life in which there is a movement toward decontextualized, uncommonsense meaning making.

Participants in semiotic interactions can occupy initiating or responding roles. In a university lecture or course reading material, the initiation lies with "the authorities"; the extent to which a student is an active and critical thinker in response to these forms of visible semiotic mediation is the extent to which they become a semiotic initiator themselves. In a seminar, while the teacher is clearly scaffolding the mediation, more initiative is deliberately passed to the student. In assignment writing, while recognizing that the assignment is prompted by "the authorities," the initiation of semiotic mediation lies with the student up to the point that the teacher provides feedback on the assignment. In all these

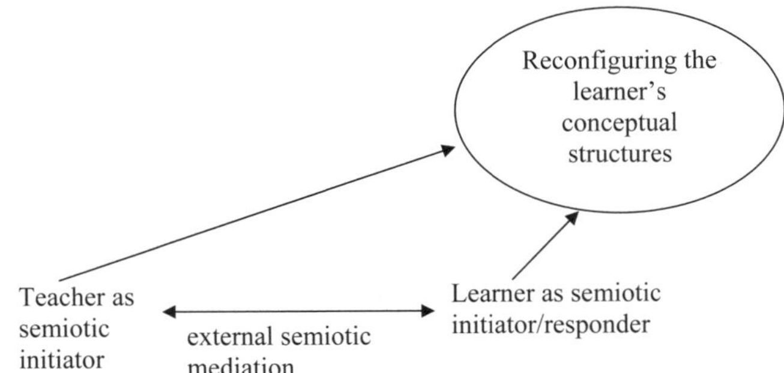

Figure 5.1 The roles in visible semiotic mediation: Teacher as initiator.

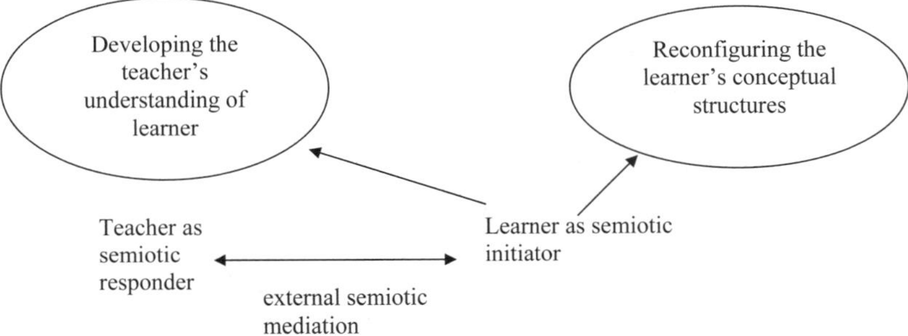

Figure 5.2 The roles in visible semiotic mediation: Learner as initiator.

situations, the purpose of the mediation is the same: it is to reconfigure the conceptual formations and goal-oriented processes of the student. Figures 5.1 and 5.2, first presented in Chapter 2, represent this reciprocal relationship between the teacher and learner in visible semiotic mediation processes, in which they alternatively take up initiator and responder roles.

In Chapter 4 we showed how a LASS approach to the teaching of Film Studies literacy added an additional dimension to semiotic mediation that we referred to as metasemiotic mediation. This was the process of raising to conscious awareness (for all participants: students, Film Studies specialist, and language specialist) the semiotic processes and artifacts that were involved in the semiotic mediation of the *Ways of Seeing* course. The specific form of metasemiotic mediation used in the *Ways of Writing* module was referred to as deconstructing and reconstructing texts. The mediated text analysis discussions described in this chapter are another form of metasemiotic mediation (see Figure 5.3). In these discussions, HSC students commented on their own use of language in their assignment texts. In effect, we were asking these HSC students

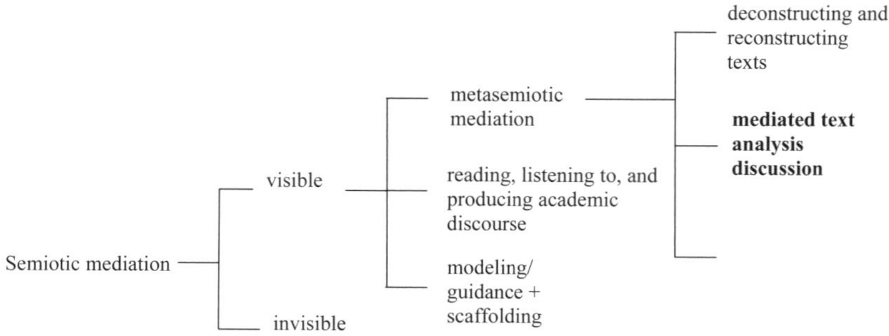

Figure 5.3 Mediated text analysis discussion as a form of metasemiotic mediation.

to take on metasemiotic mediation roles akin to the ones we had ourselves taken on in relation to the film students.

In these mediated text analysis discussions, the HSC students moved in and out of initiator roles as they explained to us their purposes in their assignment texts. And in this metasemiotic interaction, there was also the possibility that our understanding of what the text meant would be reconfigured by the student's explanation. In this chapter, we will consider what has become for us a central strand of a LASS approach: that students are semiotic mediators in initiator roles (when they write their assignments, for example) and metasemiotic mediators in initiator roles (when they articulate how they have written their assignments).

5.2 The Context of HSC Teaching and Learning

To introduce more fully the context of HSC teaching and learning, we will once again use the SFL register terms (field, tenor, and mode) informally to organize our account, as we did with the Film Studies context in Chapter 4. This representation is not based on a systematic analysis of texts and context but is built from impressions gathered through our collaboration with the staff and students of an HSC department, and following ethnographic methods, the participation of one of us as a participant observer in that department (as a registered student on a foundation HSC course).

5.2.1 Field: What Is Going On?

HSC training and education spans the institutional levels of education. Students can study care work vocational qualifications at further education college level and other care work, social work, and nursing qualifications at university.

There is a close relationship between the training or education received and the vocational or professional practice that the study is designed to underpin. In an even more pronounced way than Film Studies, HSC is an academic subject area that brings the academic and the occupational into direct contact. The field of HSC is one in which academic values are by no means the only ones; other values, such as ability in practical tasks and face-to-face interpersonal interaction, are of considerable importance.

Academic HSC is a transdisciplinary field of study, constituting its conceptual formations from the social sciences (including sociology, politics, history, ethics, geography, psychology, and economics) and applied sciences (e.g., paramedic science, exercise science, midwifery) as well as the personal and professional lived experiences of HSC workers. HSC is a field of study that is still under construction and, like Media Studies, is characterized by debates about its integrity, authority, and direction (see, e.g., McNamara, 2010). HSC academics are developing pedagogies that enable the wide diversity of students that their departments are attracting to benefit from higher education (see, e.g., Northedge, 2003a, 2003b). To some extent, caring and therapeutic orientations that characterize "the caring professions" are replicated in the learning environment of the HSC university subject area. This combines with a critical perspective on the value of academic knowledge for the day-to-day practice of HSC as a vocation to constitute a strongly marked practice/academic context where academic knowledge construction is an enterprise that is subject to considerable scrutiny. Power and the imposition of powerful paradigms on the less powerful are subject to explicit critique within the conceptual formations that both constitute HSC knowledge and inform HSC pedagogy. This is reflected in the high value placed on various forms of "critical" and "reflective" writing and thinking.

5.2.2 Mode: How Is Language Being Used?

Like Film Studies, HSC brings together a wide range of semiotic resources. Study materials can include written legislative documents, government information leaflets, health advice websites, audio recordings of interactions between care recipients and caregivers, video recordings of a community meeting, interviews with care providers, historical records of institutional practices, social surveys, investigative reports, academic articles, and many more. As with Film Studies, the mundane and everyday—the contextualized—can be placed alongside the abstract and specialized—the decontextualized. In the course that was investigated for this chapter, teaching materials adopted an informal conversational style interspersed with extracts from texts originally produced for any of the range of contexts suggested by the list of texts above. The communication styles of HSC professional contexts clearly flow across and influence academic HSC communication styles, particularly the counseling, person-centered, and empathetic style which characterizes much HSC professional practice.

In this context, written assignment tasks could draw on text types which are commonly found in HSC professional environments, such as case notes, community newsletters, and reports. In fact, in the course we investigated, students were required to produce a significant number of traditional essay texts, as well as tabulated responses to practical problem-solving tasks. As will be discussed more extensively in the next chapter, HSC students also participated in online discussion forums of various kinds.

5.2.3 Tenor: Who Is Involved?

HSC practitioners are not necessarily attracted to academic study because of a strong commitment to academic knowledge, though of course many are. More than some other subjects, HSC can be studied for instrumental purposes. This is most obvious where HSC employment is dependent on first obtaining a professional qualification required by the profession. There has long been a requirement for social workers to obtain such qualifications. Within the last 20 years, more and more nurses have been required to do the same. Most recently, universities have begun to provide courses catering for care workers, the previously least qualified area of HSC employment. This has brought into university study learners who may have limited previous experience of further or higher education. It has also increased the numbers of plurilingual learners, reflecting the high proportion of speakers of English as an additional language who work in the care sector. The HSC course investigated here also attracts nonformal caregivers and others who are interested in HSC as a field of study.

As in Film Studies, academics can come from both academic and professional backgrounds. Learners are positioned as both experienced and responsible. As mentioned above, this is associated with a high level of person-centeredness in the educational culture.

5.3 Sentences in Context

The research behind this application of a LASS approach was prompted by the expressed concern of the HSC department with the coherence of students' writing at the sentence level. Without a systemic approach to language it can be difficult to respond meaningfully to sentence-level meaning-making, which can too easily become detached from the overall meaning of a whole text. Systemic functional linguistics offers a grammar of the word choices that are made at the clause level. However, it is also a grammar that recognizes that clauses make meanings in the context of the whole text and ultimately in the context of the social and cultural situation in which the text is produced.

At the beginning of this chapter, we presented a short extract from Zuna's assignment text in order to provide an example of the sentence-level meaning making that the HSC department was concerned about. The whole text is reproduced in full in Appendix 5.1. In the chapter, we are going to examine Zuna's text as an illustration of one student's engagement with the study of HSC. We will compare this text with another one written by Andrea and consider what the comparison shows about the ways students make meanings in this HSC course. As with the two film students' assignments discussed in Chapter 4, the comparison suggests differences in the ways these HSC students are oriented toward making meaning in academic study. In Chapter 4 we took the Film Studies teacher's conceptual formation and evaluation of students' writing as our point of reference. In this chapter, we start from the HSC department's evaluation of students' texts but we move on to examine how students' configurations of meaning in written language are evaluated by students themselves. Our overarching purpose is to elaborate on the nature of semantic orientation and metasemiotic mediation and on their place in a LASS approach to teaching and learning.

In Chapter 4, we focused on a single genre from among all the Film Studies assignment genres. In this chapter, we will focus on several genres, which we will locate on a map of all the assignment genres students on this HSC course were expected to engage with. We will then turn to the students themselves, drawing on the mediated text analysis discussions we had with them about their assignments. Our objectives will be to extend our understanding of the texts these students wrote and how the texts relate to the learning of HSC subject matter: the conceptual formations of HSC. We will then consider how the theory of semantic orientation provides many insights into differences between the texts and the associated learning of each of the students. In the process, we will explore some applications of genre and register analysis to the teaching and learning of the HSC course, paying special attention to the sentence-level coherence issues that the HSC department expressed concern about. The chapter will therefore seek to relate word choice at the clause level up through the levels of text and context to include some aspects of professional and personal life worlds associated with semantic orientation. Details of the research on which this chapter is based can be seen at the end of the chapter.[2]

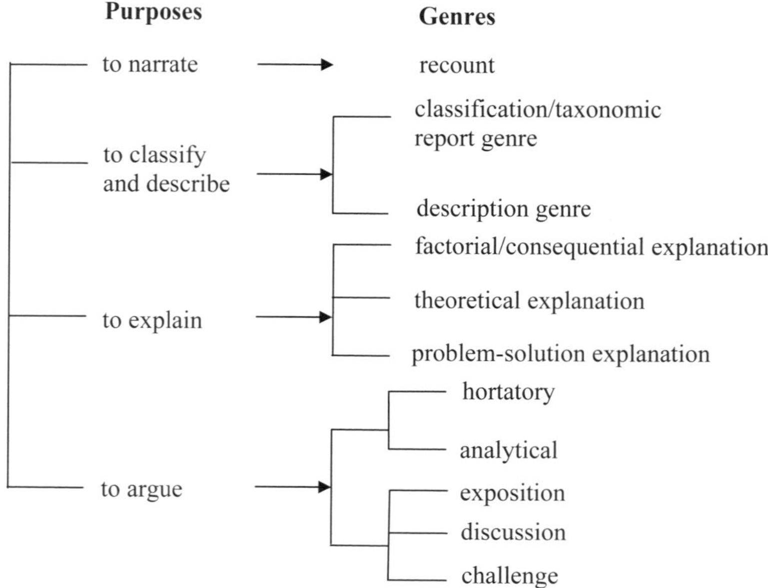

Figure 5.4 Key purposes and genres in introductory Health and Social Care: A system perspective.

In order to provide the background for the remainder of this chapter, we suggest that, at this point, readers skim the two student texts in Appendices 5.1 and 5.2.

5.4 Mapping HSC Study: Genres and Decontextualized Meanings

5.4.1 Mapping the Genres of HSC Study: Social Purposes in HSC Assignments

A LASS approach focuses on the purposes that language performs in the contexts of teaching and learning. Language purpose can be identified for every level in a text, from word through clause to sentence, and then upward to paragraph, genre stage, and whole text. Purposes for any item or level will always be related to other items or levels above or below the one that is being considered. Ultimately, purposes are grounded in the context of the language used: in the field, tenor, and mode of the situation.

In Chapter 3, we presented the key HSC genres that we identified through SFL genre analysis of 2 years of HSC assignments. The genre system is reproduced in Figure 5.4.

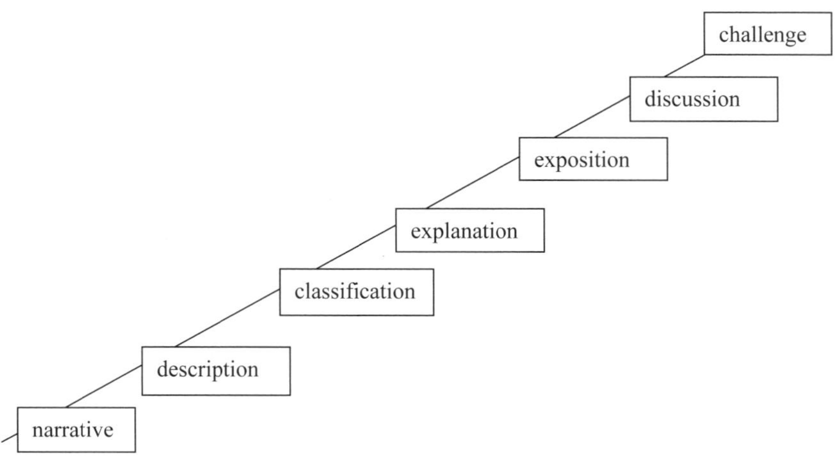

Figure 5.5 A genre trajectory.

As explained in Chapter 3, from the point of view of SFL genre theory, genres are configurations of meaning, and in a university context are directly associated with the development of subject knowledge. Assignments can be arranged along a genre trajectory, which runs from genres (such as recounts and classifying reports) that could be regarded as more basic, through the explanation genres to more complex exposition and discussion genres. The complexity arises because later genres, like discussion, can entail genres from earlier in the trajectory, like classifying reports. Figure 5.5 represents this trajectory, moving up the cline from more basic genres on the left to more complex ones on the right.

Part of what makes the trajectory one of difficulty is the movement that it entails from expressions of *categorical* meaning in description and classifying reports toward expression of points of view, which we will call *perspectival* meaning, in argument genres.

Applying the genre system presented in Figure 5.5 to the assignment prompts and the accompanying student guidance notes, we drew up a map of the genres that appeared to be prompted by 24 assignment tasks across 2 years of the HSC course's life. Despite the course's avowed intention to scaffold students' writing development along a developmental trajectory, there was a considerable contrast between the sequence of genres in the genre map for these 2 years of the course's life (see Table 5.1) and the sequence represented by the genre trajectory in Figure 5.5.

The distribution of genres was not only different from the genre trajectory, but also varied across each of the years. So, for example, macrogenres were

Table 5.1 Map of the genres prompted by the assignment tasks in an HSC foundation-level course across the years 2008 and 2009

Assignment number	2008 assignment tasks prompted the following genres	2009 assignment tasks prompted the following genres
1	Macro genre: classifying report + consequential explanation	Classifying report
2		
Option 1	Macrogenre: analytical exposition + hortatory exposition	Theoretical explanation
Option 2	Analytical discussion	Problem-solution
3		
Option 1	Macrogenre: analytical exposition + hortatory exposition	Factorial explanation
Option 2	Analytical exposition	Classifying report
4		
Option 1	Factorial explanation	Problem solution
Option 2	Factorial explanation	Problem solution
5	Macrogenre: consequential explanation + analytical discussion	Consequential explanation
6		
Option 1	Macro genre: classifying report + factorial explanation + hortatory exposition	Factorial explanation
Option 2	Factorial explanation	Factorial explanation
7		
Option 1	Factorial explanation/analytical discussion	Factorial explanation/ analytical exposition
Option 2	Factorial explanation/analytical exposition	Factorial explanation/ analytical exposition

very common in 2008 but did not appear in 2009; similarly, problem-solution explanations appeared in 2009 but not in 2008. As genres are configurations of meaning which constitute the knowledge of a field of study, genre theory would suggest there would be value in considering, first, whether sequencing genres from the "easier" to the "more difficult" would support students' writing development and, second, whether recognition of how different genres configure the meanings that constitute the field of knowledge differently would lead to a more systematic and possibly more effective development of subject knowledge.

Not surprisingly, our research indicated there was a correlation between those texts that received higher marks and those where we could clearly recognize the nature of the genre being performed and identify typical genre staging. The sequencing of stages may be altered, and stages may be reiterated, but for the assignments we examined, texts that were organized broadly in line with the staging suggested by SFL genre theory appeared to be recognized by HSC teachers as doing the kind of work that was prompted by the assignment rubric. Among mid- and low-scoring assignments, it was much harder to identify genre stages or to relate stages to the ones associated with the genre the rubric seemed to be prompting. (This will be exemplified below in relation to theoretical explanation and discussion genres.)

In mapping assignment genres using assignment tasks and guidance notes, it quickly became apparent that the wording of the task and of the guidance notes plays a key role in prompting the intended genre. According to research (e.g., Clanchy & Ballard, 1998, p. 4), relevance to the task is one of the four aspects of a text that teachers look for when marking an assignment. Central to this relevance is engaging with the genre that is prompted by the task and expected by the teacher. It was therefore significant that we found the wording of assignment tasks and assignment guidance was not always unambiguously aligned with the genre that was being prompted. For example, the word "discuss" was used in assignment tasks to mean *explain*, *describe*, *classify*, and *report*—but often not *argue*. From a LASS perspective, it seems likely that students would be helped by consistent linking of assignment instruction words to assignment purposes.

5.4.2 Mapping the Field of HSC Knowledge: Contextualization and Decontextualization

In mapping the genres of HSC assignments on this course we recognized an important configuration of meanings that cuts across all genres. In order to successfully produce a classification report or a discussion in this HSC course, students are expected to manipulate conceptual formations of concepts and relate them to real-world case study material. In other words, they are expected to move between more decontextualized and more contextualized meanings. Such a movement between abstract concepts and case study illustrations of these concepts is comparable with the similar movement between abstract concepts and illustrative film details outlined in Chapter 4. However, the film plays a different role in the process of film analysis: it is the object of the analysis. In HSC, the case study material is not the object of analysis; it is

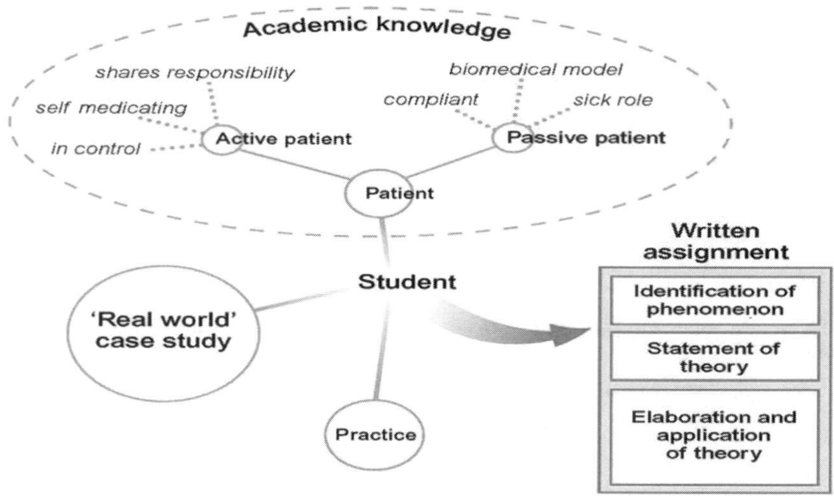

Figure 5.6 An example of an HSC theoretical explanation genre.

used to illustrate understanding of the concepts and a more general process of analytical thinking. (We have observed that, in the field of Business Studies, the case study constitutes the object of business case analysis just as the film constitutes the object of film analysis in Film Studies.)

Across assignment genres, students were expected to develop and demonstrate their understanding of the field through phases in which they frame the case study by means of their developing conceptual formations (see Chapter 3, Section 3.2.3, on the relationship between phases and stages). A characteristic of lower-marked HSC assignment texts is that they are more likely to describe or narrate case study material rather than frame it by reference to the conceptual formations of the course material. Examples of these contrasting approaches are presented below for the assignment:

> In what ways did the role Anwar Malik played as a hospital patient contrast with the expert patient role he had been encouraged to play by the Hilltop diabetes clinic?

From an SFL genre perspective, this assignment prompts a theoretical explanation. (See Chapter 4, Section 4.4 for a previous introduction of this genre in relation to taxonomic film analysis.) At the level of genre staging, theoretical explanation is a three-stage configuration of meaning. In Figure 5.6 this is represented by the schematic representation of staging in the right-hand

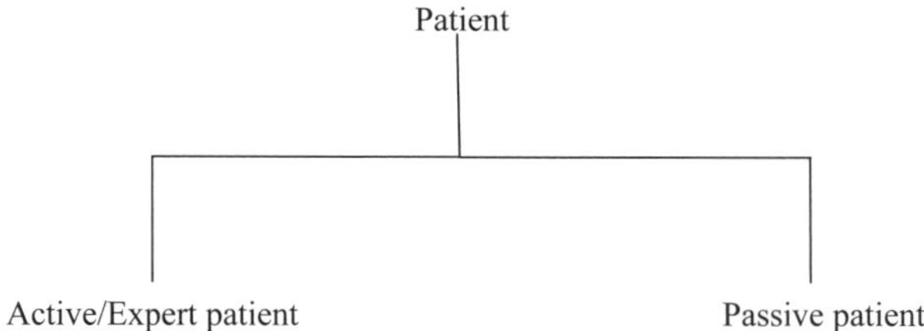

Figure 5.7 A binary taxonomy of patients.

bottom corner of the diagram. The phenomenon in this instance was Anwar's experiences in the hospital and diabetes clinic. The theoretical explanation is based on a Health Studies conceptual formation that includes the concept of *the biomedical model* and associated concepts such as *the active* and *passive patient.* Figure 5.6 presents some concepts from this conceptual formation that are central to the assignment. In the elaboration and application of the theory. students are expected to draw on the conceptual formation to think analytically about the concept of *patient role*, illustrating their thinking by reference to incidents from the case study of Anwar's experience. As the diagram shows, a student may also draw from their own personal or professional practice, though this is not explicitly required by the assignment task.

Although this genre is a theoretical explanation and not a classification report, the assignment task requires students to frame the explanation with a binary taxonomy such as those that configure classification reports (this is an example of a more complex genre entailing a more basic one). The taxonomy is of *types of patient* (see Figure 5.7).

Around this simple binary taxonomy of *expert and passive patient* is a set of patient qualities and behaviors that students may or may not have incorporated into their own conceptual formation.

The extract below shows Anne explicitly using concepts from her conceptual framework of *active/passive patient* to frame the case study (concepts underlined).

> **Extract A, from Anne's text:**
> To enable me to give examples why the hospital patient role contrasts with that of an expert patient role and why the biomedical model approach can affect these roles, I am using the case study of Anwar Malik (Block 1, Unit 2, Sections 5.3 and 5.4 and Resources 3 and 4). Anwar is 54 years of age and was diagnosed with diabetes. This is a chronic, long-term disease, which for Anwar, is controlled with insulin injections.

> . . . Previously Anwar was an expert patient, but after entering the secondary health care of a hospital he will now be expected to take on the role of hospital patient.

In this extract, Anne is moving between more contextualized, material representations of reality and less contextualized, abstract ones. This can be seen as the fundamental configuration of a classification report—so, emerging earlier in the genre trajectory than theoretical explanation—but it appeared to be required for all HSC genres along the genre trajectory.

The extract from Brian's assignment below shows a less explicit framing phase, in which Brian does not focus on active and passive patient *roles* but instead announces his intention to focus on *the issue* of whether Anwar is a passive or active patient (a purpose which converts the genre from an explanation to a discussion genre) but then embarks on a long recount of Anwar's experience (which converts the genre to a recount one).

> **Extract B, from Brian's text:**
> In this assignment I am going to discuss whether or not Anwar Malik is a passive or active patient. Anwar is a muslim man who owns a greengrocers with his wife. Anwar has been unwell for a while, after his wife and the optician said that he needed to go and see his GP. Anwar then went to see his GP and after some tests Anwar discovered that he had diabetes. After a while Anwar's GP noticed that he was not coping with his condition and was not following his diet plan that he was given. Anwar then ended up being rushed into hospital . . .

Meanings in recounts like this one by Brian are at the more contextualized, material end of the contextualized-decontextualized cline. At the university level, student assignments are unlikely to have recount as a central purpose, although students do read recounts (and descriptions) in the form of case studies. In their assignment texts they are expected to reproduce extracts from these recounts and descriptions in the framing phases but, as with Film Studies, teachers are less interested in the particulars of the real world events than they are in how students use these to illustrate their explanations, analytical thinking, and critical argumentation.

As with the Film Studies texts examined in Chapter 4, among the various textual features for configuring a phase as an analytical frame rather than as a recount or description, one of the key ones is the hyperTheme. This is exemplified by another extract from Anne's text below. The underlining hyperTheme begins with the material circumstantial clause *On entering hospital* suggesting the beginning of a recount, but this is immediately framed with the abstract Participant, *role,* as the Identified in the Theme of the subsequent relational main clause (*Anwar's first role*):

> **Extract C, from Anne's text:**
> On entering hospital, Anwar's first role is as a passive patient and is expected to become compliant with all the health professionals instructions. The hospital role is the extreme version of the sick role (Unit 2, P90) . . .

In contrast, the hyperTheme in the extract from Brian's text below orients to the individual in the case—presented as an Actor in a material clause—rather than to the concepts being illustrated. As a result, the "story" element of the case study is foregrounded and the concept of *role* is not thematized as an organizing concept.

> **Extract D, from Brian's text:**
> Anwar visited Nurse Richards, the specialist diabetic nurse who is part of the primary care team within his surgery. The nurse observed that Anwar was wearing an open-toed slipper. . . .

Other linguistic features for framing case study material will be presented in the discussion of Zuna's and Andrea's assignments below.

5.5 Semantic Variation Among HSC Students

As with the Film Studies research in Chapter 4, in this HSC research we continued analyzing student assignments from the perspective of what teachers valued when they responded to students' texts. This gave us a number of genre descriptions that can be used in genre-based pedagogy with HSC students in ways comparable with the ways we used the taxonomic film analysis with film students in Chapter 4. The map of genres for the entire HSC course presented above, and the insights into how the wording of the task prompts particular responses to the task, have been exploited by HSC academics in designing assessment on the HSC course. Another use of a genre mapping approach that has not yet been tried in this context would be to provide schematic representations of the genre staging of assignments or parts of assignments in the assignment guidance notes. This metasemiotic mediation procedure will be illustrated later in the chapter where some of these ideas will be taken up again. For now we will turn our attention to the students who produce these assignment genres.

In his accounts of the curriculum design and pedagogic strategy of the HSC department, Northedge (2003a) emphasizes the diversity of professional, academic, social, and linguistic backgrounds of students on the course. The fact that all students in this distance learning environment receive the same course material and assignment guidance and are not required to read anything outside the course material creates an interesting context in which to consider the impact of students' diverse backgrounds on their study. Despite their common dependence on the same guidance notes and source material, in the year we carried out this research, students' marks ranged from 83 (a distinction) to 42 (a bare pass).

Traditionally, as mentioned in Chapter 1, differences in students' performance have been attributed to differences, for example, in students' motivation, application to work, intelligence, time management, commitment, and other *individual* characteristics or attributes. There are, undoubtedly, factors in individual students' circumstances that impact on their performance in a particular assignment—whether they have time to write the assignment, have access to a computer, are experiencing difficulties in their personal or professional life, and so on.

However, in language-based approaches to teaching and learning it has long been suggested that differences in attainment may be attributable to differences in cognitive and linguistic *social experience*. From this perspective, students' circumstances are in large part created by their own internal context: the cognitive, affective, linguistic, and other resources that they bring to the learning situation and that they have developed throughout their lifelong interaction with others in their external social, cultural, material, and economic contexts. An example of this is James's suspicion that he has had "48 marks knocked off" as a result of the particular background he brings to his study of the HSC course and the differences between his own expectations and the expectations of the course and his teacher.

In Chapter 2, referring to Hasan's (2009) research on mother–child interactions, we proposed that socially attributable differences in linguistic and cognitive resources can be seen, in part, as differences in semantic orientation. Central to the distinctions between mother–child interactions was the extent to which they promoted the development of decontextualized or contextualized meaning making and language use by children. In Chapter 4, we considered contextualized and decontextualized language use among university students writing taxonomic film analysis genres. In this chapter we will extend our consideration of contextualized and decontextualized language use to argument genres from the HSC course. In doing this, we are particularly interested in students' explanations of the choices they have made in designing their texts

To investigate students' perceptions about the design of their own assignment text, we adopted the approach we introduced in the opening section of this chapter, called mediated text analysis. This involved prompting students to explain the purposes of an assignment text they had recently written. The prompts focused their attention, in turn, on all levels of their text, from overall assignment purpose down to individual sentence and word choice purpose. In return for their contribution to our understanding of their assignment text, at different points in the discussion, we shared our perception of their text from an SFL genre perspective. The interaction was thus a reciprocally informing one that we have come to see as a form of metasemiotic mediation in which they as students and we as teacher-researchers helped each other to make more sense of this particular assignment task and text in context.

Through this process we gained an impression of how students could be differently oriented to the task, could interpret the context differently, and brought different linguistic experience to the performance of the task. These differences in students' orientation to the context and text have implications for a LASS approach to teaching and learning. In the Film Studies context our primary purpose was to scaffold students in their engagement in Film Studies language and learning by drawing their attention to linguistic features of the texts and tasks they were involved with. In this HSC context, students drew our attention to features of the texts and tasks they were working with and in the process revealed information about how they were engaging with these texts and tasks. This process seems to be more appropriately referred to as *reciprocal* metasemiotic mediation.

In contrast with the Film Studies classroom where we worked with groups of 70 students, in the HSC research we worked with individual students, which from a teaching point of view is a rare opportunity. However, the insights this generated have relevance for any teaching and learning context we want to approach as if it were a form of semiotic mediation. Treating semiotic and metasemiotic mediation as *reciprocal* reminds us that whether teaching is explicit and didactic or implicit and facilitatory, it depends on students' engagement in learning. This engagement is a function both of the semantic orientation of the teacher or the teaching and learning materials and of the semantic orientation of the student. Semiotic mediation can really only be engaging if it is reciprocal. This is the point attributed to Hasan in Section 5.5 of Chapter 2. The mediated text analysis process that led us to this view will be drawn on in the remainder of the chapter.

5.6 The Assignment Texts

Two examples of the assignment texts we discussed are presented in the appendix and have already been mentioned. They are a response to the following prompt:

> Do outreach approaches and advocacy always improve the delivery of care services for people who are socially excluded?

From an SFL genre perspective, this prompts either an analytical exposition or a discussion. The typical genre staging of each of these genres according to SFL genre analysis is as follows (parentheses mean a stage is optional):

Discussion:
(Background) ^ Issue ^ Arguments for ^ Arguments against ^ Position

Exposition
(Background) ^ Position ^ Arguments for ^ (Concession) ^Reinforcement of position

These stages were reflected implicitly in the assignment guidance notes provided for students by the department, but there was no explicit reference to them. Table 5.2 reformats the department's assignment guidance notes to bring out the correspondence between the notes and the SFL genre staging for discussion and exposition genres. An abbreviated version of the guidance notes is presented in the middle column. The two outer columns relate particular parts of the notes to the stages of the discussion and exposition genres. Key concepts in the guidance notes have been highlighted in bold. Significantly for these two genres, there was no guidance in the notes about establishing an issue or position at the beginning of the assignment.

In view of the close alignment between the guidance notes and the genre schemata, it is not entirely surprising that there was a close correlation between the grade that a student received for the assignment and the degree of alignment between their assignment text and the genre staging represented in the columns on either side of Table 5.2.

In order to demonstrate what a LASS-based approach to teaching and learning brings to an understanding of two students' responses to this assignment task, we will present some short extracts from mediated text analysis discussions with Zuna and Andrea, two of the students who were introduced in Section 2.2 of Chapter 2.

Table 5.2 HSC assignment guidance notes mapped against SFL genre stages for discussion and exposition genres

Discussion	Assignment Guidance notes (an abbreviated form of the notes provided for students along with the assignment task)	Exposition
Background	Explain social exclusion, outreach, advocacy Find examples of why socially excluded have difficulty using care services Consider how being excluded from social networks affects informal support	Background
Issue		Position
Argue for	(How they improve delivery of care) Give some examples: i) Community Access project; ii) Sussex Travellers Women's Health Relative merits of independent advocacy and advocacy as part of care workers role.	Argue for
Argue against	(How they do not improve delivery of care) Think about the limitations Think about how contact would be made with Simon, or Gypsy Traveller Women? Are advocacy and outreach readily available; if not, why? Possible limitations of advocacy as part of careworker's role	Concession
Position	Bring to conclusion Looking back, try to sum up whether outreach and advocacy improve care services for socially excluded.	Reinforce Position

5.7 Mediated Text Analysis

After students shared some initial biographical details, the mediated text analysis discussions followed a simple pattern. Our question prompts were always focused on the student's sense of purpose. For the assignment task, the assignment text, and each of the paragraphs of the text, we asked the question (in one form or another):

> What was the purpose of this assignment task/text/paragraph?

We followed this with other prompts depending on the response. We then focused on sections of the text where we hoped the student could explain word choice at sentence level. On these selected sections of text we asked the question:

> What did you want to say with this sentence? Why did you choose these words to say that?

We followed these with other prompts depending on the response.

It is a principle of mediated text analysis discussion that, if students want, the interaction can have a teaching dimension in which we share with them our understandings of the assignment task and text. It was important to try to offer our understandings in ways that did not influence or obstruct their explanations of their text. An illustrative extract from the mediated text analysis discussion with Zuna (whose words are in bold) can be seen below (see Figure 5.8). Because it is the term that is most familiar to students, we refer to the text as an essay throughout the discussion.

5.8 Zuna's Assignment

Discussion with Zuna confirmed that her assignment reflected considerable investment of time and intellectual effort. Yet it received only a bare pass. Her teacher's feedback indicated that the reasons lay in her engagement with the HSC subject matter and with the organization of her text. A LASS approach to teaching and learning seeks to explicate how these two aspects of the assignment are related and offers students and teachers ways of talking about the relationship.

Before the discussion with Zuna, our attempts to identify argument genre staging in her text left us with a number of uncertainties about the purposes of sections of her text. Our initial analysis is presented in Figure 5.9, followed by a commentary. Question marks in square brackets indicate our uncertainty about the purpose of parts of the text. (The full text is presented in Appendix 5.1.)

In line with the guidance notes, Zuna's Background stage refers to the concepts of *social exclusion, outreach,* and *advocacy*. However, we could not see how these concepts were obviously related to an issue or a position, and this partly explains our sense of the ambiguity of purpose for many of the paragraphs in the background stage. Paragraph K makes a distinct shift to a new stage, but contrary to our expectation, this does not seem to constitute an argument for or against stage; instead, it is a taxonomic description of a

Essay purpose

JD (researcher/teacher): There are various kinds of essays. For example, you can have a description essay or an explanation essay or compare and contrast or problem solution or discussion. What kind of essay is this one, do you think?

Z (student): I think this is a kind of asks you to explain about why some people have been excluded. Because if we talk at the beginning of my essay I said in our society people are excluded when they are not part of the network.

JD: Yes.

Z: Yeah. The reason why they are excluded and about they not in community through what they've been doing, through try to eradicate those been excluded. The activities and things that they are introducing and I think at the close end I concluded that, ok, with all that the definition – because I have, to me, I have to make sure I explain what exactly the meaning over because anybody can want to read it and want – if they don't know what's, after he sees, approaches this, it would be difficult then for them to understand what it is.

JD: I understand.

Z: Yeah.

JD: We're going to have a look more closely in a minute, but just going back to what you just said, you said that you think the title is asking you to explain why people are socially excluded?

Z: Yeah.

JD: I'm going to ask you Z to check this thing, that idea, have a look back at the title carefully and show me, just from the title, where you think it's asking you to say why people are socially excluded?

Z: OK, the question is saying "Do outreach approaches and", ok, it's not why, it's the include and the delivery of the car services.

JD: That's right. So do you think then it's not explain why, that's not what it's asking you to do?

Z: It's not actually what, I can put and explain

JD: You can put explanations in there as well, yeah, exactly. So it's about the improvements. So actually this is what I would call a discussion essay.

Z: OK.

JD: This is what I call a discussion essay where you have to put forward an argument about do the outreach approaches improve the delivery or not? So for me this is a discussion essay.

Z: OK.

JD: Have you heard of discussion essays before?

Z: Yes I have because [teacher] said to us that when we are being given that kind of a question you don't have to say "Yes I think it's that" you have to be in between.

JD: OK.

Z: Yeah, you have to back it up to be in between. And that is what ideally. I didn't really say, yes it's not being improved or it is being improved, yeah.

JD: Yeah, yeah. And do you know why [teacher] said that? Do you understand the reason for [teacher's] advice?

Z: Yeah, the reason is that it's not for you to say why, it's for you to just understand.

JD: Yes, yes. So you have to look at all sides of the question?

Z: Yes, yes, to understand both sides.

JD: Yes.

Z: Yeah, it's not for you to conclude.

Figure 5.8 Mediated text discussion with Zuna: The purpose of the text.

Paragraph	Stages and Phases (Phases in italics)
	Background
A	*"Social exclusion"*
B	*Elaboration*
C	[Purpose?]
D	*Description: "Outreach+advocacy"* *+ Examples*
E	[Purpose?]
F	[Purpose?]
G	[Purpose?]
K	Description (a taxonomy) of care service organizations [Purpose?]
	Organization 1
L	*Organization 2*
M	*Organization 3, etc.*
Q	*Example of outreach*
R	*Examples of causes of social exclusion*
S	*Restatement of essay title*
T-W	[Purpose?]

Figure 5.9 An analyst's view of staging in Zuna's assignment.

number of community organizations. Paragraphs Q and R provide case study illustrations of activities an outreach worker might do, but there have been only two previous mentions of the term *outreach* so it was difficult for us to establish how this links with the preceding text. Finally, it was evident to us that paragraphs S-W were intended to provide a conclusion, but the position they presented was difficult to interpret.

Despite the ambiguity of purpose for us that this analysis reveals, it was obvious from the discussion with Zuna that she had read the course material actively, covering it with annotations, and that she believed she had a strong grasp of the key concepts of the assignment. Zuna's analysis of her own text in the mediated text analysis provides some insights into how she intended the text to be read and some explanation of why this proved difficult both for us as analysts and for her own teacher. This misalignment between Zuna's perception of the meanings her text was making and the likely meanings that a teacher would make of it was repeated in several other mediated text analysis discussions with other students.

5.8.1 Mediated Text Analysis Discussion With Zuna: The Assignment Purpose

For Zuna, the main purpose of the assignment was to explain rather than to discuss:

> Yeah, they want us to really explain that those outreach approaches advocate always include the delivery of care service for people who are socially excluded.

In SFL genre analysis, explanation genres deal with configurations of meanings that center on cause and effect relationships. A contrast between an explanation genre and a discussion genre is what we have referred to previously as a contrast between the categorical ("this leads to that") and the perspectival ("it could be argued that this leads to that"). In the extract above, Zuna is using the term "explain" in ways that align with the categorical quality of the cause–effect relations in an explanation genre. In her statement of purpose, the polarity of the title ("Do outreach approaches always . . . ?") is replaced by a categorical statement (" . . . outreach approaches always . . . ").

5.8.2 Mediated Text Analysis: Paragraph and Sentence Purpose

The overall meanings of an assignment text are created by the linguistic choices that are made at the paragraph and sentence levels as a writer engages in their reconstruction of the conceptual formations of the field of study in response to their interpretation of the assignment task.

In the mediated text analysis, Zuna described the opening paragraphs of her text as background. She explained that she had selected some information about social exclusion from the course material, which, because she felt it was well expressed, she mostly reproduced in the original wording in her own text. The second paragraph of this background stage, with its ambiguous final sentence, was presented at the beginning of this chapter in order to illustrate the kind of sentence that HSC teachers found difficulty in responding to. It is reproduced below. It is fairly clear that the first three sentences and the first clause of the fourth sentence of this paragraph are taken directly from the original text. It is in the transition from the source text wording to Zuna's own wording in the final clauses of the fourth sentence that the ambiguity occurs:

Paragraph B of Zuna's assignment

In practice, the idea of exclusion is mainly used in three contexts. The first is financial: exclusion is identified with poverty, and its effect on a person's ability to participate in normal activities. The second is exclusion from the labor market: exclusion is strongly identified with long-term unemployment though there is some research evidence to question whether long term unemployed people are really excluded. Third, there is exclusion in its social sense, which identifies exclusion partly with alienation from social networks, and partly with the circumstances in Thornhill community for example, advocacy for socially excluded people is also poor in this community.

The fourth sentence in paragraph B moves from an abstract taxonomy of *exclusion* to the material *circumstances in Thornhill*, and ends with an example that illustrates the circumstances and mentions the new concept of *advocacy.* Zuna's comment on this sentence comes at the end of the second extract from the mediated text discussion, which follows in Figure 5.10.

Zuna's comment on the final sentence of paragraph B is:

With that I think the reader would be able to understand what advocacy is.

Zuna was aware that a purpose at this stage of the assignment is to begin to present the conceptual formation that centers on the concept *advocacy,* since this will frame the text that follows. In the first three sentences, she has already established *social exclusion* as part of the framework. However, in our reading of the text, the fourth sentence did not perform the function that Zuna intended, of introducing advocacy. In that sentence, the concept, advocacy, appears at the end of the paragraph as an illustration of the poverty associated with exclusion rather than as a way of responding to social exclusion. The final sentence of Zuna's paragraph B reads:

Third, there is exclusion in its social sense, which identifies exclusion partly with alienation from social networks, and partly with the circumstances in Thornhill community for example, advocacy for socially excluded people is also poor in this community.

The ideational analysis of the sentence presented below confirms a misalignment in the taxonomies that Zuna is creating.

Purpose of paragraph B

JD: And I think you've told me what is in there, what it is about, and I think was it for you the purpose was that you are introducing the essay, was this your purpose?

Z: Yeah, yeah, yeah, yeah.

JD: Yeah.

Z: Yeah because I could, I say, part of the idea of it is merely using three concepts. After introducing what it is [in paragraph A] then I now start saying what exclusion is identified as [in paragraph B].

JD: Yes, ok, so that's your next paragraph.

Z: Yeah.

JD: So your next paragraph [paragraph B] is what? What are you doing in the next paragraph?

Z: I'm trying to explain what exclusion is about, yeah.

JD: OK that makes sense, yeah. Would you call it a definition?

Z: I don't want to put it in a form of defining what exclusion is.

JD: No.

Z: Yeah, I just want to explain so that the reader will understand what exclusion is about. So I wouldn't say I'm defining, yeah.

JD: Can you show me, do you think you have explained outreach and advocacy yet or is that coming later?

Z: No I think I just, OK I can remember that. I said "advocates for social exclusion, people who is also poor in the community" because I really, I don't know how I'm going to explain that. So I really put it in to let them understand that. That's why I said "exclusion partly with *[inaudible]* **for social service and partly in the psychom...***[inaudible]* **services** *[inaudible]* **For example advocacies for social excluded people is also poor in this community"**

JD: Yes.

Z: So with that I think the reader would be able to understand what advocacy is.

JD: I see, you want the reader to see that as a kind of explanation of advocacy?

Z: Yeah.

Figure 5.10 Mediated text discussion with Zuna: The purpose of paragraph B.

Third, there is exclusion in its social sense,
Existent
which identifies exclusion partly with alienation from social networks,
Pr: relational Identified (abstract) Identifier (abstract)
and partly with the circumstances in Thornhill community
Identifier (material)

In the subtaxonomy of *exclusion* that Zuna is constructing, two different orders of experience are represented as hyponyms: the abstract concept of *alienation from social networks* and the generalized but more material entity, *circumstances in Thornhill community.* The taxonomy is destabilized by the difference in the nature of these members of the taxonomy.

Zuna then appears to move into another level of the taxonomy with the conjunction, *for example*, signaling that what follows could be expected to be an illustration of the taxonomy she has just set up (see paragraph B above). While there is clearly some cohesion between the terms of the preceding taxonomy and the illustration of the taxonomy that follows—*socially excluded* and *community* co-occur in both the taxonomy and the illustration—in fact, the Identified which represented social exclusion has now acquired a new head noun, *advocacy,* so an entity which is not obviously a member of the exclusion taxonomy has been introduced. *Advocacy* is one of the key concepts of the conceptual framework that informs this assignment so is undoubtedly relevant to the assignment, but this first mention of it as an *example* of the category of *social exclusion* rather than as a response to social exclusion is a misrepresentation of the conceptual framework that advocacy is at the center of:

for example, advocacy for socially excluded people	is also poor in this community.
Carrier (is different to the previous Identified, *exclusion* and does not belong in the same taxonomy)	Attribute (equates falsely with circumstances in Thornhill)

It is apparent in this sentence that Zuna is trying to move between abstract concepts and material illustrations in ways that HSC assignments require her to. It is also apparent that her linguistic resources for manipulating the concepts are emerging, in conjunction with her understanding of the concepts.

From a textual perspective, rather than an ideational one, the issue is partly one of thematic development, the management of the peaks and troughs of information that determine what is foregrounded and what is backgrounded in a text. This same issue was identified in Section 5.4.1 as determining whether a case study is framed as an illustration of a decontextualized conceptual formation, or is presented as a contextualized recount of events or description of states. Zuna's comments on the next paragraph suggested that a similar tension occurred for her as she wrote paragraph C:

> **Paragraph C of Zuna's assignment**
> Thornhill community was qualified for government funding because it was among the area with a high level of deprived neighbourhoods in England. Compared with other other parts of Southampton and southeast England, people in Thornhill experience lower level of health and wellbeing needs.

Zuna's analysis of this third paragraph was:

> It shows why there is advocacy and outreach in Thornhill: it's because of poverty and government response.

While the paragraph is clearly about deprivation in Thornhill, it was not obvious to us that this was tied to the concepts of advocacy and outreach. Thematic development, for us, is highly dependent on the hyperTheme of a paragraph, as illustrated previously for the Anwar Malik hospital patient assignment. For Zuna, this was not necessarily the case as the following exchange suggests.

> JD: Have you explained Outreach and Advocacy?
> Z: Yes, (pointing to the final sentence of paragraph B)

Although the final sentence in paragraph B was ambiguous to us, it was central to Zuna's purposes in this part of the text where she was beginning to build the network of concepts to frame the case study examples. Zuna's analysis of her own text was that the final sentence of paragraph B had conceptually framed the more contextualized meanings of paragraph C. She elaborated on this more contextualized perspective with the following comment:

> This is introducing what is happening in England

For Zuna, the final sentence in paragraph B introduced the key concept of advocacy and also provided the transition from the concept network of social exclusion to the case study illustration of social exclusion provided by Thornhill. This is a complex set of functions for a single sentence to perform and goes a long way to explaining its ambiguity.

Despite our difficulty in recognizing the fact, in writing paragraphs A-C of her assignment, Zuna is attempting to realize a number of phases that are highly appropriate for the background stage of an exposition or discussion text:

i) Naming concepts
ii) Defining concepts
iii) Relating concepts in taxonomic relations and moving from general to specific/abstract to concrete
iv) Describing a situation or Recounting events.

It seemed to us, with our predispositions toward how this assignment task was intended to be interpreted and responded to, that realizing these phases of the background stage required a more elaborated configuration of meanings than was possible in a single sentence. It also seemed that the background needed to constitute the background to an issue. Constructing such background and issue stages appeared to us to require at least a paragraph. An example of how to reconfigure the meanings in Zuna's original paragraph B and C so they orientate less ambiguously to the task is presented in Figure 5.11 as a further type of metasemiotic mediation. The plagiarized material in paragraph B has not been rewritten for this exercise. Paragraph C in this version is a new paragraph that replaces the final clause of Zuna's original paragraph B. Zuna's original paragraph C now becomes paragraph D.

The rewritten paragraph C in Figure 5.11 performs all the functions that Zuna had attempted to perform in the single final sentence of paragraph B. The hyperTheme (first sentence) of paragraph C makes the transition from the abstract taxonomic description of *social exclusion* in paragraph B and leads into the introduction of the two key concepts from the assignment title, *advocacy* and *outreach*. Each of these is defined and they are therefore established as key concepts. Finally, paragraph C makes a statement of intent about the assignment that directly links the key concepts, *advocacy* and *outreach*, to the ensuing discussion, announcing which case study is going to be exploited in the assignment. Paragraph D is still in Zuna's original words, but as a result of the framing in paragraph C, it is now clear that this is a descriptive introduction to the case study. As Zuna herself recognized in her analysis of her original paragraph, it is the preceding text that establishes its purposes.

This revised background and issue stage now functions more clearly (for us) as the macroTheme for the whole assignment: it announces what the assignment will be about. The similar announcing function of the hyperTheme of the revised paragraph C is crucial to the information flow through these two stages of the text. As well as announcing what paragraph C will be about, it is "dual facing"

Genre stages (in normal type) Phases (in italics)	**Do outreach approaches and advocacy always improve the delivery of care services for people who are socially excluded?**
Background *Taxonomic description and definitions of a key conceptual formation*	B. In practice, the idea of exclusion is mainly used in three contexts. The first is financial: exclusion is identified with poverty, and its effect on a person's ability to participate in normal activities. The second is exclusion from the labor market: exclusion is strongly identified with long-term unemployment though there is some research evidence to question whether long term unemployed people are really excluded. Third, there is exclusion in its social sense, which identifies exclusion partly with alienation from social networks.
Issue *Framing: Definitions of key concepts; linking to case study*	C. Because socially excluded people are outside the normal social networks, it can be difficult for the normal care services to reach them. That is why advocacy and outreach approaches may be useful in these situations. Advocacy is/means ….. Outreach is/means…. In this essay I am going to look at how successful advocacy and outreach are by using examples from the Thornhill community case study.
Describing case study details	*[The original paragraph C now works as paragraph D]* D. Thornhill community was qualified for government funding because it was among the area with a high level of deprived neighbourhoods in England. Compared with other parts of Southampton and southeast England, people in Thornhill experience lower level of health and wellbeing needs.

Figure 5.11 Modeling text-redesign on Zuna's text: another form of metasemiotic mediation.

(see Ravelli, 2004), and links back to paragraph B. Its announcing and dual facing functions establish the context in which the key concepts of advocacy and outreach can be introduced within the remainder of paragraph C.

5.8.3 Contextualized and Decontextualized Meanings

Zuna is oriented strongly toward contextualized—and categorical—meanings. Her control over decontextualized meaning making is still developing. This becomes particularly significant as material illustrations from the case studies are introduced into the text as they are in paragraph D, which reads as follows:.

> **Paragraph D of Zuna's assignment**
> Programs like Thornhill Plus are part of government's response for the socially excluded people. Some organizations are helping the socially excluded people to get better services delivered to their door steps. There are different types of organizations, such as communities' programs in Thornhill Health and Wellbeing project offer advocacy. Most of this

> Advocacy Network in Thornhill agree to work to the advocacy code of practice. As well as family support project and THAWP have been able to provide a better service to the community.

Zuna's declared intention for this paragraph was to frame the community organizations by the conceptual formation of *social exclusion, advocacy, and outreach* and to focus on the benefits of advocacy and outreach. Although it is not obvious without reference to the source material, the organizations in paragraph D are not all examples of *advocacy and outreach organizations*.

5.8.4 Explanation and Contextualized Meanings

Along the genre trajectory from classification lies explanation, with a configuration of meanings in cause–effect patterns. In explanations, these cause and effect relations are categorical rather than perspectival. Throughout the mediated text analysis discussion, Zuna referred to the importance of cause–effect in both the course and her workplace:

> Causes are very important in essay writing. They make you know more about what the question is. When you know the causes you know what you will have to do to improve it. Causes are a very important part of the course. It gives you insight into the work I do and the impact. Although I do this work I don't know what surrounds it. I can learn what is supposed to be.

The categorical quality of cause–effect is indicated by Zuna's final words, *I can learn what is supposed to be.*

In this assignment, explanation is required to relate the delivery of certain types of care (outreach and advocacy) to the effects of this delivery. However, as the genre is not explanation but exposition or discussion, the relationship between delivery of care and its effects is expected to be perspectival rather than categorical. The issue or position that the assignment is addressing is therefore key to the cause–effect explanations that are established. Interpreting the Issue to be other than "effects of certain kinds of delivery of care" will lead to an assignment that does not "answer the question." Although the purposes of paragraphs E–J were unclear to us, Zuna was clear in the mediated text analysis that these paragraphs are about causes. The mismatch in our perceptions appears to have come from our different identifications of the Issue being addressed. As Zuna says in her analysis of the overall purpose of the assignment:

I think this is a kind of asks you to explain about why some people have been excluded.

It is evident from the hyperThemes of paragraphs E–J that explaining why people have been excluded by establishing causal relations (see the causal nouns or verbs highlighted in bold in the hyperTheme sentences below)—rather than discussing the pros and cons of outreach and advocacy as responses to social exclusion—is central to Zuna's purposes in the assignment:

E. These housing problems in Thornhill have a disproportionate **impact** on particular groups
F. Poor housing is often **associated with** urban areas
G. low aspiration is **a product of** living in a place which has become associated with failure
H. **The causes** of unemployment are complex
J. **The impact** of poverty is wide ranging and **can affect**[3] children

To keep the assignment focus on the Issue of delivery of care to socially excluded people, the explanation depends on firm control over the concepts of *deprivation, social exclusion*, and *social care*, the interaction of these in cause–effect relations, and the use of case study material to illustrate the concepts and their interaction. The challenges of doing this will be demonstrated by an analysis of paragraph F, presented below.

Paragraph F of Zuna's assignment
Poor housing is often associated with urban areas, where the issues of overcrowding poorly designed large-scale estates and associated social problems are well known. Also living in a second floor flat without a lift makes it difficult to get out, especially if his or her illness affects his mobility. However, the lack of affordable housing has also been identified as one of the biggest social problems in Thornhill. Problems of isolation and poor access to public services are also more common, for example Jill can't get her wheelchair into shops.

As with the final sentence in paragraph B, there is ambiguity in this paragraph in the transition from concepts to material examples. Sentence 1 sets up a general causal relation between poor housing and social problems. Sentence 2 provides a material example of such a relationship: the conjunction *also* in sentence 2 actually functions as *for example.* Sentence 3 sets up a slightly adjusted version of the Sentence 1 abstract causal relation for the concrete situation in

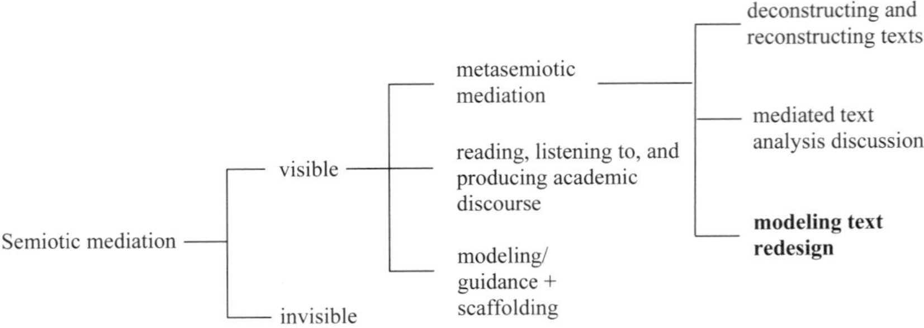

Figure 5.12 Modeling text redesign as a form of metasemiotic mediation.

Thornhill: *however* in sentence 3 is probably a causal conjunction functioning as *for this reason.* Sentence 4 provides another material example but it is difficult to identify the link to the preceding text. In general, it is difficult to trace the chain of identification on which the causal relations depend through the paragraph.

Zuna is trying to bring together conceptual framing, cause–effect explanation, and argumentation. This requires her to move among categorical, perspectival, contextualized, decontextualized, and causal meanings; it results in difficulty in maintaining a coherent information flow through the text. Reciprocal metasemiotic mediation was used to produce this analysis and could be further used to explore alternative configurations of meaning, drawing on the genre trajectory, associated phases, and related linguistic features. As an illustration of an alternative configuration of meanings for paragraphs E–J, see Appendix 5.3, Figure A5.1.

Reconfigurations like the ones presented in Section 5.8.3 and Appendix 5.3 are not simply an exercise in improving sentence-level grammar. They entail a whole text approach to ambiguities in meaning at the sentence level. By developing them through reciprocal metasemiotic mediation, they can bridge the conceptual formations, the genre knowledge, and linguistic resources of a student and a field of study, recognizing the predispositions of both. A LASS response to the HSC department's request for support with developing students' writing at a sentence level cannot be achieved by focusing exclusively on "how sentences are written." As illustrated here, supporting sentence-level writing depends on a recognition of the function of individual sentences from a text in context perspective. Figure 5.12 includes "modeling text redesign" as a third metasemiotic mediation process.

5.8.5 Argument and Decontextualized Meanings

As established previously, according to our analysis, the structure of Zuna's text did not contain an argument stage. However, in the mediated text analysis, Zuna proposed that, for her, an argument stage began with the taxonomy of social care organizations in paragraph K. She described these as "clearly showing the reader the benefits of outreach and advocacy." It was apparent to us that these paragraphs constituted a shift from the less contextualized conceptual framework to the more contextualized details of the case study. However, as discussed earlier, the conceptual framework of advocacy and outreach had not been securely established up to this point, and the absence of hyperThemes linking the case study details to the conceptual framework or to an Issue made it difficult for us to see how these paragraphs constituted an argument. Paragraph L will be used to illustrate this difficulty.

> **Paragraph L of Zuna's assignment**
> The Thornhill plus you program began by consulting local residents. It produces a range of free publications including a bi-monthly newsletter, News, a series of regularly updated factsheets and posters in shop windows continually urge resident to join committees. There are also regular training courses, monthly outreach information sessions and outings for old people. Sandra Jordan, who lived in the estate became a member of the of the community health Group. Sandra knew, from her experience in the estate all that was missing and need to be in place. Thornhill plus You project set up community Access which provide a combined advocacy and outreach services for isolated and excluded people living in Thornhill. The case study of Gypsy Traveler was later to be accepted in neighborhood although community services were not use by the traveler instead the family support and youth worker visit the caravan.

The sources of ambiguity in paragraph L lie in framing, thematic development, and conjunction. A number of community organizations are presented and their connection to advocacy and outreach is mentioned. However, there is an absence of key concepts (such as *benefits*) or a prosody of evaluative language to establish how the community organizations impact on the socially excluded. As mentioned earlier, from the mediated analysis discussions, it seemed that Zuna regarded community organizations as *necessarily* associated with benefits. As a result, for her, benefits are not evaluated but assumed. Such a categorical representation is aligned more with explanation than with discussion.

The mediated text analysis discussion with Zuna suggested that ambiguities in Zuna's text could be traced back to: the meanings she extracted from the course reading material; her overall predisposition toward description, recount, and explanation rather than to discussion; and an unfamiliarity with configuring the meanings in all these genres, especially with using the text-forming devices that underpin the genres (such as thematic development for foregrounding and backgrounding information, and evaluative language for creating linkages across text) and the phases of naming and defining concepts, relating concepts to each other, and framing illustrative case study material.

It appeared that Zuna was more oriented toward the material and categorical rather than toward the abstract and the perspectival. In terms of the APPRAISAL system of ENGAGEMENT (see Chapter 3, Section 3.4.2.2), this suggests her linguistic resources are more aligned with MONOGLOSSIC representations of phenomena than to HETEROGLOSSIC ones. Although we did not have access to the background experiences that might have led to these predispositions, it seemed quite possible that they can be explained by Hasan's concept of semantic orientation, that is, predispositions toward configurations of meanings and ways of making meanings established through earlier socialization experiences. Such differences in semantic orientations could in part explain why the same communicative situation (such as an assignment task and its guidance notes) is interpreted and engaged with differently by students.

5.9 Mediated Text Analysis Discussion as Metasemiotic Mediation

Our comprehension of Zuna's assignment text was mediated by Zuna herself. Without her metasemiotic mediation we (and her teacher) were left with ambiguity. Our revision of her text in Figure 5.11 is the product of our dialogue with her, that is, her metasemiotic mediation of our understanding of what she was seeking to achieve. Students come into university study with predispositions—their semantic orientations—toward that study. For teachers not to engage with those predispositions may limit the semiotic mediation that we are proposing constitutes university teaching and learning. In order to engage with agentive learners we need to develop our awareness of their semantic orientations and enter into reciprocal relationships of semiotic mediation (see Figures 5.1 and 5.2). The model paragraphs we have presented in Figure 5.11 probably come closer to what is valued in the field of HSC study than the paragraphs Zuna wrote. However, these cannot simply be imposed on her for that reason. What Zuna wrote represents what she knows. How and how far she takes on the knowledge that is reflected in the remodeled version depends on how she relates that knowledge to her own knowledge of content, genre, and language. In this view, we are following Hasan's proposal reported in Chapter 2 that teachers have a responsibility to seek to understand the cultural and linguistic backgrounds of their students, particularly as these are reflected in their semantic orientation. This is not to suggest that a teacher abrogates responsibility for classifying and framing knowledge according to the recontextualization rules that they are following. But it is to recognize that both semiotic and metasemiotic mediation are reciprocal activities that depend ultimately on a student's appropriation of what is being mediated.

Taking this into account, a modified form of the teaching and learning approach that was presented in Chapter 4 can be proposed. In a reciprocal mediated text analysis approach, features of text can be brought explicitly to Zuna's attention through metasemiotic mediation. The relationship between sentence and paragraph structuring and how she makes meanings that are recognized and valued in HSC study can be explored. In the process of doing this, her understanding of the conceptual formation will come into focus and may send her back to the course reading material to reestablish the concepts she is working with. Her whole assignment text may take on a different configuration, more aligned with the typical features of a discussion genre since the remodeled paragraphs have a clearly expressed issue that will need to be addressed. This would involve her in reconfiguring information from the source material. It is this reconfiguration that constitutes the legitimate peripheral participation in the discourses of academic HSC, referred to by Northedge as an objective of the course (2003a, 2003b). Zuna expressed strong awareness, for example, of the significance of an introduction in setting the direction of an assignment, obtained from her feedback on previous assignments. What she is still learning is how to write such an introduction.

5.10 Andrea's Assignment

Our initial analysis of the stages and phases of Andrea's assignment text (Figure 5.13) revealed a strong orientation toward argument and genre staging very similar to the schematic version of the assignment guidance notes presented in Section 5.6 above (Table 5.2).

In Andrea's assignment, there were few ambiguous stretches of text, although the concluding position statement was not clear (a point which was commented on by her teacher).

Paragraph	Stages and phases (in italics)
A	Background
B	Issue
C-F	Background: *Definition of "social exclusion"*
C	*Taxonomy of effects*
D	*Description of effects*
E, F	*Elaboration of definition + effects*
G	Argument For (1) *("benefits")*
H	*Case study (1) illustrating concepts*
I,J,K	*Case study (2) illustrating concepts*
L	Arguments For (2)
M-P	Argument Against (1)
Q	Argument Against (2)
R-T	Argument Against (3)
U	Argument Against (4)
U	*Problem*
V	*Solution to problem*
W-Y	Conclusion [Purpose? not entirely clear]

Figure 5.13 An analyst's view of staging in Andrea's assignment.

5.10.1 Mediated Text Analysis Discussion With Andrea: The Assignment Purpose

For Andrea, the purpose of the assignment was to argue:

> So they are asking you to explain first of all what the services are, how they work, and if they are useful. So it's like an explanation. It's a critical, to give a criticize because they are asking "Do you think that these always work?" . . . So yeah I think it's that kind of like more expressing your own opinion on them and everything.

Genre stages	Do outreach approaches and advocacy always improve the delivery of care services for people who are socially excluded?
Background	A. Since the early 1930s there have been many changes in the lives of people who live in the UK. We have observed how the population moved from being in absolute poverty to being in relative poverty, where citizens are no longer lacking in the resources to satisfy their basic needs. (Faculty of Health and Social Care, Diverse communities and resources for care, 2008, unit 9)
Issue Position	B. However we still have cases where poorer communities are in a difficult position and some of the residents may experience social exclusion and be in need of outreach services and advocacy. During this assignment I will define the meaning of these concepts and develop their policy and function in the society. Moreover I will focus on the success that they can have in improving the delivery of care services to socially excluded service users and their limitations.

Figure 5.14 Background and Issue in Andrea's text.

Although Andrea uses the term *explain*, she emphasizes the perspectival and argumentative nature of the assignment with her use of the words *criticize* and *expressing your own opinion*. Throughout the mediated analysis discussion, Andrea showed an orientation toward argumentation and a critical perspective on HSC. In terms of the APPRAISAL system of ENGAGEMENT (see Chapter 3, Section 3.4.2.2) Andrea's linguistic resources appear to be more aligned with HETEROGLOSSIC representations of phenomena than to MONOGLOSSIC ones.

5.10.2 Mediated Text Analysis: Paragraph and Sentence Purpose

Andrea does not attempt in the first few paragraphs of her text to perform all the functions that we proposed in Section 5.8.2 are typical phases of the background stage:

i) Naming concepts
ii) Defining concepts
iii) Relating concepts in taxonomic relations and moving from general to specific/abstract to concrete
iv) Describing a situation or recounting events.

Instead, she restricts herself to naming the concepts of *social exclusion, advocacy,* and *outreach* and signals she will carry out the defining and taxonomizing of these concepts in the subsequent paragraphs, which she does in fact do. This allows her space to establish the issue in paragraph B (see Figure 5.14). In fact, she also proposes a position in that paragraph that SFL genre analysis would see as more appropriate for an exposition genre than the discussion one she is writing, where an issue for discussion is all that is needed in the background stage.

5.10.3 Contextualized and Decontextualized Meanings

Andrea's explicit reference to *outreach and advocacy* as "concepts" in paragraph B (see Figure 5.14) indicates her recognition of the role of concepts in the discussion she is embarking on, which she clearly intends to organize in terms of concepts. This constitutes a powerful cohesive device that ensures that even as she explores arguments for and against the benefits of outreach and advocacy, the concepts themselves become and remain clearly established. In other words, Andrea is oriented toward decontextualized meaning making. Andrea had not written such assignment introductions before this course. She had learned to write them in the course. The fact she had learned so well reflects, in our view, her predisposition toward the perspectival meanings of argumentation.

5.10.4 Argument and Decontextualized Meanings

Throughout the mediated text analysis discussion and throughout her assignment text, Andrea demonstrated her predisposition toward making decontextualized (i.e., abstract, conceptual) meanings alongside the contextualized meanings that the case studies represent. These extracts from the mediated text analysis discussion illustrate this.

> Yes as I say from theory to practice. You have shown the theory now show you know how it works in practice.
>
> I find once you understand the concept you can relate it to the case study. *[She tries to think about the case of Anwar but can't remember his name.]* You see I remember the concept but can't remember the case. I could have put the case of Simon as contraposed to the case of Anwar.

Below, in Figure 5.15, is an example from Andrea's assignment text of how she manages the transition from a more abstract and decontextualized conceptual formation (the effects of social exclusion) to the more material contextualized meanings of the case study. It is a comparable transition to the one in paragraphs B and C of Zuna's assignment, which we discussed in Section 5.8.2.

As well as framing the case study with the concept of *social exclusion* in Figure 5.15, Andrea also establishes a cause–effect relationship chain:

Movement between contextualized-decontextualized	**Text**
Decontextualized (Abstract Participants in bold)	D (HyperTheme). These **effects [of social exclusion]** are interlinked and can lead to **a physical sense of exclusion** where people are drawn to live in the margin of their community and they lack the support necessary to lead healthy lifestyles. . . .
More contextualized (Generalized, human Participants, in bold, engaged mostly in material Processes, underlined)	F (HyperTheme). Even if good social care services are provided **socially excluded individuals** do not feel comfortable to approach **the services** by themselves therefore it can be challenging for **service providers** to deliver care.
Most contextualized (After the generalized human Participants in the hyperTheme (*outreach team, project workers, people in need of service*) Participants that predominate are an individual human (*Simon, a young man)*, a number of material places (*his house, local places*), and human conditions that Simon is subject to (*signs of physical, psychological and mental disabilities*), some of which include other, generalized human agents (e.g., *difficulties with other citizens)*. These are the details of the case study story representing "real" experiences of particular Participants, illustrating the concept of *social exclusion* and *outreach*.)	G (Full paragraph) For this reason **an outreach team** is formed where **project workers** are required to look for **people in need of service**. In the case study explained in the course text we have analyzed the situation of **Simon, a young man** who is socially excluded **by his community** and delivers **signs of physical, psychological and mental disabilities** but is scared to approach **public figures** due to **maltreatments by other citizens**. **Simon** lives alone since the death of his father and **his living conditions** are **very poor** as **his house** has being vandalized and **he** is **the victim of harassment from other people. His mental conditions** are **dubious** as **he** is prone to talk **to himself** but even though **he** is not **dangerous he** has been banned from **local places** to prevent **difficulties with other citizens**.

Figure 5.15 Movement between contextualized and decontextualized meanings in Andrea's text.

> These effects . . . can lead to . . . even if . . . do not feel . . . therefore . . . For this reason . . . .

By means of these causal connections, this causal chain moves logically to a point where it is coherent to introduce the case study with the words: *In the case study explained in the course text.* The shift from abstract decontextualized meaning (*social exclusion*) to concrete, contextualized meaning (the case of Simon) is foregrounded as being what the following stretch of text is about.

However, while explanation is entailed in the purposes of the assignment task, as Andrea knows, the assignment is not an explanation genre but a discussion. What distinguishes it from explanation is perspectival, as opposed to categorical meaning making. Andrea was strongly oriented to the genre of discussion. The explanation and classification features identified in paragraphs E–G were embedded in the higher order genre of discussion in Andrea's text.

The schematic structure for her assignment text demonstrated her understanding of discussion stages and phases. Closer attention to how she configures these stages and phases shows her using text-forming devices that progress the logic of the discussion. At the beginning of each of her arguments a claim is foregrounded, drawing on the conceptual formation she is building in the text.

> Claim: *For this reason an outreach team is formed where project workers are required to look for people in need of service*

This is followed by an illustrative description from the case study as evidence for the claim.

> Evidence: *In the case study explained in the course text we have analyzed the situation of Simon a young man who is socially excluded by his community . . .*

The logic of the argument is reinforced by an evaluative prosody that establishes links between the claim and the material reality of the case study (see Chapter 3 on tenor and APPRAISAL).

> Evidence (evaluative language underlined): *For this reason an outreach team is formed where project workers are required to look for people <u>in need of service</u>*

APPRAISAL language used in the case study recount links back to the claim and builds the argument:

> *is <u>scared</u> to approach public figures*
> *<u>maltreatments</u> by other citizens.*
> *living conditions are <u>very poor</u>*
> *mental conditions are <u>dubious</u>*
> *been <u>banned</u> from local places*

The interconnectedness of each of the sentences in the configuration of meanings that make up Andrea's argument again emphasizes the importance of considering single sentences from within the context of a whole text.

5.11 Nimet's Text

To conclude this consideration of the reasons why students using the same source material and guidance notes produce different assignment texts, we will briefly consider the extract from Nimet's assignment, which was presented as Extract A at the beginning of this chapter, as an illustration of coherence problems at the sentence level. The first sentence of the extract is reproduced in Figure 5.16. Like the previous two texts (written by Zuna and Andrea), this was written by a speaker of English as an additional language. However, it is important to stress that the challenges of writing texts in the context of HSC assignment tasks are by no means confined to additional language speakers of English. They are equally significant for first language speakers of English.

One of the key features of the context of university assignment tasks is that they are essentially *reading-into-writing* processes, as has already been pointed out in the case of Zuna. The mediated text analysis discussion with Nimet led to the recognition that the ambiguities in her writing were deeply rooted in this reading-into-writing process. This becomes immediately obvious when the source text from the course reading material is put alongside the extract. A short illustration is provided in Figure 5.16.

At her current stage of language development, Nimet stays close to the source text during the reading-into-writing process. In this process, many ambiguities in how meanings are configured emerge. These ambiguities at the sentence level, like the ones we have considered in other texts in this chapter, do not reside in individual sentences but emerge from a matrix of forces. Nimet is actually operating at the discussion end of the genre trajectory. She is seeking to argue and is reading and writing meanings that are perspectival. The single sentence in Figure 5.16 connects directly with the genre of arguing. In it, Nimet is seeking to express "in her own words" the view presented in the source material, which was written by Shameem Nawaz. She has attributed the view to Nawaz as university writing conventions expect her to (although the wording of the reference does not conform with such conventions). Placing the source material alongside Nimet's rewording reveals, first, how close to the original her rewording is. In the longer run, supporting her to make meanings from source materials that more authentically reword the source material meanings

Extract from Nimet's assignment	Source text
Shameem Nawaz (Resource 13, p65 to p70) about black and minority ethnic for disabled children short break care shows us important for a disabled child to have an ethnically matched placement as they are not aware of cultural differences and short break doesn't involved children living away from home for long period of time.	Some people may think it is not important for a disabled child to have an "ethnically matched" placement as they are not aware of cultural differences and short breaks do not involve children living away from home for long periods of time.

Figure 5.16 Extract from Nimet's assignment compared with source material from the course.

would be useful. But metasemiotically mediating the rewording as it stands would offer a step in this direction.

In her attempt to both present and contradict the viewpoint that *some people* hold (that it is not important for a child to have an ethnically matched placement), Nimet has lost the focus on who the Senser is that holds this view (*some people*), who it is that is contradicting it (*Nawaz*) and who the view is about (*a disabled child*). This confusion reaches a head with Nimet's use of the pronoun *they* in the clause *they are not aware*. With the possibility that this pronoun refers back to any of the three Participants above, Nimet's rewording needs to establish clearly which of the three Participants is responsible for the view *they are not aware of cultural differences.* The fact that it does not do this clearly creates opportunities for metasemiotic mediation on a number of fronts: how Nimet understands the reading material; how she understands her own rewording; and, more broadly, what her linguistic repertoire provides her with in terms of linguistic resources.

In view of what has been argued in this chapter about semantic variation, differences in linguistic repertoire and all the other factors that constitute the particularity of students' genre knowledge and their responses to assignment tasks, the prompt for Nimet's HSC assignment carries a message that is relevant for a LASS approach to learning and teaching:

> Treating everyone the same won't meet everyone's needs. Discuss this statement in relation to Health and Social Care work and suggest some ways in which care workers can respond sensitively to diversity.

This chapter has explored some of the ways that reciprocal semiotic mediation constitutes an approach that is sensitive to semantic variation in the context of HSC academic study.

5.12 Implications

When writing an HSC assignment, a student is interpreting the context in terms of assignment purposes and genres: they are using their linguistic resources to extract or make meanings from source material and to form texts that configure meanings that are valued in the context by their teachers and themselves (through explaining, arguing, naming and defining concepts, relating concepts, and framing case material). They do this by means of text organization (staging and phasing), and managing their representations of conceptual formations, causal relations, information flow, and evaluative links through the text.

Diversity is already a well-recognized principle in the HSC course. Students are seen to come with different affective predispositions, practices (ways of studying, for example, or of performing their professional roles), knowledge of the subject matter, sense of self, sense of purpose, responsibilities, and availability of time. Recognizing semantic variation among the participants in this academic community of practice connects diversity directly with ways of making meaning.

Responding to individual sentences like the ones presented at the beginning of the chapter requires awareness of the role each sentence plays in the text in its context, a context that will be interpreted, experienced, and expressed differently, to greater or lesser extent, by a student and by a teacher. The "extravagant theory" of SFL (Halliday, 1994, p. xix) makes a good contribution to developing such awareness.

Intervention can be carried out through reciprocal metasemiotic mediation drawing on SFL genre knowledge to explore a student's purposes in configuring meanings the way they have. Reciprocally, genre stages and phases can be modeled with students. At the end of the mediated text analysis discussions carried out for this research, students were shown the schematic representations of the assignment guidance notes presented in Table 5.2 and expressed great enthusiasm for such modeling. Mediated text analysis discussions like this are more than simply explorations of a single text. They build a semiotic and metasemiotic repertoire which students and teacher can take forward into subsequent reading-into-writing or text evaluation processes.

A schematic representation of a single assignment can be used in various ways to raise awareness of genre and can then be located on the genre map for the whole course. Models of configurations of meaning at the level of stage and phase—either schematic diagrams of the stages as demonstrated in Table 5.2, or texts themselves labeled for their stages—can be provided for awareness raising. As with the assignment task itself, semantic variation will influence how students interpret and implement such models. Semantic orientation, diverse interpretations of context, and diverse linguistic repertoires all need to be taken into consideration in providing feedback to students on their texts in context and in designing a pedagogy overall. This is what constitutes reciprocal semiotic mediation.

5.13 Conclusion

Like Chapter 4, Chapter 5 has illustrated the dual research and teaching strands of a LASS approach. Mediated text analysis discussion informed by SFL provides both a research and a teaching approach to the semantic variation that characterizes participants in the semiotic mediation that constitutes teaching and learning in contemporary higher education. This SFL-based exploration of HSC student writing leads to the conclusion that student guidance and student feedback that draws on a LASS approach to teaching and learning should be from the perspective of text in context and also entail recognition of semantic and other variations in the meaning-making processes of individual participants in the context.

Underpinning the approach should be three principles:

i) Semiotic mediation is the responsibility of students as much as teachers, although the objectives of each are different. Teachers are seeking to support the reconfiguration of students' conceptual formations. Students are co-participants in that reconfiguration. Despite their co-participation in semiotic mediation activities, because of their different objectives, students and teachers perform different roles in the interaction. Broadly, these can be seen in terms of who initiates and who responds.
ii) Metasemiotic mediation that entails bringing to awareness the semiotic resources that are being deployed and developed in semiotic mediation activities is a means of enhancing such semiotic mediation at both an initiating and responding level. In effect semiotic mediation is the activity whereby interactants develop conceptual formations and genre and register knowledge. Metasemiotic mediation enhances that activity by bringing to awareness the semiotic resources involved. Mediated text analysis discussion and remodeling students' writing in collaboration with them are two examples of metasemiotic mediation. The impact goes beyond the immediate text and provides tools and insights that can be exploited in subsequent reading-into-writing and text evaluation processes.

iii) How students make meaning from the source material and then subsequently in the texts they write reflects their semantic orientations toward the contexts in which they are reading and writing. Semantic orientations encompass both the predispositions that participants have toward making particular kinds of meaning and the language and other meaning-making resources they have at their disposal. Differences in semantic orientation mean that assignment tasks, guidance notes, and course material may all be interpreted and responded to differently by students on the same course.

In order to implement a LASS approach to the HSC assessment design and feedback, the focus on text in context should address genre and register. The focus on content should deal with conceptual formations and their relationship with illustrative case material. It should be anticipated that students' diverse semantic orientations will result in various interpretations and implementations of this approach.

If sentence-level meaning making is seen from this text in context perspective, then sentence writing (and reading) takes its place among the meaning-making practices that constitute the participation of HSC professionals in university based HSC communities of practice. Reciprocal semiotic and metasemiotic mediation is an important way to support that participation.

Notes

1 Please note that all student texts that we draw on throughout the book are presented exactly as written by the student, including any errors of grammar, vocabulary, or referencing.

2 In part one of the research, assignment tasks, guidance notes, and marking criteria were collected for 24 assignments across 2 years of the course in order to develop a genre "map" of the course. Seventy-two student texts were then collected from across the assignment tasks and subjected to an initial genre analysis to see how well they matched with the predictions. Genre stages were identified by reading the texts and generalizing or abstracting the purposes of parts of the text. A total of 40 high-, mid-, and low-scoring assignments were then selected for closer analysis with linguistic features being used to test our identification of the purposes of texts and text stages. In part two of the research we carried out "mediated text analysis discussions" with 10 students about an assignment they had written, prompting them to explain why and how they had written the text the way they had. We asked students to comment on global text, paragraph, and sentence level features. Then we showed them a genre schema we had created, and sought their opinion about its

usefulness. Ten student discussions of up to 2.5 hours were recorded and transcribed (average length of discussion was 1 hour 54 minutes; average length of transcript, 15,000 words) and an SFL-based genre analysis was carried out on the student's written text before and after the discussion. In this stage of the analysis, closer attention was paid to the relationship between the purposes of sentences and the linguistic features realizing these purposes. We did not subject the transcripts of the discussions to an SFL analysis but instead treated them as a source of insight into how students perceived their own texts. The objective was to develop ways of using genre analysis that would support students to write HSC assignments more effectively, with particular reference to sentence level meaning making. For a more detailed account of the research behind this chapter, see Donohue and Coffin (2012).

3 The hyperTheme for paragraph I, *Exclusion from the labor market takes many forms*, is taxonomic, not causal.

Appendix 5.1

Zuna's assignment text

Assignment: *Do outreach approaches and advocacy always improve the delivery of care services for people who are socially excluded?*

A. In our society people are excluded when they are not part of the networks which support most people in ordinary life networks of family, friends, community and employment. Among many others, poor people, ex-prisoners, homeless people, people with AIDS, people with learning disabilities or psychiatric patients might all be said to be at risk of exclusion. This is a very broad concept; it includes not only deprivation, but problems of social relationships, including stigma, social isolation and failures in social protection.

B. In practice, the idea of exclusion is mainly used in three contexts. The first is financial: exclusion is identified with poverty, and its effect on a person's ability to participate in normal activities. The second is exclusion from the labor market: exclusion is strongly identified with long-term unemployment though there is some research evidence to question whether long term unemployed people are really excluded. Third, there is exclusion in its social sense, which identifies exclusion partly with alienation from social networks, and partly with the circumstances in Thornhill community for example, advocacy for socially excluded people is also poor in this community.

C. Thornhill community was qualified for government funding because it was among the area with a high level of deprived neighbourhoods in England.

Compared with other other parts of Southampton and southeast England, people in Thornhill experience lower level of health and wellbeing needs.

D. Programs like Thornhill Plus are part of government's response for the socially excluded people. Some organizations are helping the socially excluded people to get better services delivered to their door steps. There are different types of organizations, such as communities' programs in Thornhill Health and Wellbeing project offer advocacy. Most of this Advocacy Network in Thornhill agree to work to the advocacy code of practice. As well as family support project and THAWP have been able to provide a better service to the community.

E. These housing problems in Thornhill have a disproportionate impact on particular groups, such as older people, children and young people, those on low incomes and those with health problems, including mental ill health.

F. Poor housing is often associated with urban areas, where the issues of overcrowding poorly designed large-scale estates and associated social problems are well known. Also living in a second floor flat without a lift makes it difficult to get out, especially if his or her illness affects his mobility. However, the lack of affordable housing has also been identified as one of the biggest social problems in Thornhill. Problems of isolation and poor access to public services are also more common, for example Jill can't get her wheelchair into shops.

G. Lynsey Hanley, a journalist who grew up in council flat estate on the out shirts of Birmingham, argues that low aspiration is a product of living in a place which has become associated with failure.

H. The causes of unemployment are complex. Some kinds are long term technical unemployment happens due to sickness or physical disability. These made people's skills redundant. Some are medium term cyclical unemployment happens because there is inadequate demand to keep production going. Some are short term frictional unemployment happens because people change jobs or locations. Seasonal work, casual employment and sub employment are patterns of work which lead to people being employed only for short periods at a time.

I. Exclusion from the labor market takes many forms some people can opt for early retirement, further education or domestic responsibility, and others cannot. If poor people are unemployed more, it is not just because they are more marginal in the labor market; it is also because they have fewer choices, and because people who become classified as unemployed, are more likely to be poor.

J. The impact of poverty is wide ranging and can affect children, how well they do in future life. Babies that are born from poor family are likely to low birth weight or were born underweight, and that could result to problem across their life span. That does not mean that it is based on a comparison with others in the same society there are some countries where most people are poor.

K. **New Deal for Community** has formed a partnership to deliver advocacy for vulnerable older people and people with physical disabilities and or sensory impairments in Thornhill, with the King fund idea of healthy neighborhood. These are to improve people's health, housing, and physical environment. Also increase educational achievement and skills, and it increases number of people in work and reduces crime.

L. **The Thornhill plus you program** began by consulting local residents. It produces a range of free publications including a bi-monthly newsletter, News, a series of regularly updated factsheets and posters in shop windows continually urge resident to join committees. There are also regular training courses, monthly outreach information sessions and outings for old people. Sandra Jordan, who lived in the estate became a member of the of the community health Group. Sandra knew, from her experience in the estate all that was missing and need to be in place. Thornhill plus You project set up community Access which provide a combined advocacy and outreach services for isolated and excluded people living in Thornhill. The case study of Gypsy Traveler was later to be accepted in neighborhood although community services were not use by the traveler instead the family support and youth worker visit the caravan.

M. **The Family Support Project** provides better services to you mothers such as home visit to help the family. It also show relationship in which support or care is provided on a reciprocal basis. Shelly and her friend looked after each other child in case an emergency. At the same time, these develop relationship with other people who live in the neighborhoods. Shelly and Cheree valued the cooking Pot section; these involve the family support worker who engages the children while their parents are in the kitchen.

N. As Cheree says "We can focus on our cooking and know that our children are OK and they're in happy playing''

[Paragraphs N-P omitted. They continue the taxonomic description of more community organizations]

Q. Outreach predicated on developing a trusting, meaningful relationship between the outreach worker and the homeless person with Traveler. The case study of Simon is afraid of people around him and does not have contact with other people. The outreach worker would have to go out and find Simon perhaps near the community center or shops. Simon needs help, but he is not coping on his own.

R. Other issues include people who are unaware of services and people may have literacy or language skills to response to leaflets or poster placed for advertisements. With the support of the outreach worker's encouragements help people to overcome the barrier to accessing care services.

S. Do outreach approaches and advocacy always improve the delivery of care services for people who are socially excluded?

T. Conclusion in this essay, I began with defining the meaning of social excluded people and advocacy. Social networks can be the significant source for support, and the benefit and well being. However, the system has disadvantages to people who may have lack the means to develop supportive network.

U. Finally I have reviewed the success of neighborhood renewal projects and saw their benefits over their long term, and their planning to ensure they continue beyond their life of short term funding.

V. The case study of Sarah who joined the program to ensure that the planning is careful for continuality. I explained the approaches to outreach and advocacy and its limitations.

W. To top it all socially excluded people has benefited and these has improved Thorn hill community

Appendix 5.2

Andrea's Assignment Text
Assignment: ***Do outreach approaches and advocacy always improves the delivery of care services for people who are socially excluded?***

A. Since the early 1930s there have been many changes in the lives of people who live in the UK. We have observed how the population moved from being in absolute poverty to being in relative poverty, where citizens are no longer lacking in the resources to satisfy their basic needs. (Faculty of Health and Social Care, Diverse communities and resources for care, 2008, unit 9)

B. However we still have cases where poorer communities are in a difficult position and some of the residents may experience social exclusion and be in need of outreach services and advocacy. During this assignment I will define the meaning of these concepts and develop their policy and function in the society. Moreover I will focus on the success that they can have in improving the delivery of care services to socially excluded service users and their limitations.

C. As defined by the Centre for Public Policy and Management, Robert Gordon University; being "socially excluded means lacking opportunities and experiences that are taken for granted by the general population." Furthermore this definition explains how exclusion develops in three main ways: financially, in the employment field and socially. Financial exclusion is associated with poverty and its effects in daily involvement to activities, thus the inability to access service and the network of the community; long term unemployment define the labor exclusion which can lead to poverty, depression and health problems; social isolation occurs when individuals lacks access to standard education, housing, health, employment and income. (Centre for Public Policy and Management, Robert Gordon University, undated)

D. These effects are interlinked and can lead to a physical sense of exclusion where people are drawn to live in the margin of their community and they lack the support necessary to lead healthy lifestyles.

E. Socially excluded individuals have considerable difficulties to access main stream care services because they may have given up following negative experiences, they may have low self esteem and intimidation issues with care workers, there might be communication's barriers, a lack of skills and confidence to pursue options or simply for an unwillingness to join groups in the fear of being publically exposed.

F. Even if good social care services are provided socially excluded individuals do not feel comfortable to approach the services by themselves therefore it can be challenging for service providers to deliver care.

G. For this reason an outreach team is formed where project workers are required to look for people in need of service. In the case study explained in the course text we have analyzed the situation of Simon, a young man who is socially excluded by his community and delivers signs of physical, psychological and mental disabilities but is scared to approach public figures due to maltreatments by other citizens. Simon lives alone since the death of his father and his living conditions are very poor as his house has being vandalized and he is the victim of harassment from other people. His mental conditions are dubious as he is prone to talk to himself but even though he is not dangerous he has been banned from local places to prevent difficulties with other citizens. (Faculty of Health and Social Care, Diverse communities and resources for care, 2008, pp 87–88).

H. Simon represents a good example where an outreach team can help the situation by applying their policy and procedures. As outreach teams are supposed to look for patients to provide practical support, to be a first point of contact and be flexible enough to work around their needs; they would be able to assist Simon to access medical and mental support, improve his housing and financial situation contributing to minimize his exclusion.

I. Other examples of cases of outreach services are provided in the case of the Sussex Traveller Women Health Project. In this example we have seen how the female gipsy travellers were helped to improve their health and condition with targeted services such as craft sessions, cooking and training which enabled them to be more healthy and useful to their community. (Friends, Families and travellers, 2005, pp. 2, 6)

J. Practical help by the outreach team is provided by advocating the service user's needs therefore by helping them to speak for themselves while also trying not to influence them in their actions and opinions.

K. In many cases it is the social worker himself that provides the first contact for an outreach service and advocacy, like cases with the Community Access Project, which consist in helping the patient to express his views and opinions freely and effectively, to involve him in the decision making process of his care, to listen and provide a voice, to guard his rights and freedom of choice, to challenge services to make sure improvements are made, without influencing or overacting his rights and opinions. (Source: Thornhill Plus You, undated)

L. In the case of Simon having a social worker from the Community Access Service to help him would mean having someone who can assist him to access the community services, to be involved in decision making processes in his own care plan, to listen to his opinion and requirements for his situation, to understand his rights, challenge services to make real improvements to his physical conditions, without making decisions on his behalf and influencing his opinions.

M. However offering an advocacy and outreach service can have some limitations and challenges.

N. One of the main difficulties in advocating for patients can be found in the case of the nurses whom are required by the Nursing and Midwifery

Council to "act as an advocate for those on your care, helping them to access relevant Health and Social Care, information and support." (Nursing and Midwifery Council, 2007).

O. This advocacy works well when it is just a case of referring patient's wishes and opinions, but when the patients asks to the nurse to challenge hospital policy it can be difficult to maintain impartiality without putting the career at risk. (Faculty of Health and Social Care, Diverse communities and resources for care, 2008 pp 98).

P. For that reason specialist organizations are required even though services may not be broadly available.

Q. Another difficulty for outreach services is the limitation to funding. As it drains its resources from public funding which is limited to a period of time, outreach services are at risk of being stopped. Even if service users and project workers would find new methods to fund the services it would still be a difficult situation.

R. Moreover there can be conflict of interest in the social workers job because they need to provide the best options of care without contravening their employers' policy and procedures. Limitation in the availability of resources could be another challenge as it has been identified that many individuals in the poorer areas are in need of outreach resources but often there are not many services available. (Faculty of Health and Social Care, Diverse communities and resources for care, 2008 pp 99)

S. More practical barriers can be found in the first stages of outreach projects where engaging the service users can be difficult.

T. In the case of Simon the main difficulties could have been physically approaching him as he refuses contact with most people. In this case the bridge of contact could have been George Tailor, one of Simon's neighbors, who had known him for long time.

U. Even in the case of the gypsy travellers the main difficulty was making the volunteers to participate to the meetings even though reminders were used and child care was provided. This lack of participation was caused by the differences of culture and language between the service providers and the service users. Furthermore another reason was the discomfort of the travellers on being at the center of attention and their difficulty with official individuals.

V. The solution was found when one of the workers managed to access the caravan site and deliver the services to the community instead of waiting for the community to go to the meetings. As she had the same background it was easier for her to establish a connection with the travellers.

W. As demonstrated the use of outreach services and advocacy is very useful for people who are socially excluded. By overcoming the first difficulties of approach by building up stable relationships between service workers and patients, they are able to provide users with the ability and confidence to approach services by themselves; by delivering the service to the users they are able to close the gap between the individuals in the main society and those socially excluded.

X. Even if there are limitations and barriers in their job such in funding, culture and language; the outreach project workers are a part of every community and their job is often accessed by most individuals even if they are not socially excluded. (Faculty of Health and Social Care, Diverse communities and resources for care, 2008 pp 99)

Y. An example can be found in the cases of Health visitors and Midwives who offer an outreach service with home visits and provide assistance to access support and services in the care environment and nurses who provide advocacy to patients in their daily routine.

Appendix 5.3:

Illustrative Modeling of Zuna's Paragraphs E-J

Zuna's text	Illustrative feedback	Illustrative modeling
E. These housing problems in Thornhill have a disproportionate impact on particular groups, such as older people, children and young people, those on low incomes and those with health problems, including mental ill health.	Are you wanting to tackle causes of social exclusion? If so, probably best to keep it short since it is only the Background to the real Issue which is: delivery of care to people who are socially excluded.	There are various reasons why people are socially excluded and why advocacy and outreach may be necessary in order to deliver care to them. These include poor housing, unemployment and poverty.
F. Poor housing is often associated with urban areas, where the issues of overcrowding poorly designed large-scale estates and associated social problems are well known. Also living in a second floor flat without a lift makes it difficult to get out, especially if his or her illness affects his mobility. However, the lack of affordable housing has also been identified as one of the biggest social problems in Thornhill. Problems of isolation and poor access to public services are also more common, for example Jill can't get her wheelchair into shops.	What are the important influences of poor housing that affect delivery of care? This paragraph seems to be mostly about mobility. If so, suggest you make that your theme. How is 'affordable housing' a relevant concept to the problems of delivering care to the socially excluded?	Mobility problems can be increased by poor housing and are a factor which leads to exclusion. For example, living in a second floor flat without a lift makes it difficult to get out, if there are mobility problems. Jill is an example of someone who can't access public services or even the shops because of her wheelchair.
G. Lynsey Hanley, a journalist who grew up in council flat estate on the out shirts of Birmingham, argues that low aspiration is a product of living in a place which has become associated with failure.	The key concept here seems to be low aspiration. Is that the concept you want to link to difficulties of delivering care to the socially excluded? If so, suggest you make that clearer	Poor housing conditions can also lead to low aspirations. Lynsey Hanley, a journalist who grew up in council flat estate on the out shirts of Birmingham, argues that low aspiration is a product of living in a place which has become

Figure A5.1 Illustrative modelling of Zuna's paras E-J.

		associated with failure. This can mean that people do not try to take advantage of social care.
H. The causes of unemployment are complex. Some kinds are long term technical unemployment happens due to sickness or physical disability. These made people's skills redundant. Some are medium term cyclical unemployment happens because there is inadequate demand to keep production going. Some are short term frictional unemployment happens because people change jobs or locations. Seasonal work, casual employment and sub employment are patterns of work which lead to people being employed only for short periods at a time. I. Exclusion from the labor market takes many forms some people can opt for early retirement, further education or domestic responsibility, and others cannot. If poor people are unemployed more, it is not just because they are more marginal in the labor market; it is also because they have fewer choices, and because people who become classified as unemployed, are more likely to be poor.	Which aspects of unemployment are most relevant to social exclusion and the delivery of social care from paragraph H and I?	Unemployment is another cause of social exclusion. It can be a result of long term sickness or disability, medium term changes in demand, or short term because of job change or moving home. Some people are unemployed because of early retirement, further education or domestic responsibility. An important effect of unemployment is that people become poor and have fewer choices. Such people may not access social care as easily as people in employment.

Figure A5.1 (Continued)

J. The impact of poverty is wide ranging and can affect children, how well they do in future life. Babies that are born from poor family are likely to low birth weight or were born underweight, and that could result to problem across their life span. That does not mean that it is based on a comparison with others in the same society there are some countries where most people are poor.	If you want to bring children into the picture again suggest you make a clear connection with the Issue you are addressing: delivering care to people who are socially excluded	Children can be particularly affected by poverty and by the social exclusion which goes with it. The impact can last their whole life span. So it is important to find ways to bring social care to the children of peoples who are socially excluded

Figure A5.1 (Continued)

Language Learning ISSN 0023-8333

CHAPTER 6
"I Feel Very New to It and Very Inexperienced": Semantic Orientation, Semiotic Mediation, and the Genres and Registers of Online Discussion Forums

6.1 Introduction

> I am sure there is a way that I could do this better and that's, I am interested in finding out, I feel very new to it and very inexperienced about it and I feel as if I have been fumbling around in the dark with it.
>
> – Naomi, teacher in Health and Social Care

As contemporary universities increasingly blend different forms of distance or virtual learning with traditional face-to-face, brick-based learning, both teachers and students face the challenge of how to make best use of the learning opportunities afforded by computer mediated communication (CMC). For many secondary school graduates, text messaging, e-mail interaction, and blogging are now commonplace in their social and personal lives. However, the continuing lack of integration of social and digital media into school learning (Kearney, 2013) means they are often less experienced with the use of computer mediated talk as a tool for learning. Furthermore, among mature and nontraditional students there may be a range of experiences in the use of CMC, not only in educational settings but also in their social, personal, and workplace lives. Similarly, like Naomi (quoted above), some university teachers may be unsure as to how best to integrate virtual modes of communication into meaningful learning activities. The following interview extracts concerning the use of online forums for academic discussion illustrate some of the challenges from both the teacher and student perspective:

> [T]here is a permanent record, so they would be hesitant about sticking their necks out I think . . . emails are a very difficult medium in general, it is so easy to get the wrong end of the stick, it is so easy to cut someone

DOI: 10.1111/lang.12042

> dead, snub one just because you haven't bothered with the niceties of how you begin and end . . . Of 17 students, active contributors are about four and they are the best students and very computer friendly . . . Of the others I think about half are following what is going on and occasionally will put something up and some I don't even find they are aware of what is going on, they have stopped listening in all together . . .
>
> – Lucinda, teacher in Health and Social Care

> I think what upset me was most of the others would respond if you wrote anything in and I got no response. So at least at a face-to-face tutorial you would get a response, you know if what you were saying was right or wrong. I mean because nobody wrote back . . . I sort of lost my confidence and I thought I haven't got anything valuable to say so I didn't write anything.
>
> – Dagmar, undergraduate student in Health and Social Care

We found that concerns such as those expressed by Naomi, Lucinda, and Dagmar are not unusual. Indeed, despite claims in the literature that online forums open up the floor for all students to participate more equally (due, for example, to reduced competition in entering the discussion), our investigations have found that, in many ways, online spaces replicate the educational inequalities that abound in traditional learning contexts: students whose semantic orientations dispose them to interpret the context and deploy their meaning-making repertoire in ways that are valued and endorsed by both teacher and peers tend to participate in the learning activity, and those whose semantic orientations dispose them to interpret the context and deploy their meaning-making repertoire in ways that are not valued or endorsed may engage only minimally. Like Dagmar, they may lose confidence altogether and become marginalized (at best engaging as "read-only" participants in the online world). Others may never participate in the first place.

Despite the concerns outlined above, in this chapter, we will argue that there is huge potential for online discussion[1] to provide the kind of semiotic mediation that can support students' learning—both learning the language of their field of study and (in so doing) learning their field. This is partly achieved through the fusing or recontextualization of the more traditional academic activities of reading, writing, and speaking as a form of written dialogue. The affordances of written dialogue for a LASS approach to teaching and learning is the focus of this chapter. A key point will be that practitioners need a better understanding of how online discussion forums are structured and how language in this environment functions as a blend of informal dialogue (akin to spontaneous face-to-face interaction) and more formal academic writing. Such understanding can provide a firm basis for teachers and students to best exploit the opportunities for semiotic mediation offered by online forums.

6.1.1 A LASS Approach: Review and Preview

So far in this monograph, we have shown that, from a LASS perspective, context and language are deeply implicated with each other. We have used this perspective to analyze the nature of language use in relation to the teaching and learning of academic subjects, focusing particularly on those contexts where more everyday, contextualized meanings from outside the academic environment are interacting with the more decontextualized meanings of academic study. As well as describing the language that teachers and learners are called on to use in making academic meanings we have begun to identify the diversity of semantic orientations that teachers and learners bring with them based on their previous language experiences. In particular, we have proposed that the patterns of language use that all members of society engage in throughout life establish different kinds of semantic orientations. These orientations may position those embarking on tertiary-level learning more (or less) closely to the kinds of meaning making and learning that are valued within the academic context.

In Chapters 4 and 5, we considered how (language) interactions and experiences within both the wider culture (e.g., film viewing) and the workplace (e.g., the person-centered interactions of HSC professional practice) may influence semantic orientation. In those chapters our attention was on how such interactions may influence students' orientation to academic sources of knowledge as well as their reconfiguring of such sources in their own written texts.

In this chapter, we will maintain a focus on the influences of prior social experiences on meaning making, but we will also consider the influence of students' and teachers' previous experiences and use of digital and social media. We will consider how these may influence the kinds of interactions and learning that take place in online forums.

While the hybrid nature of CMC, and more specifically, discussion forums has been explored in a number of studies both within the SFL literature (e.g., Landers, 2013) and more broadly the linguistic literature (Crystal, 2006; Herring 2012; Thurlow & Mroczek, 2011), its affordances as a teaching and learning technology have been less well explored (but see Coffin et al., 2009, 2012). In this chapter we will bring to the fore what we regard as the most significant implications of CMC, which we are describing as written dialogue, for a LASS approach to teaching and learning:

i) teachers have unique opportunities for semiotic and metasemiotic mediation as they observe (in frozen form) students' understanding and learning and have greater opportunities for judicious intervention and modeling (enabling students to learn language and learn about language)
ii) through teacher-guided interaction, students can simultaneously develop knowledge about language and subject knowledge (learning through language)
iii) students can actively rehearse and extend academic meaning-making through engaging in a slowed down, semi-formal dialogue which involves reading and responding in writing
iv) online forums can serve as a bridging environment, a hybrid "third space," which can support students in the movement from reading subject knowledge to constructing (in written assignments) their own arguments and perspectives on it.

6.2 Online Discussion Forums in the Fields of HSC and Applied Linguistics

The two contexts of learning that we will be drawing from in this chapter are a second-level undergraduate course in HSC and an Applied Linguistics course forming part of a master's in education.[2] This section outlines key academic and pedagogic features of both contexts. With its primary focus on computer mediated written dialogue our discussion is, however, relevant to a wide range of academic learning areas.

As discussed in Chapter 5, HSC is a transdisciplinary field of study, drawing on the social sciences and applied sciences as well as on the personal and professional lived experiences of HSC workers. The data examples in this chapter are drawn from a second-level undergraduate course—*Perspectives on Complementary and Alternative Medicine* (CAM)—where the main disciplinary base is the social sciences. The combined theoretical and professional dimensions and aims of the course are represented in the following two learning outcomes. Students are expected to gain knowledge and understanding of:

> theoretical and professional rationales concerning health interventions in relation to orthodox medicine and Complementary and Alternative Medicine.

as well as develop their cognitive skills to:

> reflect upon and critically evaluate personal and lived experiences of health in relation to Complementary and Alternative Medicine.

In order to help meet the learning outcomes of the course, teachers use online discussion forums. Discussion forums are used for a variety of purposes in educational and other contexts and are not reserved for the exchange of opinion and perspective. However, this is a common purpose in a wide range of university programs and was the motivation for their use in both the HSC and Applied Linguistics courses we investigated.

Typically, online forums last for approximately 2 to 3 weeks and are organized around discussion tasks designed to prompt debate relevant to students' prior reading and future written assignments. More broadly, they are designed to encourage students to reflect on and discuss various aspects of subject knowledge, including the relationship between theoretical knowledge and (in the case of CAM) the real-world context of health provision and day-to-day care or (in the case of Applied Linguistics) the everyday realities of classroom teaching. Below is the task from the opening tutorial in the CAM course (referred to as Module 1 below). This is designed to prompt students' thoughts on the changing context of health care and thus inform the follow-up writing task (also set out below):

Tutorial online forum task: Outline one reason or factor which you think has led to an increase in the choices available when it comes to making decisions about our health.

Written assignment task: The following description is of an encounter between a reiki practitioner and a fictional person (Mrs. Bannister) who goes to see her. Think carefully about this encounter and write a report on the interactions that took place in the light of your learning throughout Module 1. In particular, your analysis should focus on the context of the interaction: how does the interaction fit into the way that society and health care is changing, along with any ethical considerations for both the provider and the consumer of health care in this situation? (*The case study of the reiki practitioner and Mrs. Bannister follows*).

The Applied Linguistics course to which we refer was designed to make connections between students' professional experience (with the majority of students being practicing English language teachers) and theories of language (linguistics) and language learning. In a number of ways, Applied Linguistics follows a similar pattern to Film Studies and HSC, and indeed, many areas of applied study that span the world of theory and the world of professional practice. It tends to attract students with varied orientations toward academic knowledge with many (including at the graduate level) finding the crossover from the practical to the theoretical a challenge to their current ways and preferences for meaning making (i.e., their semantic orientations).

As in the case of HSC, online forums in Applied Linguistics are designed to prompt argument and debate relevant to students' prior reading and future writing. The data we draw on in this chapter comprises online forum interaction in which students discuss the factors that affect second language learning. The follow-up written assignment required them to write a review of an academic journal article on this topic.

6.2.1 Reading, Writing, and/or "Speaking"? The Hybrid Nature of Online Meaning-Making

Throughout this monograph we have emphasized that a LASS approach construes learning at the university level as primarily learning about, and through, language and that this is generally in written form. In other words, tertiary learners need to be able to make meanings from course reading material and original academic sources and rework these meanings in their own written texts. Being an independent reader and writer with the capacity to produce written texts that make the meanings that constitute the field of study is, we would argue, what is most at stake for a student to be academically successful. At the same time, we have seen, in Chapter 4, how in a field of study like Film Studies, viewing and interpreting visual material is also an important study activity and, in general, listening and speaking play important roles in mediating written source material. Indeed, developing and practicing the skills of listening and speaking—in the form of lectures, tutorials, and seminars—has always been an integral part of traditional university programs. In this chapter, however, we will show that CMC brings new ways of "listening and talking" and of engaging with academic knowledge.

To do this, we will use the concepts of genre (in Section 6.3) and register (in Section 6.4) to shed light on how the structure and language of online forums can develop students' subject knowledge. The discussion and text extracts show how, in many ways, participating in an online forum is akin to interacting in a face-to-face academic seminar or tutorial and, at the same time, similar to writing an academic assignment. Across Sections 6.3 and 6.4 we will highlight the main pedagogic opportunities and challenges of written dialogue for both teachers and students. In Section 6.5 we will consider the influence of semantic orientations on how students and teachers manage such interaction. We conclude the chapter by summarizing the potential of online forums for a LASS approach to teaching and learning and make several recommendations.

6.3 In What Ways Can Online Forums Support Teaching and Learning? A Genre Perspective

As first introduced in Chapter 3 (Sections 3.2–3.3) and further illustrated in Chapters 4 and 5, within SFL, text structure or design can be investigated using the concept of genre, with genre being defined as a staged, goal-oriented social process. As we exemplified in those chapters, genre analysis identifies the functional stages (as realized through particular lexicogrammatical patterns) that students move through in order to achieve their learning purposes within different fields of study.

In this section we use the concept of genre to show how online forums are functionally structured and discuss how this structuring has considerable potential for teaching and learning, but at the same time raises issues concerning how focused a discussion should be and what kinds of contributions and interactions constitute a satisfying and effective learning experience. Such issues are indicated in the following student comments:

> With respect, are these sessions supposed to be brief replies to [tutor's] questions or complete essays which, along with study stuff for K221 we're expected to plough through? Enthusiasms one thing but some of you peeps are getting carried away!!!
>
> – *Comment posted by Kristina within online forum*

> The discussions reveals aspects and personal experience which are not covered in the course material, but sometimes the discussions go in different directions which are only indirectly linked with the assignment. This is very interesting, too but it is not always useful for the assignments.
>
> – *Comment by Robert on research questionnaire*

> I like reading peoples views about the topics but not quite sure what to contribute myself.
>
> – *Comment by Lina on research questionnaire*

In essence, Section 6.3 will show that online discussions draw on the structuring principles of both face-to-face discussion and formal academic writing to produce a unique learning environment. First, we will outline how the online forums in our HSC and Applied Linguistics data were structured, and then we identify key features that are of pedagogical significance.

Task ^ Argument * Discussion * Challenge * (Explanation) * (Report) * (Recount) * Procedure * Solidarity stage * (Summary)
Key: ( ) = optional ^ = followed by * = recursion

Figure 6.1 Online discussion macrogenre: A synoptic perspective.

6.3.1 The Online Discussion Macrogenre

In conducting a genre analysis of the online forums in the two disciplines of HSC and Applied Linguistics, it became clear that online discussions do not equate with any one elemental genre such as an exposition or discussion (Chapter 3, Section 3.3.1). This is the case even where the stated pedagogical purpose is to debate an issue and where the task is designed to prompt argumentation. Rather, while argument, or arguing, genres are a core component, other elemental genres such as explanations, recounts, and descriptions run in parallel. These genres interrupt and cut across the stages that make up arguing genres. They may be more or less topically relevant but are not directly integrated into the core arguing genres (hence, we refer to them as nonarguing genres). Also occurring across all forums are procedural genres and those with a community-forming purpose. These also run in parallel and interrupt the sequential unfolding of the core argument genres. Since these are not academically focused, we refer to them as nonacademic genres.

We decided that the combination of, and relationship between, arguing and nonarguing genres is best represented by the notion of an *online discussion* macrogenre. This macrogenre structure is represented schematically (and at the highest level of abstraction) in Figure 6.1. Figure 6.1 demonstrates the relative absence of any fixed sequencing principles: most of the genres may occur in any order and most occur recursively. The figure also shows how some genres are optional, whereas others are obligatory. Also included is what we are referring to as a *task* genre (discussed below), *summary* genre (discussed in 3.4), and *Solidarity* stages, which are designed to build community.

What Figure 6.1 does not show is the complexity of the internal unfolding of each of the elemental genres comprising the macrogenre whereby, as we have already mentioned, the stages within an exposition genre may be interrupted by unrelated elemental genres or Solidarity stages. This complexity is driven by:

i) the asynchronous nature of online forums and
ii) the multi-party, dialogic nature of online forums, whereby written genres are often co-constructed and shaped through interactive sequences (as they

Participants	Argument Genres – Central to task	Argument genres less central to task	Non-argument genres not central to task	Non-academic genres/ stages (Solidarity and procedure)
Teacher	Task			
Laura	**Exposition 1 Thesis:** modern thought rejecting paternalism of orthodox medicine is the main reason			
Karalena	**Arg For 1 (relating to Exposition 1)** **Claim + Explanation** embedded as evidence (relating to Mrs. Banister case study)			
Laura	**Arg For 2 (relating to Explosition 1)** **Claim + Explanation** embedded as evidence (relating to Mrs. Banister case study)			
Charlotte	**Agree (Exposition 1)** **Exposition 2 – Thesis:** consumerism is the main factor			
				Solidarity
Charlotte	**Exposition 3 - Thesis:** media is the main factor			
Abbie	**Arg For 3 (relating to Exposition 1)** **Claim + Explanation** embedded as evidence			
Karelena		**Exposition 4 Thesis:** wider choice means people are conned		
Karelena		**Exposition 5 Thesis:** some CAM treatments are unfounded		
Karalena			**Exemplum** (own use of CAM)	

Figure 6.2 A genre perspective on the unfolding of an online discussion forum in a CAM course.

might be in speech). For example, an argument may be confirmed or reinforced through an *Agree* stage or it may be questioned or criticized through a *Refute* stage.

To illustrate how an online discussion macrogenre is typically instantiated in online forums, Figure 6.2 provides a representation of the first section of a discussion in the CAM course. The initial genre in this macrogenre is a task genre that consists of an (optional) background, argument prompt, and (optional) preview stage, as outlined below:

Task genre: (Background)—here the teacher provided a summary of relevant course concepts with references to course materials (e.g., *Chapter 1 suggests why we have more choice when it comes to health*).

Argument Prompt—this comprised the issue for discussion: *outline one reason or factor which you think has led to an increase in the choices available when it comes to making decisions about our health.*

(Preview)—this directed students to the nature of the evidence they should draw on, i.e., the course concepts, the course case study of Mrs. Bannister, who chooses to visit a Reiki practitioner rather than her own doctor, and their own lived experience of healthcare choice.

In the left-hand column of Figure 6.2 are the names of the students and in the remaining columns (reading downward) are their chronologically ordered contributions to the construction of the macrogenre (summarized for the purposes of the figure).[3] As the labels in the top column indicate, some genres were more central to the discussion task in terms of closeness to the issue/topic required by the argument prompt, others less so. By including the names of students, the nature of individual students' contributions is revealed as well as the nature of nature of an online discussion macrogenre.

In combination, Figures 6.1 and 6.2 bring to the fore several features of online forums that serve as evidence of what we would argue is their unique potential as a teaching and learning site for developing students' academic meaning making. In the following sections, we discuss these features in turn.

6.3.2 Fluidity in Online Discussion Macrogenres

The absence of any fixed sequencing of the majority of genres that comprise the online discussion macrogenre provides evidence of a social process that is relatively unplanned and, in its spontaneity and fluidity, structured in ways similar to conversation. This feature thus provides students with opportunities to engage in the kind of academic exchange more traditionally confined to the seminar room though the asynchronous aspect makes the exchange distinct. That is, as shown in both Figures 6.1 and 6.2, students may respond to an argument prompt by constructing an exposition or discussion genre, but equally they may contribute a relatively unrelated recount or a Solidarity stage. They could also unpredictably change tack by constructing an exposition that is not directly linked to the argument prompt stage within the task genre. And they could disrupt and cut across an unfolding exposition genre by interpolating a disconnected genre or genre stage.

In general, the pattern for how texts unfold in online forums is a movement away from the starting issue and a dispersal of ideas. This potential for an expansion of focal points and a tolerance for multiple lines of discussion and argument contrasts with the contraction and narrowing of scope that typically occur in individually authored written academic genres.

It could be argued that such freedom of movement whereby, in rhizomatic fashion, ideas spark new avenues to explore and so become increasingly distant and disconnected from the original argument prompt may be a rich stimulus for learning. By rhizomatic, we refer to Deleuze and Guattari's (1980) use of the rhizome metaphor to describe unpredictable movement in thinking; that is, thinking that goes in various directions, forming surprising connections and that is in contrast to any unified, static plan or organized discussion. It certainly brings written dialogue closer in form and function to face-to-face discussion and to classroom talk where teachers can capitalize on unexpected but meaningful turns in the line of argument. As Twiner's (2012) research has revealed, "deviations from a planned path can offer valuable responsive, dialogic, and cumulative teaching-and-learning opportunities" (p. 185). This feature was positively recognized by some of the teachers interviewed. Bethany, for example, commented:

> it provides an opportunity for me to go on and say, yes that is very interesting I am glad you brought that point up, it was very valid to have it in a tutorial . . . Or for one of their own peer groups to say you know – oh we are taking this off on a tangent, this is interesting let's explore it since we can't explore it in the essay because we haven't been asked to.
>
> – Bethany, HSC teacher

It could also be argued, however, that changes in topic direction may simply represent an unfocused meandering with students misunderstanding the purpose of the discussion or subverting and digressing from the original task prompt to align with their own interests rather than the learning outcomes of the activity and course, a point made by Robert, quoted earlier. Digression and dispersal may also prevent ideas from progressing and may mean that the discussion does not culminate in a clearer understanding of, or more informed position on, an issue. As one of the CAM students, Abbie, commented (somewhat critically) at the end of the first online forum in relation to her teacher's lack of involvement:

> I thought as a group it was easy for us to wander off the subject and chat, perhaps more input from you would help us (me) to be more focused.

In sum, a balance may need to be struck between, on the one hand, fluidity and spontaneity and, on the other hand, accumulation, direction, and focus.

6.3.3 Restructuring in Online Discussion Macrogenres

On the one hand, the fluid, open-ended design of the online discussion macrogenre may make it difficult for participants to keep track of multiple unfolding lines of argument and information and to make sense of and position themselves in relation to these. On the other hand, unlike in face-to-face discussion, online forums have features that facilitate the tracking and review of the various elements. These include message headers, threading devices, and the capacity to reassemble messages (i.e., posts sent by individual students) in relation to message headers or contributors. More significantly and uniquely, the archived, frozen nature of online discussions makes them amenable to review and to restructuring. The analysis of our data, for example, showed that a contribution which might start life as a story genre could be retrospectively taken up and embedded within an argument stage of an exposition or discussion genre.

Thus in Figure 6.2 we can see how an exemplum (first discussed in Chapter 3 Section 3.2.2.1) stands outside the main discussion. Here is the exemplum:

```
The only experience i have ever had regarding CAM would
be buying a bottle of aromatherapy massage oil to try
and help relax my youngest child to encourage her to
sleep all night IN HER OWN BED! (advice from morning
show) however after nightly massages for 2 weeks she was
still waking up, eventually i resulted back the old way,
good old bribery no sleep no mcdonalds
```

Albeit anecdotal personal evidence and therefore relatively academically weak, this exemplum could have been linked into the arguments made as part of both Exposition 2 and 3 in Figure 6.2. Although in this particular case this potential was not taken up, we found that, across the data, nonarguing genres were sometimes retrospectively recontextualized and woven into the line of argument.

Our analysis also showed that arguments sometimes grew out of explanations or recounts following an inductive line of reasoning. In other words claims were derived from specific examples. For example:

Recount (evidence of CAM practitioners having a positive effect and the failure of conventional drugs)	Hi Glad to see Ive stirred things a bit. Yes, actually a number of CAMS help arthritis. Thats one I do know about because I used to be severly affected myself. Had very bad reactions to NSAIs so stopped taking them. Now have no problems at all, and have had none for over 2oyears, thanks mainly to homeopathy. I have also seen accupuncture help sciatica beautifully fast and well and have seen nutriton and herbal remedies make a big diffeerence. Homeopaths treat chronic pain including arthritis and migrains every day, and often have very good results. Not always of course. One of the big pharmaceutical companies recently published a report in which they said conventionally prescribed drugs fail in 50% of cases.
Claim (CAM practioners can have better results with lower risks than orthodox medicine)	I think that at least some CAM practiotners do better than that, with less risk.

The movement above—from evidence to claim—contrasts with the more typical pattern in written academic genres where the movement tends to be from high-level abstract generalizations to more detailed elaborating evidence following deductive lines of reasoning (as illustrated in Chapters 4 and 5). This pattern might in part be explained by the applied nature of the two courses in

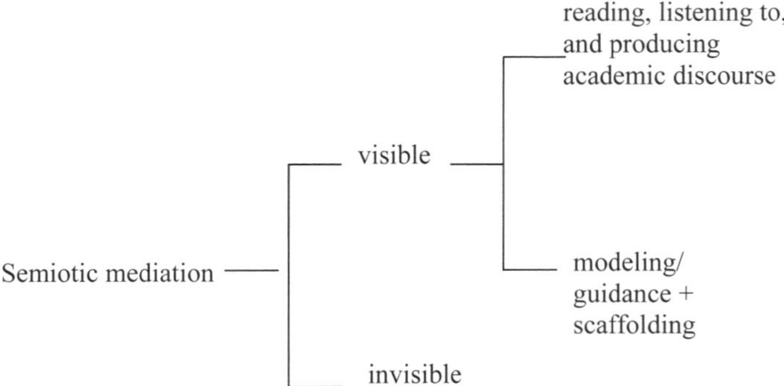

Figure 6.3 Visible semiotic mediation in online forums.

combination with the fluid open structure of the online discussion macrogenre. However, it would seem to us that the drive to tell personalized stories, out of which more general positions can be drawn, is also likely to be explained by the need to assert individual identity in the depersonalized environment of online forums. Most significantly, the presence of detailed evidence provides an important opportunity for visible semiotic mediation (Figure 6.3, first introduced in Chapter 2) in that either the teacher or a student can model or scaffold the movement from specific data to high-level generalized claims. Given that such a movement is a key feature of all knowledge building, this is evidence of the structuring potential of online forums to support students' academic learning.

6.3.4 The Summarizing Genre in Online Discussion Macrogenres

As commented on above, partly because of the unplanned, dynamic construction of the online discussion macrogenre, contributions to a discussion tend to accumulate in a relatively unplanned manner and hence may be more or less relevant and more or less integrated into an argument or discussion genre. This may make it difficult for students and teachers to recognize how the diverse contributions ("the jigsaw pieces") fit together as a whole. Some argument stages, for example, may be distant in time and space to the thesis stage with other genres rupturing and breaking up any continuous smooth unfolding. Figure 6.2, for instance, shows how two thesis statements in relation to Expositions 2 and 3 cut between the thesis for Exposition 1 and Abbie's argument (Argument 3) supporting Exposition 1.

The frozen archived nature of online forums does, however, make it possible to view the flux and flow synoptically and for a teacher (or indeed student) to impose a hierarchical structure retrospectively, if not prospectively. In doing this, they model for other participants how the more general significance and meaning of the discussion can be extracted and made prominent. That is, linguistic resources such as nominalization and densely packed nominal groups (see Chapter 3, Section 3.4.1.2) can be used to synthesize ideas in the form of a summary genre. Summary genres work at a high level of abstraction to give shape to the preceding discussion. They identify and consolidate the overall positioning that has emerged across the genres that make up the online discussion macro genre. Here are two examples of contributions by a student and teacher, in which their ideational grammar is largely constituted by nominal groups and nominalizations (as underlined). These resources serve to bundle together in condensed form the many individual points made in the preceding discussion and realized in more free-flowing clausal form (i.e., in the first example, the different reasons for difficulties in second language learning, and in the second example, the reasons for changes in health care choices).

> As <u>so many factors</u> are inter-related, it's difficult to isolate <u>the effects of a single factor</u>. Also, <u>individual variations</u> are often more significant than <u>specific factors.</u>
>
> *(Applied Linguistics data—student contribution)*

> To summarize what I see as the ''story so far'' drawn from preceding emails I suggest the following :
>
> 1. <u>Increased information available to ''all''</u>
>
> (a) media -- TV, radio etc.
> (b) internet
>
> 2. <u>Unpleasant ''side-effects'' of orthodox medicine</u>
> 3. <u>Dissatisfaction with the NHS -- economic / political strands</u>
>
> MRSA
> long waiting lists
> <u>impersonal approach (of orthodox medicine)</u>
>
> 4. <u>more autonomy / independent thought</u>
> 5. <u>orthodox medicine's inability to solve certain conditions.</u>

```
Choice may be restricted by:

1. Economics.

private medicine
government budget/priorities for NHS

2. Poor CAM practitioners exist too (Ch4
   professionalization/ethics).
3. Opposition of orthodox sector (also historical
   /political, see Ch3).

Feel free to build on or chall these thoughts...
```

(CAM data – teacher contribution)

In our data we found that summary genres were extremely rare (on average, only 2 instances in each of the 16 CAM forums) and therefore it would seem that their pedagogical potential is rarely harnessed. It would thus seem advisable to encourage teachers and students to occasionally step back and review the discussion and to build in a textual hierarchy of hyperNews and macroNews (see Chapter 3, Section 3.4.3.3) in which multiple discussion threads are disentangled and the main points summarized. The practice in synthesizing, integrating, and remapping represents, we argue, an important pedagogic potential that should be more systematically exploited than was the case in the data we examined.

6.3.5 Dialogic Argumentation in Online Discussion Macrogenres

> It is useful to share views and others perspectives. Reading others comments often makes me see things from a differing viewpoint.
>
> *– Verity, CAM student*

> the discussions can point you in a direction you may not have considered or help you to focus when you have lost your way.
>
> *– Polly, CAM student*

A key aspect of the pedagogical potential of the online discussion macrogenre is the occurrence of multiple points of view through the recursive presence of exposition, discussion, or challenge genres. As Polly and Verity (quoted above) recognize, this provides an opportunity for students to confront and navigate differing viewpoints and, in the process, consolidate their own (possibly shifting) position. In other words, following Vygotsky (1978), we would argue

Table 6.1 Genre contributions to online discussion by lower- and higher-scoring students

Average no. of stages contributed	Counter-claim	Challenge	Concession	Agree	Argument prompt	Claim	Evidence
Higher-scoring students	0.3	0.3	0.6	2.4	0.3	3.5	4.9
Lower-scoring students	0	0	0	0	0	0.5	1

that, as a social process, public dialogic argumentation (as in the case of the online discussion) is likely to create (or at least facilitate) in learners an internal dialogue between different perspectives and hence support critical reasoning and reflection (cf. Hasan's 1996 call for reflection literacy discussed in Chapter 2). In turn, we would argue that this internalization of alternative voices and perspectives is likely to support students in their own individually authored discussion or argument genre. Certainly this was the view of Bethany, one of the CAM teachers:

> you need to learn to explore giving reasons and backing those reasons up, acquiring flexibility, being able to change your point of view if evidence is produced that points somewhere else. Being able to hold to your point of view in face of disagreement if you feel that you have the evidence to justify this. There is a very useful tool that can be learnt in the to and fro of discussion which will be harder to do in the more one way work as an assignment.

If we look at the online and assignment data, we see evidence of the relationship between dialogic argumentation in the online forum and in students' individually authored assignments. That is, we found that, as a general pattern, those students who produced assignments with marks of 57% or below (lower-scoring students) engaged minimally with the argumentation taking place in the online discussion. They put forward relatively few claims and did not directly negotiate with other participants' claims by contributing counterclaim, challenge, concession, argument prompt, agree, or evidence genre stages. Table 6.1 shows how, in comparison, higher-scoring students (who produced assignments with marks of above 70%) contributed on average all these stages, and in the case of the claim and supporting evidence, a far greater number.

We cannot, of course, necessarily claim any causal relationship between students' meaning making in online forums and in their written assignments. It is likely that higher scoring students already have a greater control of argumentation in both environments, rather than the online discussion directly contributing to their greater success in their written assignments. However, it could be argued that the online forum acts, on the one hand, as a consolidating space to engage with conceptual formations and, on the other hand, as a rehearsal space for students to develop their position on these issues in preparation for their written texts. Our analysis of higher-scoring students' assignments does, for example, show that they have greater understanding of the conceptual nature and organization of an argument genre as well as the arguable nature of any claim put forward (and therefore the need for evidence). Our analysis of lower-scoring students, in contrast, shows that typically their argument structure is undeveloped, claims are not located within the conceptual formation of the course material, and evidence is almost entirely of the personal recount type. Furthermore, explanation and recount genres are often free floating and remain disconnected from any line of argument. To illustrate these points we will compare extracts from two HSC students' assignments.

The first extract is taken from Charlotte's assignment (which scored 88%) and attracted the following feedback comments (among others) from her teacher, Lucinda:

> ... it is well structured, flows and has a good introduction and conclusion. You have obviously got to grips with the material.

The extract shows how Charlotte replays a key abstract concept taken from the course material (*power disequilibrium*) and then supports this through an explanation genre that consists of case study material (i.e., professional knowledge). In this way, Charlotte is mediating lived experience and framing it with concepts from the course, thus demonstrating the valued rhythm of relating professional/personal experience to a conceptual formation from the field of study (and moving up the ladder of abstraction from more contextualized to more decontextualized knowledge). (We previously considered this in relation to Andrea and Zuna's assignments in Chapter 5).

Extract 1	
Claim	There is always a power disequilibrium between patient and therapist
Evidence/ support phase (embedded explanation)	As her therapist points out, Mrs Bannister may have problems dealing authoritatively with her life. She is worried about consulting the doctor as she feels a 'bother' which suggests that she has a very unequal relationship with the GP.

The structuring of Charlotte's claims in her assignment was preceded by extensive practice in the online forum where she contributed the highest number of claims (seven) as well as eight evidence stages, one concession, three agreements, and one counterclaim.

Extract 2 is taken from an assignment by Zoe, which was given 55%. The following comments (among others) were made by her teacher, Bethany:

> You have failed to make any references to course material or other reading. You have made a number of assertions which are not evidenced.

The extract exemplifies a key pattern in Zoe's assignment: statements of fact (i.e., statements given in the case study) are made with no reference to a conceptual frame and tend to be elaborated in the form of personal/professional judgments, rather than evidence from the course materials. There is no movement from higher-order claims to the detail of lived experience. Much of the material stays at the level of contextualized lived experience and there is an absence of engagement with alternative perspectives.

Extract 2	
Explanation	Mrs. Bannister felt that she did not understand many of the things explained and knew nothing of any side-effects, [Personal Judgment] this to me suggest the therapist was assuming the lot of Mrs. Bannister's knowledge and not taking the time needed to make sure the user felt safe and secure within the treatment. (APPRAISAL: negative JUDGMENT)

In many ways Zoe's assignment structuring is prefigured by her contribution to the online discussion where her only input—aside from Solidarity stages and procedure genres—consists of two evidence stages and two personal assertions (a type of claim which expresses a personal, affective response).

In sum, genre analysis sheds light on the disparities in how the two groups of lower- and higher-scoring students design and structure argumentation in both the online forum and written assignment (as exemplified by Charlotte and Zoe but played out across the data sets as a whole). This raises the question of how students' participation in online discussion could be more effectively supported so that the opportunities for visible semiotic mediation and its affordances as a consolidating and rehearsal space for dialogic argumentation are maximized. In Section 6.5, we will make some suggestions in relation to this point.

6.3.6 Solidarity Stages as Part of the Structure of Online Discussion

As the structure of the online discussion macrogenre shows, Solidarity stages occur recursively throughout online forums. These stages function to build solidarity and community by, for example, encouraging and motivating peers, teasing and using humor, and showing deference, as illustrated by these extracts.

> `I do feel that Reiki for your car is abit mad, having said that might give it a go due MOT tomorrow eck.`[4]
>
> *(CAM data)*
>
> `Well, due to circumstances beyond my control, I'm starting into the course quite late. Nevertheless, I'm excited and full of anticipation! You all sound like such an interesting lot of people!`
>
> *(Applied Linguistics data)*

Our analysis showed that Solidarity stages occurred frequently and at all points throughout the online forums (see Coffin et al., 2009, for similar findings in school history online forums). In one of the Applied Linguistics forums, for example, they occurred more frequently than argument genres and, as an overall pattern across both sets of data, they occupied on average approximately 50 percent of the discussion space. While in some research studies the presence of nonacademic chat has been seen as having a negative impact on the discussion topic (e.g., Williams, 2002), we would argue that, based on our genre analysis, Solidarity stages should be seen as a necessary prosodic element in the structure of online forums, encouraging and motivating students to exchange opinions and engage in academic exchange.

Because in face-to-face academic discussion Solidarity stages might be rare and even discouraged, it seems likely that it is the remote and disembodied environment of virtual learning environments with their absence of visual and gestural supports that motivates their use. In other words, less contextualized environments call for greater contextualizing behavior, building solidarity alongside epistemic knowledge. The degree to which online forums are used as an accompaniment to face-to-face contact as opposed to being the sole form of student interaction may be one reason for the degree of frequency of Solidarity stages. A further explanation may lie in the kinds of transitions students are making in any particular cohort. For example, as discussed elsewhere, the shift from school learning to more specialized university-level learning places certain pressures on students particularly where their semantic orientations do not predispose them to an abstract decontextualized world of theory. Solidarity stages may therefore serve as an important mechanism to keep in play the personal, "here and now" worlds they inhabit alongside the "anywhere and anytime" worlds of decontextualized knowledge. Once more, the structuring principles of online discussions in which there is an intertwining of the social with the academic provides evidence that they may be an important environment for softening the identity conflicts and learning transitions experienced by students and for motivating them to engage in the kinds of discourse experiences that will develop their academic language and hence subject learning.

6.3.7 Summary

In Section 6.3 we have discussed a number of features concerning the structuring of online discussion macrogenres that make them both similar and different to academic written genres and face-to-face discussion genres (see Tanguay, 2012, for research on spoken academic discussion genres). On the one hand, their design is nonlinear and nonhierarchical, their production is collaborative, and their unfolding is relatively dynamic, fluid, and unpredictable. This makes them akin to casual, spontaneous spoken conversation. On the other hand, the interaction is in written form and there are opportunities for reviewing and abstracting out key points and, in doing so, representing the discussion synoptically in the form of summary genres. While such potential may not always be taken up, this type of structuring aligns online text with formal academic writing. In combination, therefore, it could be argued that forums combine in complementary fashion the text structuring and organizing principles that underpin both academic writing and speaking. Participating in online forums can thus simultaneously support and build students' skills in online interaction, face-to-face academic debate and academic writing. It is for this reason that unevenness in patterns of participation (as exemplified by Zoe and Charlotte) is of concern, a point that we will return to in Section 6.5.

6.4 In What Ways Can Online Forums Support Teaching and Learning? A Register Perspective

In this section we will continue to look at aspects of online forums that serve as evidence of their unique potential as a teaching and learning site for supporting students' learning of, and through, academic discourse. In this section, we will draw on the concept of register as a lens for looking more closely at the detail of how participants engage in semiotic mediation.

As discussed in Chapter 3, register refers to the three contextual features of field (the social activity/topic), tenor (social roles and relationships), and mode (the nature of the text as a communicative event). These three contextual features (or register variables) are systematically related to students' use of lexicogrammar to make ideational, interpersonal, and textual meaning. While Chapters 4 and 5 focused primarily on ideational and textual meaning, in this section we will discuss, in turn, each of the variables and related metafunctions using representative data from the CAM and Applied Linguistics research projects. Part of our purpose here is to understand the degree of register variation in online forums as a means of better understanding the different ways that students and teachers use language to make textual, ideational, and interpersonal meaning in such an environment. We start the discussion with mode, as it is the contextual feature that accounts for much of the distinctive language use in online forums, namely the combining of language resources associated, on the one hand, with spontaneous dialogue and, on the other hand, with reflective academic writing. Mode thus shapes the ways in which ideational and interpersonal meanings are made.

6.4.1 The Mode of Online Forums: Developing Textual Meaning

> you are trying to focus on the issues, but actually in a conversation kind of way – hard
>
> – *Naomi, CAM teacher*

> it has its down sides . . . because you know it could be a few days before anybody looks at your messages and you look at other people's messages, so you do lose the instant sort of answer and discussion really
>
> – *Eve, CAM student*

Mode, as set out in Chapter 3 (Section 3.4.3) is the register variable concerned with the nature of the text as a communicative event including how a text is produced and transmitted and how the information flows across it. In this section we will focus on two key aspects of mode—*interactivity* and *spontaneity*—and look at their relationship with the language resources of turn taking, nominalization, and Theme. As suggested in the teacher and student quotes above, these have particular significance for semiotic mediation.

6.4.1.1 Interactivity

The interactivity of online forums makes the language speech like: contributions involve turn taking with participants anticipating and responding to alternative views and voices (just as in face-to-face conversation). Responses may serve to endorse (through agreement) prior contributions. Equally, participants may push for further interaction by asking for clarification, probing for additional information and perspectives or challenging what has been said.

In our data there was evidence of interaction through the use of prompts, challenges, and agreement, and through the collaborative construction of arguing genres. An unexpected finding, however, was that, across all CAM forums, just over half of the claims that were made were not responded to. It is likely that where this happened there was a detrimental effect on students' motivation and confidence. Certainly comments made by students such as Dagmar (quoted at the start of this chapter) would suggest this.

Dagmar's comment about the lack of response to her contribution underlines a feature of asynchronous online interactivity that is very different from face-to-face interactivity. In a face-to-face situation it would be unusual if students were to offer ideas and perspectives and these were simply ignored and/or were followed by completely unrelated claims. In the online environment, however, the absence of a response or the lack of cohesion across messages is relatively commonplace. There seem to be two main reasons for this: (a) the asynchronous feature of forums and (b) students often responding directly to the task rather than previous responses to it.

In this sense the interactive nature of online written dialogue may appear to be counterproductive—at least in its take-up by students. Our linguistic analysis, nevertheless, showed that there is considerable potential for the facilitative functionality of online forums. However, this depends on the way teachers and students utilize the opportunity provided. For example, unlike in face-to-face interaction, the frozen, archived nature of debate makes it possible for students to re-read and reflect on different argumentative positions (particularly when directed to in the form of structured tasks) and may facilitate the incorporation of different positions into a student's own argumentative line. In the Applied Linguistics data, for example, where one teacher required students to "*read your fellow students' messages and challenge or endorse at least one of the factors they put forward*" the students from this group more frequently used language resources that endorse (by approximately three times) both in the online forum interaction and in their subsequent assignment writing (Coffin & Hewings, 2005).

Another pedagogical advantage lies in the possibility for teachers to intervene in the dialogic exchange and model for students higher-order synthesizing summaries or to pull out key positions and perspectives on an issue, particularly where these relate to students' subsequent written assignments. This kind of synoptic reworking of the to and fro of dialogic interaction into a consolidated overview can provide an important step along the path from reading to written dialogue to individual writing. It can be seen as a form of modeling text redesign (as discussed in Chapter 5). As one of the Applied Linguistics students so astutely recognized in a message posted to the forum:

> `The assignment, naturally, being an academic exercise, will be written in a somewhat different tone to our messages! In particular it will need to be effectively organized and written, hopefully, in such a way that a) the reader will not drop off to sleep and b) with the same feeling of enthusiasm and of having something decisive to discuss and compare and analyze as we did in the forum and c) importantly to successfully fit together the pieces of the puzzle we have at our disposal.`
>
> *– Michelle, Applied Linguistics student*

From a pedagogical perspective it may also be productive to require students to respond to a prior message (where they exist) rather than the task itself.

6.4.1.2 Spontaneity

> I would write then re read to make sure the meaning was clear which one doesn't do when speaking
>
> *(Applied Linguistics student)*

Text in online forums is transmitted in a way that enables both instantaneous responses and delayed ones (i.e., from minutes to hours or even several days). Contributions are produced in written form. This makes it possible to plan and edit messages or respond rapidly to messages and compose them on the fly (though these are never as instant as in a face-to-face conversation or instant messaging). Spontaneity is revealed in patterns of language use analogous to the errors of false starts, repetition, and mid-utterance changes of face-to-face chat. The following message, for instance, has typos (*mind mind*) and there is the absence of written conventions (i.e., a lack of capitalization for *i* at the start of the second sentence). There is also the use of textese (where *u* stands for you, *no* for know, etc.; in this case, *2* stands for to) and minor or abbreviated clauses (*thank goodness*, *and re CAM*).

> thank goodness !!! i also share your views on the issues of black mailing children 2 sleep in own bed and re CAM. It has cross mind mind a few times from reading peoples message as 2 whether any one else has any exp of CAM other than as a patient.

On the other hand, producing on-the-spot language is usually associated with a lower density of information packaging than in planned written text, while the example above has two long nominal groups:

> i also share **your views** on the issues of black mailing children 2 sleep in own bed and re CAM
> **any exp** of CAM other than as a patient.

Certainly, based on the data overall, there seems to be considerable evidence of students taking time to compose their contributions. For example, a large number of contributions to the argumentation shows high densities of information packaging. The following extract, where we have underlined the nominal groups, is typical in this regard:

> From:
> Abbie
> Subject: Mrs B
> A post modernity era featuring an increase in consumer culture provides Mrs B with an increase of information of alternative approaches to her health.
> Following on from the counter-culture changes in the 1960's promoting questioning of authority in health provision this led to an increase in and acceptance of CAM.

```
  So Mrs B was able to form the opinion that her GP was
busy and that her current problem did not warrant
medical intervention. She cose her own health care in
light of accepted practice and the information now
freely available.
  I think I have said much the same as others, maybe
just a little differently?? Abbie.
```

Aside from the final two clauses and signoff, the message above resembles a formal, written academic assignment from the perspective of both its organization and linguistic expression. Other data we analyzed provided a different kind of evidence of the amount of crafting and editing work that may go into the composition of a message. In the following extract Karalena accidentally posted a message followed by an edited version:

First version

```
Mrs. Bannister. There may be many factors why she did
not bother her doctor and went to a reiki practitioner
instead for instance, did she feel her complaint was
serious enough at the time, or may be lacked confidence
in her doctor due to previous meetings or even found it
difficult to arrange a consultation due to a stroppy
receptionist.
```

Second version

```
There may be many factors why she did not choose to see
her doctor and visit a reiki practitioner instead. May
be she felt her condition was not serious enough at the
time, she may have lost confidence in her doctor due to
previous meetings or even found it difficult to arrange
a consultation due to a stroppy receptionist. Factors we
all may have experienced at times or know of someone who
has.
```

It is significant to note that in her second message Karalena makes more prominent (through her selection of lexis) the concept of choice: *she did not choose to see her doctor* as opposed to *she did not bother to see her doctor*. She also changes an interrogative structure (*did she feel her complaint,* etc.) to a declarative one: *maybe she felt her condition*. Finally, in the second, edited version she moves to a high-level generalizing clause and thematizes reasoning: *Factors we all may have experienced*. These changes are significant because they suggest that students such as Karalena are exploiting the slowed-down pace of forum interaction to practice the editing and shaping skills of formal academic writing. As the Applied Linguistics student commented in the quotation at the start of this section, there is greater time for reflecting on and scrutinizing the clarity of one's meanings.

In this way, the opportunities and motivation to hone a piece of writing place the composition process of online interaction much closer to that of writing than to spontaneous speech. At the same time, the dialogic context comprising a responsive audience of peers and a teacher may have provided the motivation (or pressure) to do this.

6.4.1.3 Recap

In sum, to date, our investigations of the relationship between mode and language use in online forums show that in its written form online dialogue is not quite so unselfconscious and intuitive as it would be in face-to-face interaction. Equally, in its dialogic form, writing is not always quite so self-conscious and "designed" as it would be in a formal academic writing context. In terms of interactivity, how responsive participants are to each other's contributions appears to vary widely. The challenge that faces both students and teachers therefore lies in harnessing the complementary meaning making opportunities of, on the one hand, spontaneous spoken-like interaction and, on the other hand, the more reflective nature of written interaction. How to meet such challenges is discussed in Section 6.5.

6.4.2 The Field of Online Forums: Developing Ideational Meaning

> They didn't really address the more analytical part of the tutorial . . . I don't think it provides as much of a sort of intellectual exchange as it is hoped to, whether that is my fault as the teacher for not stimulating them enough, I don't know
>
> – *Julie, CAM teacher*

> You have got to think and sometimes you actually want somebody to pull your thoughts together or help you bring your thoughts together
>
> – *Carol, CAM student*

The register variable of field refers to the *social activity* as well as the *subject matter* or *topic* of a text and how these features of the context both shape, and are shaped by, the ideational meanings people make. Chapter 3 discussed the connections between field, the ideational metafunction, and language resources. This section will focus on the use of specialized lexis and the nominal group to construe the conceptual formations of academic fields of study. It thus continues the discussion, from Chapters 4 and 5, of ideational meaning making, but focuses in particular on how this is achieved in an online environment.

As outlined earlier, within university learning one of the most common activities in online forums is academic debate, that is, the dialogic exchange of perspectives and positions on an issue, idea, or theory. In this section we take up the issue expressed in the quotations at the start of this section, considering how far online semiotic mediation can help students to articulate their thinking in ways that are intellectually coherent and valued. To explore this, we will primarily draw on data from the CAM introductory forums.

6.4.2.1 Moving Between Decontextualized and Contextualized Knowledge

The topic of the first CAM forum, as set out in Section 6.3.1, was healthcare choice with the task itself providing a further narrowing of the topic to "the factors leading to choice." This was a topic covered in the first few chapters of the students' course monograph (text book) and therefore the teachers could assume that students would contribute a range of views on what the factors were and that these would be appropriately conceptually framed as well as supported by evidence (using, for example, the case study on Mrs. Bannister or their own professional and personal experience). What the data revealed, however, was considerable variation in students' responses and, in particular, how these were, or were not, conceptually framed. Compare, for example, the following two messages, posted in quick succession by Laura and Karalena, noting in particular their use of field specific terms and concepts (underlined).

From: Laura

Subject: choice

HERE WE GO THEN...

I feel that the rise in consumerism, depersonalization and paternalism within orthodox (biomedical model) medicine has resulted in the disempowerment of patients. In the current climate this is no longer acceptable. people have come to distrust and in my opinion, feel disattisfaction with what was once the dominant model of health. (??? chapter 3 political and historical perspectives 3.4 resurgence of CAM).

Laura

From: Karelena

Subject: Mrs Bannister

Mrs. Bannister. There may be many factors why she did not bother her doctor and went to a reiki practitioner instead for instance, did she feel her complaint was serious enough at the time, or may be lacked confidence in her doctor due to previous meetings or even found it difficult to arrange a consultation due to a stroppy receptionist.

From the perspective of field, Laura's message uses numerous field-specific, abstract concepts (*biomedical model, disempowerment of patients,* etc.) to present a response to the question, whereas Karalena's message hones in on the more concrete case study of Mrs. Bannister, where the factors are restricted to an individual case and cannot be generalized beyond this. It is significant to note that, as discussed in Section 6.4.1.2, Karalena's edited version did move toward generalization. Nevertheless, it did not reach the level of abstraction of Laura's contribution.

In many ways Laura and Karolina's responses demonstrate the two complementary means of construing HSC knowledge discussed in Chapter 5: on the one hand, the use of general and abstract concepts and, on the other hand, the use of concrete and specific examples of lived experience (usually in the form of case studies). What is significant here is that each of the two students has chosen to orient to one or other of these strands of knowledge building. That is, either the decontextualized (Laura) or the contextualized (Karalena). Given that, for both students, this is a continuing pattern throughout the forum discussion it would seem that these contrasting linguistic construals of the field reveal something important about their overall semantic orientations, both their orientations to HSC and to academia more broadly. Indeed, if we take their assignment marks for the year alongside assessment feedback as an indication of their overall academic orientations and their take up of the academic values of HSC, then Laura is more closely aligned and Karalena less so. That is, Karalena received an average mark of 57 across the year and her teacher's comments on her assignments suggested that her analytical skills required further development (this was confirmed by SFL analysis of her assignments):

> You obviously feel strongly about the ethical issues around CAM – it is great to have your own opinion, but in an assignment like this it is important to back up your statements with published evidence and also put forward both sides of the argument before drawing your conclusions. (*Comment on Karalena's first assignment*)

> in your essay, rather than simply listing the models, use them to analyze the information you got from Mrs. X. This shows that you have read them and understood them to such an extent that you can apply them yourself. (*Comment on Karalena's third assignment*)

Laura, on the other hand, received an average of 68 marks and the feedback on her assignments suggested that she was orienting to academic knowledge making (through her conceptual framing) in ways that were recognized and rewarded by her teacher.

Below are two further examples, taken from a different forum but on the same topic of choice (though with a focus, at this point in the discussion, on the limiting effect of money) and showing similar patterns to those in the examples above but also a slight and significant difference. In the first message, Chloe uses both technical terms (*post modernity, later modernity*) and abstract nominal groups (e.g., *spirituality, a move towards science and technology*) to represent the high-level generalized position that fewer people attend formal religious services and may be seeking alternatives. She then argues that choice has always been limited by money and at this point moves to a specific example whereby there is a gear shift in the language used and a specific human Participant becomes thematized (*she*). Thus within the same response we see the movement of abstract to specific. The "specific," however, is Louise, who is part of a case study in the course textbook and as such is part of the academic domain set up in the course.

Chloe's text matches the desired movement in HSC from general abstract concepts (which we have indicated with a solid underline) to specific case study material (the example of Louise). It would seem, then, that the way Chloe is using language to construe knowledge in this example is very close to the kind of language and meanings valued in HSC study. At the same time, however, it should also be noted that these are part of an interactive dialogue, hence the use of *you* and *I* (indicated with a dotted underline). The movement between more decontextualized and more contextualized meanings contrasts with the meanings that another student, Amy, makes (in a follow-up message to Chloe; see below) and how these reorient the discussion.

Chloe

`In the post Modernity or late modernity period (as named by giddens) there has been a move towards science and technology but also a reduction in formal religious attendance. As you say, perhaps people are missing this need for spirituality but instead of heading back to formalized religious are looking for alternatives that are not being dictated to them. I also believe, however, that choice is only really available if you have money to spend and I think this has always been the case even in the pre modernity period. If you take the example of Louise in the course book, she has lots of choice in theory but little money and this actually equates to no choice.`

In Amy's response to Chloe there is a further shift from a professional case study to a personal experience and a corresponding change to the use of language that has no technicality and little abstraction. The *Participants* (underlined) tend to be concrete and/or human and overall the language is more informal and conversation-like, for example, the use of JUDGMENT, AFFECT, and vocatives (*Good point Chloe, choice is great, moaned*), contraction (*it's out there*), lack of capitals (*it*), and the use of an emoticon (*:o*)).

Amy

`Good point Chloe, more money usually equals more choice. I also believe that choice is only available if you know it's out there. When I was in a lot of pain with my back I simply took painkillers and awaited my physio appointment. it never even occurred to me to I had a choice and could try a CAM therapy because I didn't know what was out there. I talked/moaned to various friends and colleagues and not one of them mentioned CAM therapies either. Choice is great but only if you realize you have it.`

`Amy :o)`

Arising out of the examples above comes a key pedagogic question: how can students be guided (in an online forum) to reclassify and conceptually reframe their personal and professional lived experience?

One possible answer lies in a pedagogic technique that the analysis of the Applied Linguistics data brought to our attention. It is a form of semiotic mediation that shifts students from a more personally contextualized world to a more generalized and decontextualized one.

The strategy was for the teacher to paste in a sentence or two from a previous student posting containing, for example, a personal recount or observation genre (see Chapter 3, Section 3.2.2.1). Solidarity with the quoted student was then achieved by the teacher offering a comparable personal experience. This constituted a preface for one or more questions that extended the topic. By participating in the exchange of personal recounts, the teacher was able to build solidarity with the students and encourage camaraderie. At the same time, he was able to model the importance of using personal or professional experiences as a springboard to extend a topic to a greater level of generality and abstraction as well as bring in key concepts. The extract shows the movement from observation to explanation/argumentation and the introduction of the key concept *motivation*. Because the causes and effects of dialect use are debatable (hence: *do you think?*) the teacher's question is also likely to stimulate dialogic argumentation.

Student observation genre pasted in (specific Circumstances of place and specific humans as underlined)	`Living here in the North East of England has been in some situations like learning a whole new language and culture for me. The accent used by some individuals has been very difficult for me to understand not to mention the abundant use of idioms.`
Implicit endorsement by teacher of student contribution (through shared APPRAISAL: JUDGMENT as underlined) This serves as preface for prompt.	`I can also attest to the difficulties of the ''Wayay, hinny, I'm gang nyaem'' strong dialect utterances sometimes heard in the North East.`

Continued

Teacher extends the topic through prompt (movement from observation to explanation/argumentation) and from specific to generalized humans (as underlined)	`But what do you think is the motivation of the user, and what effect does it have on the non-dialect-using listener?`

The type of semiotic mediation illustrated above exploits the restructuring potential of online discussions we have commented on in Section 6.3.3. That is, the teacher identifies an opportunity to intervene in the dialogue in order to model for students the way in which low-level evidence (specific, anecdotal examples) can be lifted up to construe high-level propositions (inductive reasoning). Though the extract above was not a unique example of such mediation, it was not commonplace in our data. It therefore seems to us that if the affordances of online forums are going to serve as environments in which students learn to progress their decontextualized language use, then teachers may need to play a more active and interventionist role as semiotic mediators. This, of course, benefits from an awareness of the role of language in the process (metasemiotic mediation).

6.4.2.2 Interactive Development of Conceptual Formations

Another pedagogically significant feature of field construction that our linguistic analysis revealed was the way in which students could interactively, over time, build up field-specific conceptual formations. Take, as an example, the following interaction between Abbie and Charlotte, where they clarify the concept of medical pluralism:

```
From: Abbie

While I'm online, could I ask the other students how
they understand medical pluralism?

On page 23, 3rd line down, it says that its a 'term used
to describe the wide range of complementary forms of
health care ...'

Am I wrong therefore to describe it as a wide range of
all forms of health care, including orthodox?

From: Charlotte
```

That is how I have been thinking of it -- all forms of health care, I shall have to go back and look again.

From: Charlotte (Two days later)

On page 65, about half way down it talks about the pluralistic health field, in which doctors worked alongside CAM practitioners ...so showing a meaning for pluralism as all types of medicine.

In the same sentence it talks about how this pluralism evaporated with the development of orthodoxy in the first half of the 19th century.

By which I assume it to mean more scientific observation, apothecaries and surgeons and physicians joining together etc.

Best wishes

Charlotte

From: Abbie

Dear Charlotte

Thankyou very much for your help which has enabled me to move on with my assignment!!!! Sometimes its the trivial things that get in the way of this process so i'm very grateful. Hope I can reciprocrate during the rest of the course.

In the extract above Abbie and Charlotte interactively build and check their conceptual formations relating to medical pluralism. Through dialogue they mediate the contradictory lexical meanings and relations in the course material to reach the following classification (Figure 6.4):

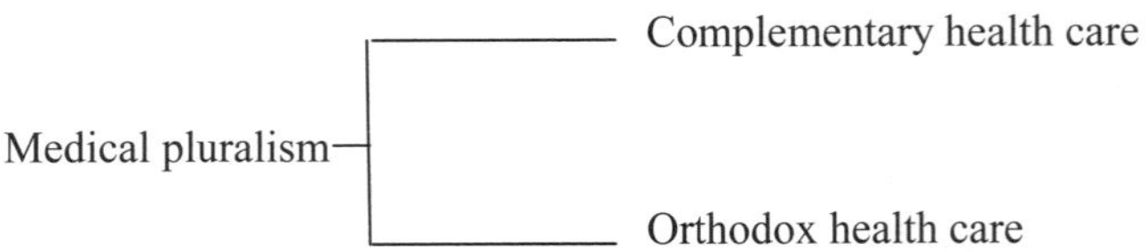

Figure 6.4 Classification of medical pluralism.

6.4.2.3 Recap

To summarize, a focus on field and ideational meaning making has exemplified some key features of the learning potential of online forums. The extracts in 6.4.2.2 show how forums provide opportunities for students to collaboratively clarify and consolidate key academic meanings—and, perhaps significantly, over time and at point of need (i.e., in relation to a piece of writing). We have also shown in 6.4.2.1 how forums provide opportunities for practicing the rhythm of moving from more abstract to more concrete renderings of HSC knowledge, a rhythm that is at the core of many applied disciplines. The extent to which such opportunities are taken up, however, is at least in part related to the teacher's skill in guiding and scaffolding students' meaning making. In this regard, the archival aspect of online forums seems to be a key affordance of the technology in that where students are at risk of remaining stranded in the world of the personal and concrete teachers can retrieve, replay and endorse their contributions and, significantly, expand outwards to the world of the general and the abstract.

6.4.3 The Tenor of Online Forums: Developing Interpersonal Meaning

> It's easier saying something to people's faces when you can actually see their faces and so you can gauge whether people will be offended or—it is much more difficult when it's a computer I found
>
> – *Eve, CAM student*

As previously discussed in Chapter 3 (Section 3.4.2), the register variable of tenor relates to the roles, statuses, and relationships of those involved in communication. Tenor relates to the interpersonal metafunction and a wide range of language resources including mood, pronoun use, vocatives, colloquial/formal lexis, and APPRAISAL.

In this section, we are interested in considering the kinds of social roles and relationships that are enacted in online forums and how these might support academic exchange and the collaborative construction of knowledge. To this end we will consider how the patterns of language are used to:

- enact particular *social roles* (and what this indicates about participants' identities and semantic orientation)
- construct relationships on familiar, friendly terms or in ways that suggest *social distance*
- construct equal or unequal relationships in terms of *social status* or *power*

6.4.3.1 Social Roles and Semantic Orientation

In terms of the social roles that are enacted in online forums there is considerable variation. Not surprisingly, in our data, one set of roles were the conventional and expected ones of teacher and student. By and large it was the teacher who took responsibility for initiating, sustaining, and concluding the discussions and for pushing students' thinking from more contextualized to less contextualized domains of knowledge building (which we have already seen examples of in 6.4.2.1). In other words, they were acting as semiotic initiators seeking to enable the reconfiguration of the learner's conceptual structures (see Chapter 2, Section 2.5.1). There was, however, some uncertainty on the part of some teachers as to the level of, and type of, intervention they should make, and as we have already commented on, the opportunities for extending students' contributions from the anecdotal to the general were not exploited as fully as they could have been. This perhaps can partly be explained by the fact that notions of learner autonomy (a dominant pedagogy in online environments) were influencing these teachers' thinking and linguistic behavior (though to different degrees). It may also be partly explained by the fact that most teachers (at the time of our study) were working with an unfamiliar communication medium and were thus attempting to develop effective patterns of interaction from the ground up.

Not surprisingly, both the CAM and Applied Linguistics data revealed considerable variation in the contributions made by different teachers. In broad terms, however, the linguistic analysis of the online data (in combination with an APPRAISAL analysis of teacher interview and questionnaire data) suggests that there were two contrasting semantic orientations at work, that is, two contrasting preferences for making meanings and, as a result, for using language in certain ways. These orientations showed differences in the degree of authority invoked and, we argue, shaped the pedagogic roles in play.

One orientation to the online teaching role was to focus on the interpersonal rather than ideational aspect of online meaning making. This suggests that some teachers saw their role as primarily one of fostering community through encouraging participation and maintaining symmetrical interaction. As part of this orientation, there was particular concern that the online medium drove a wedge between higher-scoring students who participated more and lower-scoring students who tended to be "read only" participants and rarely made a contribution. There was little focus on stepping up the discussion cognitively through the explicit guidance or scaffolding of students' learning. The following interview and online data from two CAM teachers, Naomi and Lucinda, exemplify this orientation. With regard to Naomi, she clearly sees her role as a facilitator. However, her evaluation of herself in this role is negative:

> the idea was that I wouldn't be seen to be the prime mover as it were, but actually there to facilitate . . . so it is essentially a prime mover in the beginning and initiating and then letting it flow and then bring it to a conclusion . . . which I am not very good at (negative JUDGMENT:CAPACITY) (*interview data*)

Despite Naomi's negative JUDGMENT, the following forum extract provides evidence of her attempt to construe a facilitative orientation. For example, her use of vocatives (*Hi Alex*) personalizes her interaction with students. She also positively appraises Alex's contribution and appreciates other students' future responses. Solidarity is built through her offer of best wishes to Alex (speech function: offer).

> Hi Alex
>
> Many thanks for you contribution and this certainly raises an interesting point. (positive APPRECIATION) It will be interesting (positive APPRECIATION) to hear what others have to say in response! I wish you all the very best to and your partner on your marriage -- congratulations!! (*discussion forum data*)

In a similar manner, Lucinda judges any contribution from herself in terms of negative CAPACITY while she positively appraises students' contributions:

> I actually held back from entering the tutorial discussion deliberately. This was advised by my mentor and I think, now I have read back the discussion, that it paid off. You guys have the resources amongst yourselves to have an informative and stimulating discussion (positive JUDEGMENT: CAPACITY), my contribution might have put some of you off (negative JUDEGMENT: CAPACITY). (*message to students in the first forum of the year*)

In this way, the authority of the teacher role, alongside the capacity for expert semiotic mediation, is diminished. In contrast, the expertise and authority of the student role is elevated. In our view, Naomi and Lucinda's reluctance to act in semiotic initiator role is problematic. We do not wish to diminish the importance of the interpersonal dimension of semiotic mediation and teachers' affirmation of students' capacity. However, as previous discussion in this chapter and elsewhere has shown, it is often through a teacher's active modeling, scaffolding, and guidance alongside different forms of metasemiotic intervention that a student is supported in developing their meaning making repertoire.

Further evidence of the orientations of teachers lies in the genre analysis of the data. This revealed that on average (across 2 years and four forums), of all teachers, Naomi contributed the least number of genres or genre stages (across the range of arguing, nonarguing, and nonacademic genres). Both she and Lucinda contributed about half the number contributed by Bethany, a teacher who took on a more interventionist and authoritative role. Particularly significant is the fact that Naomi and Lucinda each contributed approximately half as many argument prompts as did Bethany (argument prompts are stages designed to elicit argumentation).

As exemplified by Bethany, the other main orientation, in the group of teachers we investigated, was to be more interventionist in guiding and modeling academic meaning making. Bethany commented in her interview on the importance of

> responding to some of the students' views that do come up in ways that are empowering and intelligent, while also pointing them in the other directions and showing them other places that they might like to look.
>
> – *Bethany, CAM teacher, interview data*

The online conferencing medium is seen by teachers such as Bethany as having much potential for learning, though as SJ (another teacher, whose expert semiotic mediation in the form of comments on Karalena's assignments was discussed in 4.2.1) comments, students may need strong guidance:

> it seems to me that I need to be a little more forceful with students in insisting on the "ways and means" of online forums . . .
>
> – *SJ, Applied Linguistics teacher, questionnaire data*

Certainly, based on some student questionnaires and comments in the online forums, there was a clear expectation and desire for teacher intervention. In response to Lucinda's less directive style, the following point was made by Charlotte. In the extract it is important to observe the reversal of roles, with Charlotte adopting a teacher-like persona in her appraisal of Lucinda and in the request (in the form of a declarative) for greater intervention: *I wonder if you could join in more*. Though this kind of reversal was rare in our data, it is interesting to note the inverse relation between a teacher's reduced authority and a student's desire to reinstate it (and in the process an exertion of his/her own authority):

> `Lucinda, you made a very good point (positive JUDGMENT: CAPACITY) about half way through, that brought out the discussion, but this was your only contribution (negative JUDGMENT: CAPACITY). I wonder if you could join in more? It certainly helps to get us thinking about the subject.`
>
> – *Charlotte, CAM student, forum data*

From these comments it is clear that there are different construals and expectations of the teacher role in an online forum and that a key issue centers on what might be called under- or over-intervention. Based on our data it would seem that at both undergraduate and postgraduate levels, learners see themselves (at least in part) as occupying a student role and, as such, wish to develop their learning not only through dialogue with their peers but through interaction with, and feedback from, a teacher. Students' expectations of a teacher's role and availability may, however, be out of step with a teacher's understanding of the role alongside academic workload constraints. Therefore it would seem particularly important for roles to be clarified in advance and, rather than teachers feeling under pressure to respond to every message posted, maximize their impact by reserving input for judiciously timed interventions. Teacher-initiated semiotic mediation would, in our view, be best focused on opportunities to move students from more contextualized to more decontextualized representations of phenomena (as exemplified in 6.4.2.1).

In applied disciplines, complicating any simplistic notion of a teacher or student role (in addition to the reversals already discussed) is the fact that many students are likely to be mature professionals (such as teachers or health care workers). We found in our data that, as such, participants are likely, at different points in the discussion, to speak from their roles as professional health practitioners, users of CAM, and/or as a family member. Similarly, teachers (some of whom in our data were experienced CAM practitioners or language teachers) may wear professional as well as academic hats.

The different semantic orientations alongside the diversity of social roles in the online forums we researched can play out in pedagogically significant ways. One clear advantage is participants' movement between academic and professional viewpoints, which allows a critical evaluation of knowledge from both perspectives, a key learning outcome of the applied disciplines we researched. That is, as professionals, students can interrogate the usefulness of theoretical models when applied to practical situations and, as (novice/peripheral) members of the academic community, make sense of professional scenarios by applying theoretical concepts.

One clear challenge, however, is how to foster the interpersonal community-building dimension of online discussion without jeopardizing robust intellectual debate. Our analysis showed, in both sets of data, that the topic and choice in task design was key in this respect, particularly with a first tutorial, where bonds are often formed as much through a sharing of professional roles and identities as they are through academic ideas. In the Applied Linguistics data, for example, students were first required to brainstorm factors affecting language learning by drawing on personal experience. Thereafter, they were given a number of tasks designed to exploit the relatively permanent form of online discussions and give them staged practice in the academic discourse skills of reasoning, debating, and supporting claims with evidence. In this way, students were encouraged to initially wear their professional or personal hats as language teachers or language learners before moving to an engagement with the more abstract academic ideas presented in their course materials.

Of course, combining the interpersonal and ideational is good practice in all teaching environments, but the nature of disembodied virtual communication and the nature of learning in an applied field of study makes the combination all the more critical and a particularly useful mechanism for encouraging less academically experienced students to expand and elasticize their identity from a default professional/personal one to one that includes an academic orientation to knowledge construal.

6.4.3.2 Distance or Familiarity?

Based on our findings and, in line with our expectations, there appears to be considerable variation in how formal or informal people are in their linguistic interactions in the online forums: just as in any social encounter, people orient differently to each other and with different degrees of distance or familiarity. And given the relatively new use of online forums in tertiary learning whereby patterns and conventions have yet to be firmly established, this is likely to be even more the case in those environments.

In our data we found that, at times, participants used colloquial and casual lexis, abbreviated or elliptical forms of expression, and more familiar terms of address and were not concerned about standardizing or correcting spelling, grammar, and punctuation (as most would be when composing a formal academic assignment). This style, we suggest, construes familiarity and social closeness between participants. In the message below, for example, Laura uses textese as well as other abbreviations (*exp., prob*). She also uses repeated exclamation marks for emphasis (!!!). The absence of capitals for *I* and at the start of some sentences (*my background . . .*) and her tolerance of spelling errors/typos and nonstandard features of written language all suggest that she is participating in a casual interaction among friends:

```
thank goodness !!! i also share your views on the issues
of black mailing children 2 sleep in own bed and re CAM.
It has cross mind mind a few times from reading peoples
message as 2 whether any one else has any exp of CAM
other than as a patient. my back ground is in orthodox
health care and so i have found some of the course
material a challange to my views as i no nill about the
subject. would it be very rude to ask whether this is
also the exp of other students ?
                                                 Laura

p.s the birbery still is nt working !!!! mind prob a bit
young at 22 months to understand . ha .
```

At other times, however, we found that participants used more standardized lexicogrammatical forms. In Abbie's message below, taken from the same forum, there is no use of colloquial expressions, contractions, ellipses, or textese, and there are no indicators that she is addressing a specific flesh-and-blood (albeit virtual) community of fellow students. These differences, we suggest, construe different degrees of social closeness or distance. Whereas Laura's linguistic choices suggest familiarity and friendliness, Abbie's imply social distance:

```
A post modernity era featuring an increase in consumer
culture provides Mrs B with an increase of information
of alternative approaches to her health.
```

> Following on from the counter-culture changes in the 1960's promoting questioning of authority,in health provision this led to an increase in and acceptance of CAM.

Another variation in the use of interpersonal resources was the presence or absence of APPRAISAL realized through graphics to do the interpersonal work of increasing or decreasing social distance (interpersonal work that might be more typically achieved through intonation, gesture, or facial expression in face-to-face spoken discussion). For example, some students used smiley icons to lower the force of what might be provocative claims and in a similar way used exclamation marks to raise the force of a point being made (see Chapter 3, 3.4.2.2). The following two messages illustrate this:

> I would also agree that many treatments do not hold up to scientific enquiry :-) (APPRAISAL:FORCE-lower) That said many people get a lot of benefit from the relaxation and counselling aspects of them....

> Thankyou very much for your help which has enabled me to move on with my assignment!!!! (APPRAISAL:FORCE-RAISE)

In general, however, the use of graphics to realize APPRAISAL was relatively infrequent. This stands in contrast to the findings of a study into secondary school students' interaction in online forums where choices in color and font type and size were integral to construing social relations (Coffin et al., 2012).

The kinds of contrast exemplified in the extracts above were a general feature of the online forums and beg the question of how such variability might have a bearing on the kind of learning taking place. It seems clear, however, that language choices that create closer social bonds support rather than hinder academic exchange. This seemed to be intuitive on the part of most students with considerable switching back and forth from language that created social closeness and social bonds to language that was more formal (most typically used in discussions of more abstract, conceptual notions).

The teachers, similarly, were generally interpersonally attuned so as to diminish social distance when desirable—most typically when encouraging contributions. What became clear, however, was that there was a degree of tension between wanting to reduce social distance and create community while at the same time wanting or needing to maintain distance as academics and teachers/evaluators. Distance and formality were partly achieved through

- Hi folks,
  Just checking in to see how you're getting along.
  First, many thanks for all your contributions.
  I have found them all stimulating and interesting. [Positive APPRECIATION]
  It's been great to get to know you a bit better, [Positive AFFECT]
  and to hear your perceptions and analyses of your
  (and Mrs. Bannister's) health choices. (*Julie, CAM teacher*)
- Good to see the way this discussion is going. [Positive APPRECIATION]
  Really glad to see someone making this point [Positive AFFECT]
  about the poverty problems in our own country. (*Bethany, CAM teacher*)
- Some really interesting points of view on quite a [FORCE Positive APPRECIATION]
  tricky and very unresolved area (*Naomi, CAM teacher)*

Figure 6.5 Evaluating students' contributions.

an absence of textese in their messages (in contrast to many of the students' messages) and through their use of APPRAISAL to evaluate students' contributions, as exemplified in the underlined choices in Figure 6.5. The significant point here, however, is that there is generally under-specification in terms of the ideational meanings that are being appraised and that the appraisal may be directed as much to the community forming aspect of the forums and general discussion as to the specific ideas being put forward. There is also a tendency for the evaluation to be positive and somewhat formulaic.

6.4.3.3 Social Status and Power

> It (*online discussion*) has got potential but it is not doing it, the ones who are doing it have already got very good skills.
>
> – Lucinda, CAM teacher

Claims have been made that asynchronous discussion forums provide a democratic space in which students can interact more equally than in face-to-face seminars. Dysthe (2002), for example, argued that a key factor in the success of the electronic tutorial she investigated was its "symmetrical interaction" where "none of the participants have more authority or power than the others" (p. 341). Our findings, however, challenge this notion. For example, our interviews with the teachers pointed to a different dynamic in which certain students dominated and others were peripheral—much as they might be in a face-to-face situation. This observation was borne out through analysis of a subset of data in which we looked at patterns in the kinds of contribution made by individual students. The linguistic data revealed very clearly the different degrees of equality/inequality between participants' contributions and some of the power dynamics at play.

We found that higher scoring students (as evidenced by their written assignment grades) were more visibly present in the online forums, contributing an average of 30 genre stages whereas lower scoring students contributed an average of 11.5. Of the contributions made by the lower scoring students, in line with our predictions, we found that, for the major part, they were personal recounts, observations, and Solidarity stages. With the higher scoring students it was the inverse; the majority of their contributions were focused on the main lines of argumentation. Furthermore, we found that higher scoring students not only dominated ideationally but also interpersonally: their contribution of personal recounts and Solidarity stages (10.9 on average) exceeded those of lower scoring students (6 on average). These patterns provide clear evidence of the asymmetry of online interaction whereby higher scoring students are positioned to exert considerable power over the lines of argumentation as well as to figure prominently in the more socially oriented interaction.

Patterns such as those above reveal, quite starkly, differences in patterns of engagement and bear out the concerns of some teachers (such as Lucinda, quoted at the start of this section and below) that online participation is uneven. This raises the question of what can be done to help make such interactions more equal. While some teachers may have built up strategies in a face-to-face tutorial such as the use of encouraging gestures and other visual cues, the virtual environment can be challenging:

> I just think that face to face is so much—because just with an expression you can encourage people to sort of—come on, a bit more, yeah, come on . . . that is so much harder on email.
>
> *– Lucinda, interview data*

Of particular concern is Lucinda's earlier comment which points to the danger of those students benefitting from online interaction being the ones who have already developed skills in this environment through prior experience (either inside or outside formal learning environments). This means that students unfamiliar with either exchanging ideas in formal university-level learning environments or online environments are likely to lose out and that (as expressed in the quote from Lucinda above) part of the reason for this may be teachers' inexperience at knowing how to draw such students into online discussion.

6.4.3.4 Recap

In summary, a focus on tenor and interpersonal meaning making has demonstrated that in online forums there is a pressure to connect interpersonally and to build community. This applies to all fields of study being taught and learned in an online environment (not just applied ones) and is well documented in the literature. Using the tools of SFL to make visible the patterns of language use that work to enact social roles and power relations and to create different degrees of social distance and familiarity, we have shown that considerable effort is made by participants to create community and a positive learning environment. What the analysis of our data set has shown is that patterns of engagement are not equal for all participants and that there is a delicate balance to be drawn between interpersonal and ideational meaning making. These issues are taken up in the next section.

6.5 Teachers' and Students' Orientations to Online Forums and Patterns of Interaction: Implications for Semiotic Mediation

Based on our questionnaire and interview data, it would seem (unsurprisingly) that how students and teachers operate in an online environment is at least in part influenced by their experience of technology and of online teaching or learning. We found that, even though teachers had been given technical training in the use of online forums, their experience in the pedagogic aspects of these was generally limited. Similarly, we found that, of the Applied Linguistics students interviewed, 90% were using online forums for learning purposes for the first time. With the CAM students, experience of online learning was mixed, with a few experiencing problems even at the level of typing. In broad terms, we identified two orientations to online forums. On the one hand, there were teachers and students who had little experience of interacting in a computer environment and whose unfamiliarity produced anxiety or even hostility toward online interaction. On the other hand, there were teachers and students who had considerable experience in using virtual technologies and who embraced the opportunity for such interaction.

Returning to our discussion of Charlotte and Zoe (in Section 6.3.6) and the different kinds of contributions they made to the online forum, it is likely that their teachers' orientations may have had some impact on this. Bethany, Charlotte's teacher, for example, is an enthusiastic supporter of technology and it is perhaps for this reason that she involved herself in the debate throughout, contributing, in total, 114 genre stages. Lucinda, in contrast (Zoe's teacher), does not have a positive view of the pedagogic use of online forums and contributed 31 genre stages. Perhaps of particular significance is the fact that Lucinda rarely put forward argument prompts (2, in contrast to 31 by Bethany), a stage in an online discussion that is likely to move a discussion forward and encourage students' participation (including more reluctant students). A well-timed argument prompt also has the potential to integrate contributions that might otherwise remain disconnected from the line(s) of argument. Certainly, though we cannot make any hard claims, the fact that Bethany's group contributed a third more argumentation stages than Lucinda's indicates that the teacher's role in encouraging and stimulating dialogue is an important one.

6.5.1 Identifying Potential for Semiotic Mediation

The previous sections have shown how, in the context of online forums, language enables students to build, exchange, and manage new meanings and so develop their skills in online academic discussion. Furthermore, we have discussed some of the ways in which meanings from course materials get reconfigured in the course of online dialogue and how this may support students' meaning making in their individual written assignments. In this sense, online forums can be said to play an important bridging or mediating role as students move from academic reading to writing.

In and of themselves, however, online forums may not serve this role unless their potential is understood by both teachers and students. That is, in view of their hybrid nature—somewhere between informal, spontaneous speech and formal, academic writing—participants need to know how to take advantage of what each communication mode has to offer: on the one hand, the informal dialogic exchange of opinions and co-construction of knowledge, and on the other, the opportunity for consolidation, synthesis, reflection, and repositioning. We would argue that of particular importance in relation to these features is the design of tasks and the deployment of semiotic mediation strategies which use the online environment to scaffold students' contributions as part of the longer-term process of learning; in other words, learning through and about language in order to become more conversant in academic knowledge building. As we have noted here and elsewhere, this may involve, for some teachers, an expansion or adaptation of their skills in semiotic mediation for an online environment. For students, it may entail a semantic reorientation to meaning making.

In the next and final section of this chapter, we highlight the most significant implications for semiotic mediation in an online forum, from both the teacher and student perspective.

6.5.2 Semiotic Mediation: Supporting the Expansion of Students' Meaning Potential

How effectively teachers manage semiotic mediation in the teaching and learning environment of online forums is, of course, partly related to their experience with the technology. As previously discussed, our linguistic analysis showed that teachers contributed in a range of ways, including (i) guiding students to move from more contextualized to more decontextualized meaning making, (ii) modeling (in their summary genres) how to stand back from the detail of the argument and provide abstract position statements, and (iii) reassuring students that their contribution was valuable.

We also found through our interview and questionnaire data that teachers had a number of concerns. Of primary significance was the fact that they were unsure how to transfer the skills they had developed in face-to-face situations into an online medium. Teachers found particularly difficult the diverse semantic orientations and linguistic repertoires of the students they found themselves teaching. Time and workload was an issue as well as the feeling that online discussions did not provide a satisfying learning experience for many of their students.

Based on our SFL analysis alongside teacher and student interview and questionnaire data, we would argue that there is an important role for professional development that focuses on the pedagogic, not just technical, dimension of online forums and on how, as a medium, it is continuously evolving. Such professional development (which is already being implemented at our own institution) would raise teachers' awareness of the unique way language functions in the online discussion environment (both at the level of genre and register) and help them develop metasemiotic mediation strategies in the light of these.

One area for teachers to explicitly focus on in their metasemiotic mediation may be the way in which academic discourse varies according to context. That is, while the relatively informal nature of online forums encourages a greater personalization in the way claims are constructed and may give greater attention to students' personal and professional experience as support for a claim, it remains the case that in a formally assessed assignment, teachers expect argumentation to be located in academic reference works rather than there be a reliance on personal or professional recounts (though, as previously discussed, the integration of professional with academic knowledge is a feature of many applied fields of study). This type of knowledge and explicit instruction would help students have confidence in communicating in each medium and would prevent the inappropriate transfer of discourse conventions from one context to another.

Other factors that may contribute to the effectiveness of online forums and that teachers could be encouraged to consider are set out in the following bullet points:

- The topic chosen and the wording and clarity of the task are crucial in motivating students. In particular, opening tasks with a new group should be carefully chosen to provide for personal contact and community building as well as academic interest. It should not simply involve a challenging academic topic that might deter students not sufficiently confident to contribute to discussion with relative strangers in a written mode, nor should it be academically shallow in case students perceive online forums as tangential or irrelevant to their study.
- Given that a number of students engage in online discussions infrequently (some not at all), it may be necessary to carefully design and structure the forum discussion so that students move from more personal reflections to more academic discussion. Equally, it may be necessary to sequence discussions across the year to reflect a similar movement.
- Teachers could model effective ways that discussion and argument can unfold in an online context. For example, they could show how genres that appear to be free-floating and extraneous can be integrated into the overall argumentative thrust and could demonstrate the usefulness of higher-level summary genres.
- Less experienced students need careful support to avoid being inhibited by more articulate, experienced students.
- Students need to be convinced of how online forums will enhance their learning, their enjoyment of learning, and/or their success in course assessment.
- The tone employed by the teacher is important.
- The teacher needs to make sure students feel connected to a community and thus may need to tolerate/encourage a degree of chat and frivolity in order to create community and personalize what might otherwise be an alienating teaching and learning space.
- A focus on community building and interpersonal relations should not take priority over supporting the development of ideational meaning.
- Teachers may be best advised to save their responses for contributions that might otherwise be ignored.

To conclude this chapter we reiterate that, if discussion forums are to support students in learning through and about academic discourse (and furthermore diminish the gap between higher- and lower-scoring students), teachers need to learn how to motivate students to benefit from the online environment. The strategies outlined above are one way forward. If implemented skillfully, these would, we believe, support students in progressing from more contextualized to more decontextualized language use, an academic shift that remains elusive for some students. As we have pointed out, there is a danger that online participation could simply reflect what already exists in other modes. So it, too, like all other modes, calls for targeted semiotic mediation of a type that harnesses the complementarities of spontaneous dialogue and reflective academic writing.

Notes

1 The use of computer technologies for various types of discussion and exchange has led to the development of a range of different software packages and interfaces referred to variously as e-conferences, text-based conferencing, Web forums, message/discussion/bulletin boards, etc.

2 Details of data collection and analysis:

1. HSC data

While the data and much of the analysis derives from an HEA-funded study (Hewings et al., 2007) further analysis was required to underpin the discussion in this chapter, as well as some rethinking of the original methodology. In total, the data underpinning the claims made in this chapter (collected across two academic years) comprised:

• 8 discussion forums held at the start and end of each academic year (16 in total comprising a total of 49,223 words).

• 15 student assignments, which followed the first discussion forum. The assignments were written by students from 2 tof the 16 tutorial groups and represented all higher-scoring assignments (with marks of 70 or more out of a hundred; 11 in total) and all lower-scoring assignments (with marks of 57 or less; four in total). This subset was selected in order to make more manageable the in-depth linguistic analysis.

Aside from the data identified above that was collected and analysed linguistically, we also draw on qualitative data comprising semi-structured teacher interviews (4 in total) and student questionnaires and follow-up interviews (19 in total). This data focused on teachers' and students' previous experience of online discussion forums as well as their views and perspectives on it. Other contextualizing material (namely, the course readings and other teaching/learning materials and assessment guides) was also collected and informed the investigation.

Further understanding of the field of HSC was gained through one of the authors using the ethnographic method of participant observation. By undertaking a first level undergraduate course in HSC values, an insider (emic) perspective on meaning-making complemented the etic perspective developed through linguistic analysis (see Chapter 2).

2. The Education/Applied Linguistics data

The data collected and linguistically analyzed comprised:

• 2 online discussion forums

- These took place in two tutorial groups at the start of the academic year.

• 26 written assignments

- These were produced by all students across the two tutorial groups at the start of the academic year (subsequent to the online discussion forums)

In addition there was questionnaire data from teachers (8 in total) and students (10 in total). These explored previous experience of online discussion forums as well as views and perspectives on it. Other contextualizing material (namely, the course material and text books and the assessment guide) was also collected and used to inform the investigation.

3 Note that individual posts do not necessarily equate with a genre or even a stage within a genre.

4 "MOT" here refers to the test for a vehicle/car over three years old as to its basic roadworthiness. The test was originally set up by the Ministry of Transport, hence M. O. T. "Eck" is a colloquial expression and should be understood to have the same meaning as "yikes."

Language Learning ISSN 0023-8333

CHAPTER 7
Implementing a LASS Approach to Teaching and Learning

7.1 Teaching and Learning from a LASS Perspective

> Most of us take language for granted—it's a transparent medium in which we swim.
>
> – University Pro Vice-Chancellor[1]

Fundamentally, this monograph has been concerned with the learning and teaching that takes place in contemporary universities and the central role played by language in that process. That language is central to the process of teaching and learning may be obvious to some but far from obvious to others, as the quotation above suggests. Such a view is, however, increasingly untenable in a context of globalization, increased diversity, and widening university participation. In this context, language can no longer remain marginal, invisible, and transparent. Rather, as we have argued throughout the preceding chapters, it is both important and timely to bring language to the fore and make evident the complex language—and therefore cognitive—demands of university-level study. This includes understanding better how individual students navigate the demands and how individual teachers can support them.

In this monograph, we have shown how SFL provides us with a means of making language more visible so that it can become an object of attention not only for linguists but also for university-level teachers and their students. In relation to several applied fields of study, and in relation to a number of individual students, we have shown how metasemiotic mediation can bring patterns of language choice to the conscious attention of both teachers and students and how this can enhance the processes of semiotic mediation that constitute teaching and learning.

As we have sought to demonstrate, the most significant patterns of language for university learning and teaching purposes constitute decontextualized representations of the world. Decontextualized language is central in fulfilling diverse purposes such as explaining the impact of phenomena, arguing a point

DOI: 10.1111/lang.12043

of view, or analyzing a problem and suggesting a solution. This understanding of how language works goes far beyond the commonsense perception of academic language simply being "big massive jargon" as the student, James, put it in Chapter 2. It is, in fact, much closer to James's observation that tertiary study fundamentally changes who people are, transforming them from people who are action oriented to people who focus on ideas (although we might argue the ideal is that they do both):

> The course changes 'em, the way of thinking changes 'em to where they focus on things but don't seem to be able to make a decision. Whereas from my point of view I go and look at the problem. Address the problem, look at the problem, make a decision, you've got to do it.

James's concerns about academic language may thus have less to do with its use of "jargon" but may lie instead in a more pervasive concern about the reinterpretation and representation of the world (and his positioning within this) that comes with decontextualized language use. In her book, *Rethinking University Education,* Laurillard (2002) describes university-level learning in comparable terms:

> [T]he great majority of study time is not spent on activities in the field, but in working with analogies, historical accounts, critiques, statistics, case studies, diagrams, etc., which is straightforwardly "acting on descriptions of the world," acting on a mediated world. (p. 55)

It is certainly true that the first-level HSC course that James is studying has as one of its learning and teaching purposes the development of students' ability to recontextualize their lived (professional) experience in terms of social science theoretical frames and conceptual formations; that is, to become more proficient in "acting on descriptions of the world." In applied fields of study, however, acting on the mediated world is generally not the only purpose of university-level learning (though it may be a primary and highly valued one). Students are also expected to use the new framings of the world to make new sense of their professional situations and experiences. This was an activity that appeared to come naturally to Andrea (also introduced in Chapter 2). Andrea's engagement with university-level conventions of language, literacy, and knowledge making induced much less concern and she was successful in connecting these to her personal and professional experience. This motivated her learning.

Nevertheless, as in James's case and for many students, the relationship between acting on descriptions of the world and acting in the field may not be straightforward. Zuna (the third student introduced in Chapter 2) was motivated to make these connections, but her semantic orientation to meaning-making at that point in her studies made the transition between worlds and the capacity to act in the mediated domain a challenging one.

In the preceding chapters we have addressed the questions we asked at the beginning of the monograph:

- How can a theory of language as a social semiotic contribute to our understanding of the different ways university students make meaning?
- How can a theory of language as a social semiotic contribute to our understanding of the ways teachers engage with students' meaning-making at university?
- How do understandings gleaned from asking the questions above inform a LASS-based approach for enhancing teaching and learning in higher education?

In this chapter we will bring together our responses to the final question into a set of proposals for how to implement a LASS-based approach to teaching and learning in higher education.

7.1.2 Review

In the Chapters 4 to 6, we discussed aspects of university teaching and learning as viewed from a LASS perspective. The pedagogical implications of the account for the linguistic-cognitive development of students from diverse language backgrounds were discussed at various points in these chapters. In particular, we identified a major developmental change that occurs as students learn to shift up and down the ladder of abstraction, moving back and forth from the more contextualized material realities of professional or social lived experience to the more decontextualized theorized realities of academic learning. As previously observed, this requires students to come to terms with a second-order experience of the world: whereas everyday knowledge is located in our experience of the world, "academic knowledge is located in our experience of our experience of the world" (Laurillard, 2002, p. 21).

Establishing that academic learning involves a movement from the immediate and the sentient toward the more remote and the more abstract may seem a somewhat obvious argument. This is a point that Christie (2012) makes at the conclusion of her work on language and learning at the primary and secondary levels:

> So what? How does it help to think about the matter in these terms? What have we gained from the general arguments advanced in this book? (p. 190).

Like Christie, we have several answers to this last question, which we will offer in this final chapter.

Informing our answers is the premise that a LASS approach to teaching and learning is an approach with relevance for all university students, regardless of language background: while we accept that students' language experiences are far from identical, these do not necessarily line up with traditional categories of *English as an Additional Language (EAL), home student, EAL international student, L1 student,* and so on. It is, we suggest, necessary to develop a more finely tuned approach to identifying and targeting students' needs and we discuss this in Section 7.2. Set out below, in Figure 7.1, is a summary of some of the key points of LASS that have emerged for us through the teaching and

1) Language is a meaning-making resource and using language is a meaning-making process, performed in social contexts wherein linguistic form and meaning are fused in order to represent experience, interact with others, and construct texts.
2) Language is one semiotic resource among others, including visual, gestural, musical, physical, mathematical, and multimodal semiotic resources. Language in the context of learning, however, is central: it mediates and orchestrates other semiotic modes.
3) Taking part in a social situation involves drawing on the meaning-making resources and processes that we have developed through our participation in a lifetime of previous social situations. This constitutes our semantic orientation. We adapt our use of the resources to our interpretation of how and what meanings are made in the situation.
4) At the heart of communication in the academic learning and teaching context is decontextualized language used for constructing and managing abstract concepts and concept relations.
5) Teaching and learning are interacting processes of semiotic mediation in which both teachers and learners are semiotic mediators. At different times, teachers and students are initiators or responders.
6) The formal objective of semiotic interaction in university education is the reconfiguration of students' conceptual formations and for these reconfigurations to be evaluated by teachers. These activities constitute Bernstein's notion of the pedagogic device: knowledge construction – recontextualization – evaluation (Bernstein, 1996).
7) As well as having knowledge-construction as an objective, semiotic mediation is a site of power struggle, identity formation, and relationship building.
8) Semiotic mediation can be enhanced through metasemiotic mediation, which brings semiotic resources to conscious awareness.

Figure 7.1 Language as a social semiotic: key points for learning and teaching.

research projects that we reported in previous chapters and that underpin the proposals we put forward in this chapter.

7.2 Implementing a LASS Approach in Higher Education

University teaching and learning was once seen as a process that was understood by all its participants, with differences in achievement by students being regarded as a natural outcome of a system that was designed in part to rank student ability. Changes in the purposes of higher education, diversification of the student body, the impact of globalization, widening participation, employer engagement, and other influences have meant that student learning, progression, and retention are no longer the taken-for-granted results of teaching. Instead, teaching has come under scrutiny, and enhancements to subject teaching have been encouraged through allocation of resources to training, design of the curriculum, and other innovations. At the same time, the notion of "student support" has emerged as an important element of what universities provide. Responsibility for student learning, progression, and retention is thus divided between subject teachers, support services, and, of course, students. Throughout this monograph, we have demonstrated how a LASS approach provides insights, tools, and procedures that can enhance the work of all these participants in the teaching and learning processes of higher education. Figure 7.2 illustrates the core dimensions of LASS that we have focused on to this point: semantic orientation, semiotic mediation, and SFL analysis of meaning-making (using the constructs of genre, register, and metafunctions). Figure 7.2 adds a further dimension: institutional awareness and analysis in order to ensure effective implementation of LASS (in terms of policy, curriculum, and assessment design).

To date, the recognition of the role of language in teaching and learning has varied, both in terms of the extent and depth to which it is recognized and understood and in terms of the institutional response in the types of provision offered. For example, in a recent survey of 22 universities located in the United Kingdom, mainland Europe, Australia, and Japan, which was conducted as part of an English Language Policy Review (at The Open University, UK), we found that provision for enhancing student learning, progression, and retention through specific attention to the role of language in learning could take many forms. Such provision could be:

- Aimed at students, academics, or administrators;
- For international/additional language speakers of English, or for speakers of English as a first language;

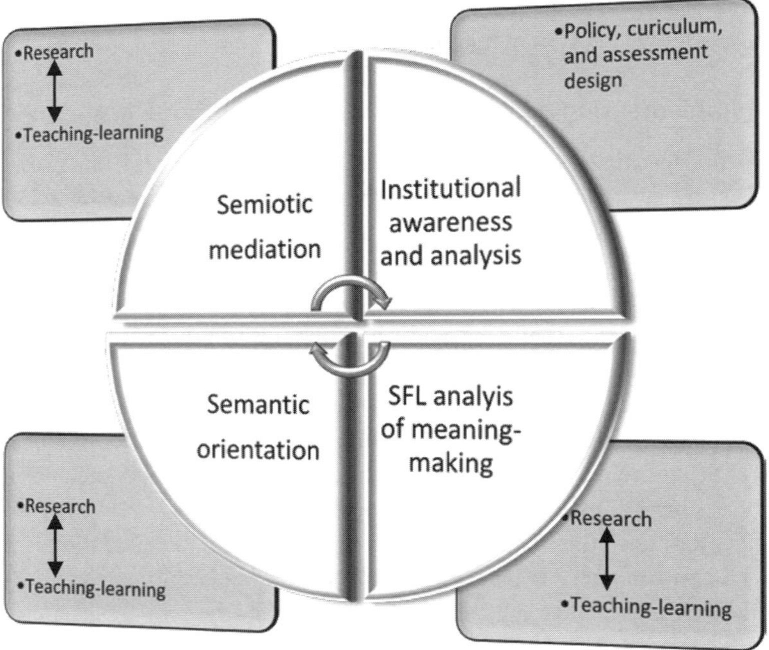

Figure 7.2 The core dimensions of implementing a LASS approach in higher education.

- For all students as part of their academic development, or for students whose academic development and success were deemed to be "at risk";
- Incorporated in disciplinary teaching by language-aware subject specialists or by collaboration between subject and language specialists;
- Provided one to one, in a workshop or a class, through self access, or at a distance;
- Provided in occasional sessions, in regular sessions, or in a full course; in presessional classes, in-sessional classes, or as required;
- Provided by language and learning professionals, student peers, or subject specialists;
- In the form of subject-teacher professional development;
- In the form of either general or subject-specific English language for academic purposes for students;
- Compulsory or voluntary;
- Fee charging or free;
- Credit bearing or not credit bearing.

Whatever the nature of the provision, it is our contention that student learning, progression, and retention can be enhanced with a LASS approach to subject teaching and student support. This section sets out the four main steps that we see as fundamental for implementing a LASS approach. These are:

i) Establishing evidence and needs through research (Section 7.3)
ii) Designing a LASS-based curriculum (Section 7.4)
iii) Developing LASS-based teaching and learning (Section 7.5)
iv) Applying LASS principles to assessment (Section 7.6)

There is a fifth step that we will not deal with in any detail in this chapter but which is vital for the implementation of a LASS approach: fostering institutional change by means of alliances, policy formation, and the establishment of institutional structures and processes. Throughout the following sections, we illustrate the points being made with examples from our own institution (The Open University, UK) and elsewhere.

7.3 Establishing Evidence and Needs

Evidence (primarily research based) is at the center of a LASS approach to learning and teaching, including evidence of need, the role of language in the field of study and the learning and teaching of the field, students' diverse semantic orientations to university learning, and current learning and teaching practices. Although there is an increasing interest in student learning, progression, and retention as mentioned earlier, students, teachers, and administrators may not necessarily see this as related in a meaningful way to language, or if they do, they may not know what to do about the relationship.

In this section, therefore, we consider evidence as the foundation for implementing a LASS approach to learning and teaching. This involves collecting data (and often conducting analysis) on the following. We elaborate on each of these areas in Sections 7.3.1–7.3.4:

- Students' language backgrounds and learning/linguistic behavior and patterns (7.3.1: Institutional data)
- Course materials and student writing, in order to identify, through linguistic analysis, patterns of meaning-making in different fields of study (7.3.2: Mapping the field of studies)
- Student writing and teachers' and students' metasemiotic mediation of their writing in order to gain insight into their semantic orientations and linguistic repertoires (7.3.3: Mapping students' linguistic repertoires)

- Course materials and records of teacher–student interaction (including online or face-to-face discussions/teaching, feedback on written assignments, etc.), in order to develop understanding of teachers' existing semiotic mediation techniques and approaches (7.3.4: Mapping semiotic mediation)

We are not suggesting that such data or evidence collection is a process that is carried out exclusively by researchers or data managers who are not directly involved in the teaching and learning relationship, although it may also be carried out by people in such roles. The purpose of data collection is to inform subject specialists, language specialists, students, and policy makers at the university, and data may be collected by any of these people and used by any of them. The ideal proponent of a LASS approach is a teacher-researcher who is a language specialist attempting to understand the semiotic mediation of another specialist's subject area or, alternatively, a subject specialist who develops an interest in the nature of language as a social semiotic. Collaboration between two or more such teacher-researchers is a particularly powerful combination. Extending this collaboration to include student-researchers enhances the combination.

7.3.1 Institutional Data Collection

Universities do not routinely collect data about students' language backgrounds and use and, where they do, the means of collecting this data, in terms of validity, reliability, and value, vary enormously. We suggest that such data collection can play a part in building a deeper understanding of the language landscape of university learning and can therefore serve as foundational knowledge for implementing a LASS approach. Below we have set out an indicative list of the kinds of institutional data that may be gathered (accepting that such collection may be currently rare or indeed nonexistent in some institutions):

- Entry tests in language for international students (e.g., IELTS, TOEFL)
- Self-diagnosis or self-access tests where students' language use is assessed in various ways
- Student retention, attainment, and progression data (though this is unlikely to have a specific language focus)
- Equity and diversity language background data collection (e.g., registering students can be asked what experience of academic language they have)
- As part of equity and diversity data collection, specific groups such as Black and minority ethnic groups may be investigated in greater depth to establish particular patterns of academic and language attainment (see, e.g., Erling & Richardson, 2011)

- Learning log data gathered from online environments (e.g., student responses to learning activities) such as virtual learning environments and content management systems. These can be subjected to "learning analytics" (see Buckingham-Shum, 2012): automated analysis in order to establish aspects of students' learning (e.g., how many, if any, attempts at a question were made; levels of participation in discussion forums; etc.)
- External examiners' comments on student writing/learning (see Chapter 4)
- Review and evaluation of existing language provision
- Evaluation of the language abilities that are needed to enter into and succeed in particular university courses. In the United Kingdom, for example, the Cambridge ESOL Examinations Board carried out analyses of the level of English language required by L1 and additional language speakers of English to enter and attain on first-year courses at The Open University using the Common European Framework of Reference for Languages criteria
- Findings from institutional scholarship[2] research (e.g., regarding students' use of digital tools and patterns of online interaction)

Though still rare, it is worth noting the reference above to some institutions' use of learning analytics, that is, educational data mining techniques, particularly in contexts where learning (or part of the learning experience) is computer mediated. Analytics are able to interrogate institutional machine-readable big datasets, sets of data that it would not be practical to deal with manually (Ferguson, 2012). Such analytics make it possible to look at, for example, correlations between large cohorts of students who studied an *English for Academic Purposes* course and their attainment in subsequent subject courses or to establish key patterns of language use associated with higher levels of attainment. The findings generated may then be used to group and classify students in more dynamic ways than simple demographic factors allow, the latter tending to categorize students into identity groupings (e.g., international, EAL, Black and minority ethnic, etc.), which may contain a great diversity of language repertoires. On this basis, extra targeted support and attention can be more accurately predicted and provided. At this point, however, although learning analytics is a rapidly growing field and there is considerable education potential, as Buckinghum Shum (2012) warns, there are limits to computational modeling and also ethical issues that need to be taken account of.

7.3.2 Mapping the Field of Studies: Genre, Register, and Meaning-Making

In order to gain insight into the meaning-making that occurs in academic study in general, and in different fields of study in particular, we propose that a systematic mapping of genres; register configurations; and interpersonal, ideational, and textual meaning is needed. This may not always be practical, in which case institutions can build on previous relevant research. However, where possible, we suggest that this type of linguistic (primary source) needs analysis provides a firm foundation for pedagogic design.

In brief, a linguistic needs analysis that maps a field of study (and learning stages within this) will work through the following steps (see Coffin, 2006, for further discussion in relation to school history):

- Collect data (language specialists guided by teachers in the field of study collect, for example, course readings and/or other course materials, examples of student writing)
- Build a corpus of texts which represent meaning-making in the specific field of studies (e.g., students' written responses to all assignment tasks within a particular year)
- Conduct a linguistic analysis of texts to ascertain the key patterns of meaning-making, using the constructs of genre, register, and metafunction and focusing in particular on decontextualized language and conceptual formations

Where a primary source linguistic needs analysis cannot be conducted, we suggest building on existing secondary source linguistic descriptions, analysis, and interpretations of academic meaning-making. As we have seen in Chapter 2, prior SFL research includes descriptions of genres and meaning making in a range of fields of study and at different levels of undergraduate and postgraduate education. Other relevant descriptions derive from complementary linguistic traditions. These include research into academic genres following the Swales/*English for Specific Purposes* model (e.g., Swales, 1990) and research into key linguistic patterns and the academic purposes they serve using corpus tools and other forms of discourse analysis (e.g., Hyland, 2004, 2009).

7.3.3 Mapping Students' Linguistic Repertoires and Semantic Orientations

Aside from traditional ways of testing and assessing students' use of English or, more specifically, academic english (i.e., using commercial tests such as those identified in 7.3.1), there exists a range of tools for mapping students' linguistic repertoires, some of which take an SFL, LASS perspective. Such tools are able to map students' meaning-making resources in more depth than generalized testing or diagnostic tools. They can also identify strengths and weaknesses in students' meaning-making as it pertains to particular academic fields of study. This diagnostic data can then be used to design supportive programs and other kinds of intervention in relation to students' needs. We thus see evidence of this type as a further important foundation for implementing a LASS approach to learning and teaching.

One SFL-based tool, which formed the basis for the diagnostic activity that generated the student texts discussed in Chapter 4, is Measuring the Academic Skills of University Students (MASUS). This tool was first developed for teaching and assessing academic writing and meaning-making at the University of Sydney, Australia (Bonanno & Jones, 2007), but has now been applied in various higher education contexts (for an example, see Chapter 4, Appendix 4.5). Criteria include:

1. Use of source materials
2. Text structure and development
3. Academic style
4. Grammatical correctness
5. Quality of presentation

The designers of MASUS suggest variations and flexibility in relation to the use of the instrument (Bonanno & Jones, 2007, pp. 4–5). Thus, modifications have been made for its use in different fields of study (see Scouller, Bonanno, Smith, & Krass, 2008 [use with pharmacy students]; Shrestha, 2010 [use as a diagnostic tool in Business Studies]).

Another SFL diagnostic tool is the *3 × 3 Framework* (Humphrey, Martin, Dreyfus, & Mahboob, 2010). This framework is more detailed than MASUS in that it collects data on students' realization of the three metafunctions (i.e., ideational, interpersonal, and textual meaning making) in relation to genre and register in specific academic contexts. To date, this framework has been used and reported on in the context of an online academic writing project referred to as SLATE (Scaffolding Literacy in Adult and Tertiary Environments; Mahboob et al., 2010).

Whereas tools such as MASUS and the 3 × 3 Framework provide rich data on individual students' linguistic patterns and meaning making, such data are collected in a formal writing context and are therefore limited in terms of insights into students' semantic orientations. As discussed in previous chapters (see Chapter 2, Section 2.6.3; Chapter 5, Section 5.7), in our own research we have therefore conducted mediated text analysis discussion as a complementary means of deepening our understandings of how students orient to academic meaning-making. It may be that, in the future, diagnostic tools such as MASUS and 3 × 3 will be developed in order to include such perspectives. In the meantime, we suggest that, where practicalities allow, some type of in-depth analysis of individual students' meaning making (through text analysis or discussion) provides an important additional layer to the evidence base needed for a LASS approach to teaching and learning. There are many examples of such investigations using an academic literacies approach (see Chapter 2, Section 2.6.3).

7.3.4 Mapping Current Semiotic Mediation Techniques

Analyzing and mapping the semiotic mediation techniques in play in any institution or university department or in relation to a particular course and student cohort is a further layer of evidence for a LASS approach. Chapters 4, 5, and 6 provide examples of how this may be done. In contexts where online interaction takes place or in the context of teaching collaborations, it may be easier to record and analyze different styles of mediation. Equally, however, assessment guidance and written feedback on student assignments can provide another relatively accessible way for a language specialist to gain understanding of how subject teachers semiotically or metasemiotically mediate in responder roles in order to support students in developing conceptual frameworks of knowledge and related meaning-making resources, including decontextualized language.

In contexts of collaboration between linguistic and subject specialists (see Section 7.4.2, below) the process of mapping semiotic mediation techniques may of course be a "chicken and egg" arrangement. While on the one hand the mapping is part of the needs analysis and the collaboration is part of the response, mapping need not be a one-time, upfront procedure but can continue throughout the collaboration. It may be iterative and fragmentary and knowledge is likely to build cumulatively on both sides.

7.4 Designing a LASS-Based Curriculum

In Sections 7.4–7.6, we describe how LASS approaches to curriculum, semiotic mediation, and assessment design can be developed on the basis of the evidence collected through the procedures proposed in Section 7.3. We introduce five types of LASS provision and a set of principles for institutional implementation. These have emerged through the research and practice of LASS-based approaches to teaching and learning that have been reported in this monograph.

To reiterate, our argument is that teaching and learning can be enhanced by the implementation of a meaningful and useable notion of language as fundamental to the university experience, for students and teachers alike. We are proposing that a LASS approach to teaching and learning is such an approach (see Figure 7.2). A LASS approach foregrounds:

i. Teaching and learning as semiotic and, where appropriate, metasemiotic mediation (i.e., teaching and learning language, teaching and learning through language, and teaching and learning about language);
ii. The semiotic system of language brought into focus through metasemiotic mediation, particularly its decontextualized features (i.e., teaching and learning about language); and
iii. The significance of semantic orientation (i.e., the impact of previous experiences of learning language and learning through language on current educational experience) and semantic variation among students and between students and teachers.

7.4.1 A Research-Informed Approach to Curriculum Design

Curriculum and pedagogic design that embody awareness of the role of language in learning and teaching depend on the kind of research and data gathering outlined in Section 7.3. Such analysis has to be tailored to suit the available resources (i.e., the capacity and will) of the institution implementing the approach. It can be adopted on a small scale, day-by-day basis in a single subject course by an individual subject teacher, in a collaboration between language specialists and subject specialists, in a collaboration by subject teacher and/or language specialist with students, and in many other action-research or teaching arrangements.

Needs identified through the initial research have to be shared in meaningful and persuasive ways with participants so that they can be used in curriculum design, semiotic/metasemiotic mediation, and assessment. The sharing of research insights may happen informally, in the course of team teaching, for example, or in more formal workshop or mentoring arrangements. To provide an overview of how research into the context of teaching and learning can be designed into LASS-based curriculum design, semiotic/metasemiotic mediation, and assessment, Figure 7.3 represents the process of developing a LASS-based Communication Skills for Business Studies course at The Open University, UK. This is a distance education course and the materials are used by students who are studying at home. The needs analysis process was carried out by language specialists in liaison with Business Studies specialists (called

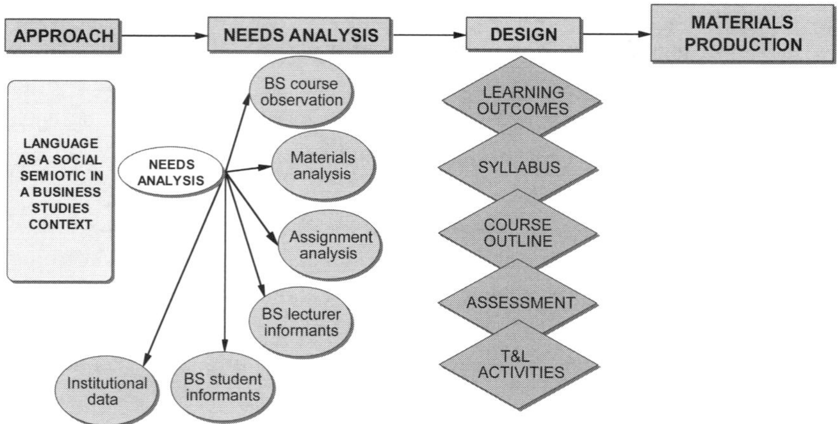

Figure 7.3 Developing a LASS-based Communication Skills for Business Studies course.

BS lecturer informants in the figure) and Business Studies students. These informants provided the language specialists with insider knowledge about the conceptual formations, genres, and registers of the Business Studies faculty and aspects of the students' experience of the teaching and learning of CAP Business Studies. The needs analysis was particularly focused on students' assignment texts from previous CAP Business Studies course presentations. This was combined with genre and register analysis of teaching and learning materials from these previous courses. More details about the course that was developed will be provided in Section 7.4.2.

7.4.2 Types of LASS Provision

There are five main types of LASS provision:

1. Language and learning awareness and development embedded within an academic subject syllabus.[3]
2. Language and learning awareness and development presented in an adjunct course running alongside a specific, related, academic subject course.
3. Language and learning awareness and development presented in a standalone course that introduces general principles of language and learning to students, making as much connection with the university curriculum as is possible but without being associated with a specific subject area or department.

4. Various kinds of individualized LASS provision for students, such as self-access online material or one-to-one language and learning counseling and coaching.
5. Various forms of subject-teacher language and learning awareness and development provision, delivered through online training material, training workshops, or academic practice development courses. These all introduce LASS principles and practices to academic subject teachers who can then transfer these to their own teaching and learning contexts.

These five types of LASS provision are elaborated further in the following sections.

7.4.2.1 Embedded LASS provision

In this case, the academic subject syllabus may be an already-existing one as demonstrated by the *Ways of Seeing* and *Ways of Writing* provisions in Chapter 4. Alternatively, a jointly constructed academic content and language development syllabus may be developed. In the Film Studies course, the context of teaching and learning was created by the academic subject teacher and the language syllabus, *Ways of Writing*, was mapped onto the well-established *Ways of Seeing* course. The collaboration led to some modifications to the content of the original *Ways of Seeing* syllabus. For example, recognizing the significance of the taxonomic film analysis genre led to taxonomic configurations of meaning in other parts of the *Ways of Seeing* syllabus receiving more attention than they might have otherwise. In a Maths, Computing and Technology (MCT) course that one of us collaborated in writing, a recognition by the subject specialists that students would benefit from developing subject-specific lexis meant that the MCT syllabus was modified to increase the amount of material designed for this purpose, and an area of technological lexis and related concept formations that had not previously been recognized by the MCT specialists—the use of analogy—were given more space.

7.4.2.2 Adjunct LASS provision

An embedded LASS approach can establish a powerful synergy between language and learning, but negotiating for metasemiotic mediation to have a place alongside semiotic mediation in an academic subject course is not always successful, and even when it is, language awareness activity can become so embedded that it actually disappears from sight. There is less risk of this in an adjunct course where there is more authority to engage in very active metasemiotic mediation and to organize a syllabus around this. An adjunct course is a CLIL course (see Chapter 1, Section 1.1.3), which is based closely on the

1. Culture of Business Studies

2. Register of Business Studies
What? (Field) Who? (Tenor) How? (Mode)

3. Conceptual formations to be developed
e.g., Porter's 5 Forces model

4. Cognitive Skills to be developed
e.g., analysis (of case studies)

5. Literacy/Language behaviors
e.g., reading and making notes on case studies

6. Genres: stages and phases
e.g. taxonomic case study analysis

7. Metafunctions (Ideational, Interpersonal, Textual)
e.g., cause-effect relations represented by means of ideational and textual resources

Figure 7.4 Main headings of a LASS-based syllabus for a Communication Skills for Business Studies adjunct course.

syllabi of one or more academic subject courses. In order to promote relevant language development, the adjunct course has to reconstruct as authentically as possible the teaching and learning context that exists in the academic subject courses.

Figure 7.4 outlines the main elements of the LASS-based syllabus that was developed for the purposes of those responsible for designing the Business Studies Communication adjunct course represented in Figure 7.3.

This was not the syllabus that was presented to students, but it informed the production of the materials and also the syllabus map that was given to students. The syllabus for students was written to reflect their core interest in Business Studies as a subject area. An illustration of this is provided in Figure 7.5, which presents the main headings of the first six units of the course. This part of the course taught a six-step *case study analysis* reading-into-writing process that created the context for metasemiotically mediating a range of Business Studies conceptual formations.

Sometimes adjunct provision cannot be as substantial as a full course and the LASS input must be adapted accordingly. The HSC collaboration described in Chapter 5 was much more closely wrapped around the existing HSC subject course and the LASS intervention was focused on making

Case Study Analysis

1. **Mapping the case**
   (Reading strategies, text structure; the U.S. airline industry)
2. **Framing the case**
   (Using Business Studies concepts: SWOT, STEP)
3. **Noticing influences and impacts**
   (Cause-effect; information flow; the credit industry)
4. **Identifying problems**
   (Problem-solution text structure; evaluation language; the clothing industry)
5. **Proposing solutions**
   (Possibility language; the motor industry)
6. **Evaluating the analysis**
   (Persuasive language)

Figure 7.5 Main headings of a LASS-based syllabus for students on a Communication Skills for Business Studies adjunct course.

very small changes to the assessment design of that course (as mentioned in Chapter 5) and the establishment of an online language and learning discussion forum for students and teachers. Despite the early limitations, the collaboration created the opportunity to carry out the research described in Chapter 5, and this in turn is leading to a more substantial collaboration where some embedding of LASS principles in the main subject course is being discussed.

7.4.2.3 Standalone LASS provision

As demonstrated by the Film Studies and HSC LASS-based research, semantic variation is a characteristic of student cohorts within an academic subject area. It is likely to be even more pronounced in standalone LASS provision catering to students from across the university curriculum. An example of a course that incorporates awareness of semantic orientation into its design is provided by a standalone online LASS course at The Open University. As this is a general-purpose cross-curriculum course, students are required to work with texts from outside their areas of academic interest. Students deal with conceptual formations, genres, and registers that they might never encounter away from this course: history students read and write science texts, science students work with history texts. To motivate this cross-curricular activity, students are asked to adopt an ethnographer-like approach, in which they explore different areas of the university environment (drawing on work by Johns, 1997). This student-as-ethnographer approach encourages students to reflect on ways of writing and making meaning across the curriculum and also on their own commitments and orientations. It creates opportunities to actively bring semantic orientation into focus.

In general, building awareness of semantic orientation into LASS provisions means creating space in which students are encouraged to reflect on the semiotic mediation and metasemiotic mediation they are experiencing during the course and to develop their own metasemiotic mediation practices in the process. It also means subject and language teachers considering the implications of semantic variation among students in their framing of any of the LASS models of teaching and learning presented here.

7.4.2.4 Individualized LASS provision for students and LASS training for subject teachers

Seeing students as ethnographers of the meaning-making practices of the academic communities that constitute higher education and recognizing that they come to their study with diverse meaning-making resources and predispositions are perspectives that can inform the syllabus of all types of LASS provision. These perspectives, combined with the principles of LASS-based teaching and learning presented in the next section and knowledge about language that has been described throughout this monograph (and is summarized in Section 7.7.2 below), are ones to exploit in one-to-one LASS sessions with students and to raise awareness of in academic subject teacher training sessions. In this way, LASS principles can feed into the semiotic mediation, and hopefully the metasemiotic mediation, of academic subject provision across a university.

7.5 LASS-Based Teaching and Learning

A LASS approach to teaching and learning is not a discrete or alternative approach that replaces other approaches. It is a perspective that can be mapped onto existing forms of teaching, contributing the insights of semiotic awareness to the semiotic mediation that already constitutes those existing approaches, and metasemiotic mediation as a further enhancement of them. It can make a contribution both to subject teaching and to the various forms of language and study skills teaching which are offered in higher education institutions (see the list of such provision at the beginning of Section 7.2). Figure 7.6 provides a list of the principles for implementing LASS-based teaching and learning that have emerged for us through the research and teaching described throughout this monograph.

1. Teaching and learning are processes of visible semiotic mediation in which teachers and students alternate as semiotic initiators and semiotic responders.
2. Visible semiotic mediation of an academic subject involves learning the language of the subject and learning the subject through language.
3. Visible semiotic mediation can be enhanced by metasemiotic mediation, in which participants learn about language as a meaning-making resource in teaching and learning the subject.
4. A central process in visible semiotic mediation is building conceptual formations, in which decontextualized meanings play a key role.
5. The language behavior that is particularly significant in building conceptual formations is *turning reading into writing.*
6. Metasemiotic mediation entails getting inside meaning-making processes by means of LASS-based textual analysis, including mediated text analysis discussion.
7. A LASS approach recognizes four interrelated elements of teaching and learning:
   i) What texts do and how they do it (i.e., genre and register)
   ii) The subject matter that texts deal with (i.e., conceptual formations and social processes)
   iii) The processes that readers and writers employ in their engagement with academic texts (i.e., language behaviors, sometimes referred to as "study skills" in the case of students)
   iv) The ways of thinking, feeling, and using language that teachers and learners bring to the academic environment (i.e., semantic orientations and identity)
8. In a LASS perspective, language has three overarching functions:
   i) to represent experience (ideational meanings)
   ii) to build interpersonal relationships (interpersonal meanings)
   iii) to construct texts (textual meanings)
9. Metasemiotically mediating language means bringing to attention:
   i) how ideational, interpersonal, and textual meanings are made in relation to the contextual variables of field, tenor, and mode (register)
   ii) how texts organize and/or construct conceptual formations for particular purposes, by means of genre staging and phasing
   iii) how thematic development and other cohesive devices support configurations of meaning in texts
10. Metasemiotically mediating learning and teaching in relation to identity and semantic orientation means seeking to explicate the diversity of interpretations and meaning-making resources teachers and students arrive with, deploy, and develop in an academic environment.

Figure 7.6 Principles for implementing LASS-based visible semiotic mediation.

Chapters 4, 5, and 6 provide examples of how these principles were applied and adapted in a number of particular contexts. In this section, we show how the principles can be applied more generally across the five main forms of LASS provision that were presented in Section 7.4.2. In order to help with this level of generalization, we exploit a well-known and widely used framework for university teaching and learning developed by Laurillard to inform the use of learning technologies in the digitally mediated university (see Laurillard, 2002, 2012). Called *The Conversational Framework*, it was Laurillard's attempt to generalize from the available research into learning, from which she identified five key elements that constitute learning and teaching at the university level. We recognize that, as with all generalizations, the five elements of the Conversational Framework oversimplify the diversity of practices that constitute real day-to-day learning and teaching and also that Laurillard's is one framework among many that have sought to represent teaching and learning at the university level. However, we are using it to demonstrate how a LASS approach maps onto a framework that is cognitive rather than linguistic in its orientation as an illustration of how a LASS perspective could enhance any form of subject or language teaching across a university.

The five elements of the Conversational Framework that Laurillard proposes are presented in Figure 7.7 and explained in the following sections:

7.5.1 Students Apprehending Structure

It is a subject-teacher's responsibility to have knowledge of how their field of study is configured as conceptual formations by means of the genres (i.e., the goal-oriented social processes) of the field. The visible semiotic mediation that constitutes teaching generally is intended to enable students to apprehend these structures of knowledge and engage in these processes. In a LASS approach, it is our proposal that awareness of the semiotic system of language can enhance the mediation processes in two ways:

The Conversational Framework
Students apprehending structure
Students interpreting forms of representation of the world
Students acting on descriptions of the world
Teachers (and students) providing feedback on descriptions of the world
Students (and teachers) reflecting on the learning cycle

Figure 7.7 The Conversational Framework (See Laurillard, 2002, pp. 60-61 and 72).

i) by illuminating the knowledge structures and social processes that teachers are mediating and
ii) by providing a language and concepts for engaging in metasemiotic mediation that articulates explicitly the ways that the structures of the syllabus are configured and the social processes realized.

Chapters 4 and 5 present a number of examples of how a LASS approach was used in apprehending the structures of knowledge that constituted the Film Studies and HSC syllabuses. In the Film Studies course, the structure of taxonomic film analysis provided a model for a wide range of structure-apprehending activities (some of which are presented in the appendices to the chapter). These include reading activities based on awareness of text structure, writing tasks that replicated or diverged from the structure of taxonomic film analysis, and end-of-lecture reviews in which students present visual representations of the conceptual formations they developed during the lecture. Underpinning this metasemiotic mediation of structure in Film Studies texts was the pedagogic procedure referred to in Chapter 4 (Figure 4.11) as "deconstructing and reconstructing genres." This is a metasemiotic strategy developed by SFL researchers in Australia and generally referred to as the "genre teaching and learning cycle" (see Humphrey & Macnaught, 2011, and Rose et al., 2008, for applications in higher education and Rose & Martin, 2012, for its origins in the school sector).

The genre teaching and learning cycle consists of the following four elements:

i) Deconstruction of a text to show how it construes, through language, ideational, interpersonal, and textual meanings in relation to its register and genre;
ii) Joint construction of a new text with similar configurations of meaning;
iii) Individual construction of a comparable text; and
iv) Critique, for example, of the choice of genre and of the meanings made.

We have not implemented this cycle systematically in the LASS pedagogy reported in this monograph, but the cycle informs the procedures we have implemented.

In the HSC context described in Chapter 5, two additional metasemiotic procedures for apprehending how meanings are structured were introduced: mediated text analysis discussion and text redesign (see Chapter 5, Figure 5.12). In mediated text analysis discussion, HSC students were prompted to apprehend the structure of their assignment texts and, at the end of the discussions, were shown the genre staging for the argument assignment they had written (see Chapter 5, Table 5.2). It was evident from their responses that this explication of the structure of the argument genre was appreciated. Once the ambiguity of the background stage of Zuna's exposition was explained by means of mediated text analysis discussion, it was possible to model a redesigned version of the stage. The purpose of such text redesign is to prompt students to notice how genre staging and phases (in this case, conceptual framing of the case study material) can reconfigure conceptual formations. A key feature of this particular redesign was to model the transition from more conceptual to more material information and through this bring to Zuna's attention the function of decontextualized and contextualized language. Such redesign, like all metasemiotic mediation, is intended to do more than simply support the apprehension of the structure of the text under consideration. It offers students (and teachers) insights into how meanings are structured by texts that they can continue to employ in their study of the subject area. As Laurillard proposes, apprehending structure is central to learning.

In each of the five forms of LASS provision, the apprehension of structure in a subject syllabus depends on collaboration between subject and language specialists, reflecting the needs analysis approach outlined in Section 7.3 of this chapter. Such collaboration can be facilitated by the use of the SFL based checklists mentioned in Section 7.3.2: MASUS (Bonanno & Jones, 2007) and the 3 × 3 Framework (Humphrey et al., 2010). The former was used in the Film Studies LASS approach we discussed in Chapter 4, and the latter is currently being adapted for use in an MCT language, teaching, and learning collaboration we are involved in. These instruments focus on the structure of students' assignment texts and, once developed collaboratively by language, subject specialists, and/or students, can be shared with students for self-analysis of the structure of their own texts.

7.5.2 Students Interpreting Forms of Representation

From a LASS perspective, students use semiotic resources (their repertoires) to interpret and represent the world in semiotic forms that correspond with (or diverge from) the representations of the world that are provided by their teachers and study materials. In 2002, Laurillard commented, "surprisingly little has been done on how students interpret teachers' language, how they read academic texts, and how they interpret graphical and symbolic information" (2002, p. 22). In fact, as our references to SFL research in Chapter 2 showed, and our accounts throughout this monograph have illustrated, a LASS approach provides a response to the need Laurillard identified. We argue that, through LASS-based research into how students and teachers create and configure conceptual formations by means of genre staging, phasing, and lexicogrammatical systems, both teachers and students are offered insights into how semiotic resources are used to represent the world. Such insights can be transferred into teaching and learning contexts where reciprocal semiotic and metasemiotic mediation activities will benefit from and further develop them.

7.5.3 Students Acting on Descriptions of the World

The semiotic resources that a student brings into the learning environment are the tools they have at their disposal to act in that environment. From semiotic interactions (particularly in the form of assignments, but also other metasemiotic interactions like mediated text analysis), teachers obtain insights into students' conceptual formations, their semiotic resources, and their semantic orientations, particularly their predispositions toward decontextualized and perspectival meanings. According to Laurillard, it is essential for the teacher to recognize alignment and misalignment between a student's representations of the world and the teacher's. We have shown how a LASS approach provides tools for metasemiotic mediation that focuses on students' engagement with teachers' descriptions of the world and also on students' own descriptions of the world, and this enhances visible semiotic mediation whether it is the teacher or the learner who is in the semiotic initiator or responder role.

It is particularly important in LASS provision that explications of representations of the world and the symbolic resources by which they are represented are mediated in motivating ways, not simply presented as information. These ways should include problem-solving investigation, hypothesis formation and testing, and experimental reconfigurations of meanings. A LASS approach depends on active semiotic mediation taking place. Without this, the apprehension of structure and the interpretation of forms of representation may be shallow rather than deep semiotic activities and conceptual formations with impoverished decontextualized meanings may be developed.

7.5.4 Teachers (or Other Students) Providing Feedback on Students' Descriptions of the World

In part, the purpose of apprehending structures is so that a learner can align their conceptual formations of the field with those presented by the teacher or in the literature. Feedback from teachers provides students with information about how aligned their descriptions are. Such feedback most obviously occurs when teachers respond to students' assignments. But it can also occur in seminars, in laboratories, in question and answer sections of a lecture, or in online forums.

Students will also be involved in giving or obtaining feedback with peers, both formally and informally.

Teacher feedback can take the form of redescriptions designed to scaffold students' recognition of how their descriptions align. Redescriptions like this were demonstrated in Chapter 5, where remodeled paragraphs from Zuna's and Nimet's assignments were presented as prompts for them to review their conceptual formations and the social processes they had engaged in. Chapter 6 contained examples of teachers intervening in and providing feedback on student participation in forum discussions. In providing feedback, teachers need to recognize that they are expert readers and writers who carry out complex semiotic processes of which they may by now be totally unaware: their complex semiotic resources are "the sea in which they swim." For teaching purposes, they need to become aware of these resources in a defamiliarized and detailed way in order to scaffold students who are not so experienced with using them.

Metasemiotically mediating interaction means looking through language at what it means and at language for how it means. These semiotic mediating processes can be carried out at the same time or separately, but it is usually better not to address the how before the what. Looking at how language means before looking at what it means will lead to a formal rather than functional understanding of language and separate language from learning. In order to operationalize this insight, we have attempted in Chapters 4–6 to show how language can be treated as both form and content at the same time. This corresponds with the position we have proposed throughout the monograph, that learning entails learning through language, learning language, and learning about language.

The challenges for academic subject specialist teacher-researchers attempting to do this is to develop sufficient insight into the LASS principles this monograph has proposed. There is a corresponding challenge for a language specialist teacher-researcher; this is to develop sufficient insight into the academic subject area to enable them to carry out the LASS analysis required. Where LASS provision is based on collaborative partnerships, subject and language specialists can support each other in this. In other provision, subject or language specialists must make the most of their own insights (for a discussion of this, see Donohue & Erling, 2012).

7.5.5 Students (and Teachers) Reflecting on the Learning Cycle

In the research into deep or shallow learning, shallow learning is often associated with students attempting to fulfill the teacher's goals in a learning task without developing awareness of the underlying problem that the task was designed to address (Laurillard, 2002, p. 60). An example of such an approach was provided during the mediated text discussion with Zuna, when she explained how she had followed closely each of the steps in the assignment guidance notes rather than engaging in the discussion process the assignment was designed to promote. Recognition and critique by students of the underlying conceptual formations and social processes their study is presenting to them is the essence of the Reflection Literacy that Hasan was quoted as proposing in Chapter 2, Section 2.6.3, and of the genre teaching and learning cycle referred to earlier in this section. Metasemiotic mediation is one process for fostering such reflection and critique.

Awareness of semiotic processes can also lead to teachers' reflection on their own role in semiotic mediation. The LASS analysis of HSC assignment design in Chapter 5 gave HSC teachers the chance to reflect on the value of the assignment genre trajectory through their course, the wording of assignments tasks seen from a genre perspective, and the desirability of providing genre schemata and register descriptions in the assignment notes. At the same time, the results of the mediated text analysis discussions, with their indications of semantic variation among students, raised questions about how assignment guidance can best scaffold learning and evaluation processes in the light of the diverse ways in which students interpret and implement assignment guidance.

7.5.6 A LASS-Based Approach to the Conversational Framework

In applying a LASS approach to the Conversational Framework, the intention was to demonstrate how the principles for implementing LASS-based visible semiotic mediation could be applied to a widely used representation of the teaching and learning processes of higher education. The synergies between the two approaches underscore the relevance of a LASS approach and its value to university teaching and learning. Laurillard is not a linguist, but it is our contention that a LASS approach is not only compatible with her cognition-based approach, but also provides metasemiotic insights that can support its implementation.

7.6 LASS-Based Assessment

In an early investigation of the criteria applied by subject and English language specialists in assessing student writing and learning (Hamp-Lyons, 1991), each set of specialists was asked to place twelve assessment criteria in rank order (see Figure 7.8). This revealed significant differences between the specialists' priorities. Subject specialists ranked "quality of content" at number 1, while

	English language specialists	**Subject specialists**
1	Organization of text	Quality of content
2	Development of ideas	Assignment requirements
3	Paragraph organization	Addresses topic
4	Addresses topic	Development of ideas
5	Overall writing	Organization of text
6	Sentence structure	Overall writing
7	Appropriate to audience	Vocabulary usage
8	Assignment requirements	Paragraph organization
9	Quality of content	Sentence structure

Figure 7.8 Priorities for language and subject specialists in marking student assignments.

language specialists ranked it 9; subject specialists ranked "assignment requirements" at 2 while language specialists ranked it at 8; subject specialists ranked "organization of text" at 5 while language specialists ranked it at 1, subject specialists ranked "paragraph organization" at 8 while language specialists ranked it at 3 (Hamp Lyons, 1991, p. 133).

This research was done at a time when there was far less contact between English language and subject specialists. We would expect to find a closer correlation between the specialists' rankings today. In a LASS approach, the correlation ought to be very close indeed. Assessment design should be based on the kinds of research outlined in Section 7.2.1, applying or refining the criteria developed for the MASUS or 3 × 3 Framework rubrics or their equivalent.

How far a department is willing to incorporate LASS criteria into their grading rubric for subject assessment will depend on their conviction about a LASS approach. In the Film Studies department described in Chapter 4, LASS criteria were used in parallel with subject criteria in formative assignments during the course but were not taken into consideration for the marking of the final assignment, which was summative. In a standalone or adjunct LASS course, LASS criteria can appear easier to apply in assessment. However, as the disparity between English language and subject teachers' priorities in the table above shows, the risk is that content slips out of sight in the assessment for such courses. As far as possible, the course and assessment design should avoid this.

7.7 Issues in Implementing LASS

In this monograph, we have presented examples of successful LASS provision. However, there are of course challenges in adopting a LASS approach, some of which are acknowledged in this section.

7.7.1 Diverse Conceptions of "Language"

We began this chapter with the suggestion that "most people take language for granted; it's the transparent medium in which we swim." To defamiliarize language, to make it an object that we look at, to turn language on its head so that rather than see it as the carrier of meaning we see it as the maker of meaning requires something of a paradigm shift. This is a shift that may be needed among institutional policy makers, teachers, and learners. One useful technique for tackling university teachers' diverse conceptual formations of "language" is to present them with a version of the list of LASS pedagogic principles presented in Figure 7.1 or 7.6. For many university teachers this represents a challenge to their preconceptions (their conceptual formations) about language and can consequently be difficult to read. In this sense it is an object lesson in that it exemplifies experientially the kind of encounter with paradigm shifting conceptual formations that their students are continuously engaged in. Through this experience, the value of metasemiotic mediation can be reinforced for subject teachers and the list of principles themselves provide practical pointers toward ways of implementing it.

7.7.2 Knowledge About Language (KAL)

Throughout this monograph, we have tried to show how SFL provides the KAL that will enhance the processes of semiotic and metasemiotic mediation. However, SFL is an "extravagant" theory (Halliday, 1994, p. xix), which means it is both extensive and complex. Using Bernstein's (1996) construct of the pedagogic device as a metaphor, recontextualizing SFL for use in university teaching and learning means reducing its scope and complexity. The nature of the reduction depends on the context and purposes for which it is being used and the expertise of the users.

As with the promotion of all conceptual formations, the conceptual formation of SFL has to be connected somehow with existing conceptual formations of the teachers and learners it is being introduced to. To a certain extent this can be achieved by building the metalanguage of SFL on metalanguage that is already in use among teachers and learners. For example, Coffin et al. (2009) attempted to add a functional grammar perspective onto the kind of formal grammar that has underpinned language study for centuries and which many teachers may be familiar with. There are two challenges to this approach: (i) not all teachers have a knowledge of traditional formal grammar and (ii) the conversion of a formal grammar perspective into a functional grammar perspective involves appropriating threshold concepts of the most transformative type. However, to ameliorate these challenges, the research in Chapters 4–6 of

Figure 7.9 The reading-into-writing process represented by using a Business Studies transformation process diagram.

this monograph demonstrate that only a limited number of concepts and terms from SFL are needed in order to carry out metasemiotic analysis and influence semiotic and metasemiotic mediation.

A different approach to KAL is to exploit terms and concepts that are already being taught and used in the field of study in which a LASS approach is being introduced. This was demonstrated for Film Studies in Chapter 4, where Film Studies terms like continuity editing or establishing shot, were transferred analogously into the *Ways of Writing* strand of the course and used to metasemiotically mediate cohesion, coherence, Theme, and so on in written text. Such an approach works particularly in fields of study where text is already one of the objects of study. In other fields, though, it is also possible to exploit field-specific terms and concepts to bring about meta-awareness of semiotic processes. In the adjunct Business Studies Communication course referred to in Section 7.4.2, the case study analysis syllabus in Figure 7.6 was presented to students as based on a model they would already be familiar with from Business Studies for representing an organization as a transformative system (see Figure 7.9). This Business Studies model was appropriated analogously in order to metasemiotically mediate the language behaviors of case study analysis.

Nonetheless, it is important to remember the paradigm shift that is entailed in adopting a LASS perspective. The knowledge about language that is needed is knowledge about language as a set of resources for creating meanings in context. As already mentioned, this entails looking *through* language for what it means at the same time as looking *at* language for how it means. This is an orientation toward language that entails defamiliarizing it so that it loses its transparency and can be examined, while at the same time it maintains its functional value.

An essential element of knowledge about language is the diversity among the meaning-making resources that have been acquired by individuals, which has been referred to as semantic variation in this monograph. How KAL is configured by each participant will depend on their semantic orientation and consequent interpretation of the contexts of teaching and learning. The students in Chapter 5 exemplify this strikingly. Despite all having studied the same metasemiotic advice in the assignment guidance notes, their interpretation and implementation of this advice varied considerably. Even where it seems the same KAL has been promoted, the conceptual formations of participants will not constitute identical representations of this knowledge.

7.7.3 Multimodality

As noted in various places in this monograph, language is one semiotic resource among many and there is a burgeoning of different resources alongside language in the new media age. In particular, the visual mode and the use of graphics are becoming more and more integrated into university teaching and learning (through the use of video clips, data visualization, extensive use of graphics, etc.). Nevertheless, we made the case at the outset of this monograph that in our view language (primarily written language) remains central to the construction, recontextualization, and assessment of knowledge. It is the primary social semiotic that mediates and orchestrates other semiotic modes.

We are nevertheless aware that there "is a clear stance in the literature that new technologies and the increasingly multimodal nature of communication are toppling a perceived dominance of text as written and spoken language" (Twiner, Coffin, Littleton, & Whitelock, 2010, p. 216). Jewitt and Kress (2003), for example, argued a decade ago that "a multimodal approach to learning starts from a theoretical position that treats all modes as equally significant for meaning and communication, potentially so at least" (2003, p. 2) and, although in the second decade of the 21st century it does not seem that any one mode or combination of modes have threatened the centrality of written communication, it is nevertheless the case that students are increasingly called upon to both interpret and construct multimodal ensembles of meaning. The orchestrated interplay among various modes is therefore an area for attention in any LASS implementation, and complementary tools of analysis (SFL multimodal discourse analysis as O'Halloran, 2008, terms it) are currently being developed for this purpose (see Archer, 2010; Guo, 2004). Developments in the genres of written language driven by online technology which were considered in Chapter 6 will no doubt continue and a LASS approach will develop in response to the changing use of language in the increasingly digitally mediated environments of higher education.

7.7.4 Other Issues

There are a number of other questions about implementing a LASS approach that we will recognize here as areas for further research but not attempt to answer.

General or specific LASS courses?

As outlined in Section 7.4.2, LASS courses can be embedded in or closely related to particular academic subject areas or they can be standalone and general. As suggested in Section 7.4.2, general LASS courses can support an understanding of the movement from contextualized to decontextualized meaning-making, the notion of threshold concepts and in general introduce genre and register awareness. However, there is also evidence that provision of language and learning development outside its immediate context of use is demotivating and risks becoming formalistic. As mentioned in Chapter 5, this was the experience of the film students in Chapter 5 before they took part in the contextualized LASS course described there.

First level of university study or throughout a degree program?

Language and learning development is traditionally treated as something for newcomers to the university. In fact, the journey into decontextualized and more and more complex configurations of meaning goes on throughout a university program.

Explicit versus implicit application of LASS?

In our approach, we have proposed metasemiotic mediation as an explication of semiotic processes, based on the sharing of language specialists' knowledge about language (from SFL analysis) with subject teachers and students. On the other hand, it would be possible for LASS insights to be used by language specialists in an implicit way, informing their collaborations with students and subject teachers without being explicated.

Politics of collaboration/partnership/teamwork?

As we observed in the introduction to this chapter, sites of semiotic mediation are sites of power, identity, and relationship formation. Introducing a LASS approach to learning and teaching at university depends on negotiating the politics of collaboration, in terms, for example, of economic resources, territory, location of expertise, and interchangeablity of staff.

The institutional challenges are complex and rather than engage with them in detail here, we offer an institutional change framework that we have developed through our LASS work (Figure 7.10). It has been used successfully to

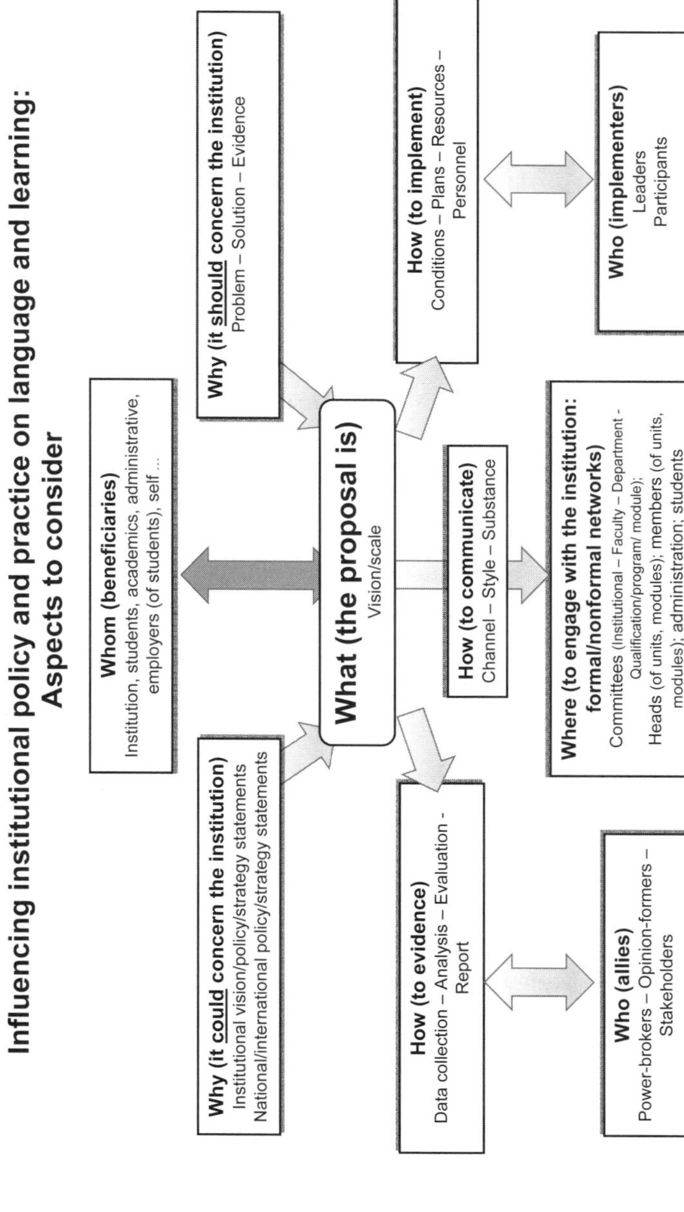

Figure 7.10 Institutional change processes for promoting a LASS approach to teaching and learning.

promote reflection in international workshops (e.g., Donohue & Ganobcsik-Williams, 2013) and informs our continuing efforts to promote a LASS approach within our own institution.

7.8 Conclusion

The theory of language as social semiotic is a complex conceptual formation composed of highly decontextualized meanings. At the same time, like the applied academic subject areas that have been the context for the LASS research and teaching we have reported on in this monograph, we propose that it is relevant to highly contextualized situations of communicative interaction and to participants of widely differing predispositions. In order to achieve its objectives, LASS uses the same semiotic tools that it is intending to investigate: it turns language back upon itself. The defamiliarization of the "transparent medium in which we swim" that this leads to makes the theory of language as a social semiotic one of the most transformative threshold conceptual formations (Meyer & Land, 2005) we can attempt to engage with. In the midst of the demands of the everyday semiotic mediation of university-level teaching and learning, the challenges of implementing a language as social semiotic approach may seem somewhat daunting. But complexity and the risk of the transformation of worldview have never been regarded as acceptable justifications for students to avoid deep learning. Neither should they be justifications for teachers to avoid deep teaching.

Notes

1 As mentioned in Chapter 1, Professor Alan Tait was Pro Vice-Chancellor (Academic) at The Open University from 2007–2012. He made this comment in an interview the authors held with him concerning language, learning, and institutional change. Because of its felicity for a LASS perspective on language we have referred to it a number of times throughout the monograph.

2 In the UK, some universities make a distinction between general research and institutionally focused "scholarship" research. The latter is usually funded internally and focuses its questions and data collection on the institution in which the scholars are working. Often it investigates teaching and learning (e.g., assessment design and progression, patterns of feedback, student motivation,etc.).

3 More accurately we should say "disembedded," since the language syllabus in fact explicates language use that is already occurring in the teaching and learning of the academic subject curriculum.

References

Archer, A. (2010). Multimodal texts in higher education and the implications for writing pedagogy. *English in Education*, *44*, 201–213.

Bakhtin, M. M. (1982). *The dialogic imagination: Four essays*. Austin: University of Texas Press.

Bernstein, B. (1971). *Class, codes and control: Theoretical studies towards a sociology of language (Vol. 1)*. London: Routledge and Kegan Paul.

Bernstein, B. (1990). *The structuring of pedagogic discourse: Class codes and control*. London: Routledge.

Bernstein, B. (1996). *Pedagogy, symbolic control and identity: Theory, research, critique*. London: Taylor and Francis.

Bernstein, B. (1999). Vertical and horizontal discourse: An essay. *British Journal of Sociology of Education*, *20*(2), 157–173.

Bhabha, H. K. (1990). The third space—An interview with Homi Bhabha. In J. Rutherford (Ed.), *Identity: Community, culture, difference* (pp. 207–221). London: Lawrence & Wishart.

Blackwell, J. (2011). *The text-compositional architecture of university lectures*. Unpublished doctoral dissertation, University of Birmingham, UK.

Bloor, T., & Bloor, M. (2013). *The functional analysis of English: A Hallidayan approach* (3rd ed.). Oxon, UK: Routledge.

Bonanno, H., & Jones, J. (2007). *The MASUS procedure: Measuring the academic skills of university students: A diagnostic assessment* (3rd ed.). Sydney, Australia: Learning Centre, University of Sydney.

Bordwell, D. (1989). *Making meaning: Inference and rhetoric in the interpretation of cinema*. Cambridge, MA: Harvard University Press.

Bruner, J. (1990). *Acts of meaning*. Cambridge, MA: Harvard University Press.

Buckingham Shum, S. (2012). *Learning analytics*. Moscow, Russia: Policy Briefing, UNESCO Institute for Information Technologies in Education. Retrieved from http://www.iite.unesco.org/publications/3214711

Chen, Y., & Foley, J. A. (2004). Problems with the metaphorical reconstrual of meaning in Chinese EFL learners' expositions. In L. J. Ravelli & R. A. Ellis (Eds.), *Analysing academic writing: Contextualized frameworks* (pp. 190–209). London: Continuum.

Christie, F. (2012). *Language education throughout the school years: A functional perspective*. Hoboken, NJ: Wiley-Blackwell.

DOI: 10.1111/lang.12044

Christie, F., & Derewianka, B. (2008). *School discourse: Learning to write across the years of schooling*. London: Continuum.

Christie, F., & Martin, J. R. (2005). *Genre and institutions: Social processes in the workplace and school*. New York: Bloomsbury Academic. (Original work published 1997)

Clanchy, J., & Ballard, B. (1998). *How to write essays: A practical guide for students* (3rd ed.). South Melbourne, Australia: Addison-Wesley Longman.

Cloran, C. (1994). *Rhetorical units and decontextualisation: An enquiry into some relations of context, meaning and grammar*. Nottingham, UK: University of Nottingham.

Coffin, C. (2004). Arguing about how the world is or how the world should be: The role of argument in IELTS tests. *Journal of English for Academic Purposes*, *3*, 229–246.

Coffin, C. (2006). *Historical discourse: The language of time, cause and evaluation*. London: Continuum.

Coffin, C. (2010). Incorporating and evaluating voices in a film studies thesis. *Writing and Pedagogy*, *1*, 163–193.

Coffin, C., & Derewianka, B. (2008). Multimodal layout in school history books: The texturing of historical interpretation. In G. Thompson & G. Forey (Eds.), *Text-type and Texture* (pp. 191–215). London: Equinox.

Coffin, C., & Donohue, J. P. (2012). Academic literacies and systemic functional linguistics: How do they relate? *Journal of English for Academic Purposes*, *11*(1), 64–75.

Coffin, C., Donohue, J., & North, S. (2009). *Exploring grammar: From formal to functional*. London: Routledge.

Coffin, C., & Hewings, A. (2005). Engaging electronically: Using CMC to develop students' argumentation skills in higher education. *Language and Education*, *19*, 32–49.

Coffin, C., North, S. P., & Hewings, A. (2012). Arguing as an academic purpose: The role of asynchronous conferencing in supporting argumentative dialogue in school and university. Special edition of *Journal of English for Academic Purposes, 11/1,* 38–51.

Coffin, C., Painter, C., & Hewings, A. (2005). Patterns of debate in tertiary level asynchronous electronic conferencing. *Special Edition of the International Journal of Educational Research*, *43*, 464–480.

Crystal, D. (2006). *Language and the Internet*. Cambridge, UK: Cambridge University Press. (Original work published 2001)

Deleuze, G., & Guattari, F. (1987). *A thousand plateaus*. London: Continuum. (Original work published 1980)

Derewianka, B. (2011). *A new grammar companion for teachers*. Sydney, Australia: Primary English Teaching Association.

Donohue, J. (2012). Using systemic functional linguistics in academic writing development: An example from film studies. *Journal of English for Academic Purposes*, *11*, 4–16.

Donohue, J., & Coffin, C. (2012). Health and social care professionals in the academy: A systemic functional linguistics perspective. *Journal of Applied Linguistics and Professional Practice*, *9*, 7–60.

Donohue, J., & Erling, E. J. (2012). Investigating the relationship between the use of English for academic purposes and academic attainment. *Journal of English for Academic Purposes*, *11*, 210–219.

Donohue, J., & Ganobcsik-Williams, L. (2013, June). *Influencing institutional policy on academic writing*. Workshop at European Association of Teachers of Academic Writing Conference. Budapest, Hungary.

Dreyfus, S., Humphrey, S., Mahboob, A., & Martin, J. R. (in press). *Genre pedagogy in higher education: (SLATE) project*. Basingstoke, UK: Palgrave.

Dreyfus, S., Macnaught, L., & Humphrey, S. (2011). Understanding joint construction in the tertiary context. *Linguistics and the Human Sciences*, *4*, 135–160.

Dreyfus, S., & Martin, J. R. (2012). Scaffolding semogenesis: Designing teacher/student interactions for face-to-face and on-line learning. In S. Starc, A. Maiorani, & C. Jones (Eds.), *Meaning-making processes in text*. London: Equinox.

Drury, H. (2001). Short answers in first-year undergraduate science writing: What kind of genres are they? In M. Hewings (Ed.), *Academic writing in context: Implications and applications* (pp. 104–121). Birmingham, UK: University of Birmingham Press.

Drury, H. (2004). Teaching academic writing on-screen: A search for best practice. In L. Ravelli & R. Ellis (Eds.), *Analysing academic writing* (pp. 233–253). London: Continuum.

Drury, H., Airey, D., & O'Carroll, P. (2010). Improving report writing for undergraduate students in engineering through an online learning environment: The case of second year civil engineering. *Proceedings of the 2010 AAEE Conference*. Retrieved April, 2012, from http://www.aaee.com.au/A-14

Drury, H., Langrish, T., & O'Carroll, P. (2006). Online approach to teaching report writing in chemical engineering: Implementation and evaluation. *International Journal of Engineering Education*, *22*, 858–867.

Dysthe, O. (2002). The learning potential of a Web-mediated discussion in a university course. *Studies in Higher Education, 27*(3), 339–352.

Eggins, S. (2005). *An introduction to systemic functional linguistics* (2nd ed.). London: Continuum.

Elliot, N. D. (1997). *Media studies in higher education: A case study of the construction and reception of pedagogic discourse*. Unpublished doctoral dissertation, University of London, UK.

Elliot, N. D. (2000). Pedagogic discourse in theory-practice courses in media studies. *Screen*, *41*, 18–32.

Ellis, R. A. (2004). Supporting genre-based literacy pedagogy with technology—The implications for the framing and classification of the pedagogy. In L. J. Ravelli & R. A. Ellis (Eds.), *Analysing academic writing*, (pp. 210–232). London: Continuum.

Erling, E. J., & Richardson, J. T. E. (2011). Measuring the academic skills of university students: Evaluation of a diagnostic procedure. *Assessing writing*, *15*, 177–193.

Ferguson, R. (2012). Learning analytics: Drivers, developments and challenges. *International Journal of Technology Enhanced Learning*, *4*, 304–317.

Frean, A. (2008, December 18). "Mickey Mouse" studies are no longer a laughing stock. *The Times*.

Freire, P. (1972). *Pedagogy of the oppressed*. London: Penguin.

Gardner, S. (2008). Mapping ideational meaning in a corpus of student writing. In C. Jones & E. Ventola (Eds.), *New developments in the study of ideational meaning: From language to multimodality* (pp.169–188). London: Equinox.

Gardner, S., & Nesi, H. (2013). A classification of genre families in university student writing. *Applied Linguistics*, *34*, 25–52.

Gibbons, P. (2006). *Bridging discourses in the ESL classroom*. London: Continuum.

Giddens, A. (1979). *Central problems in social theory: Action, structure and contradiction in social analysis*. Berkeley: University of California Press.

Guo, L. B. (2004). Multimodality in a biology textbook. In K. O'Halloran (Ed.), *Multimodal discourse analysis: Systemic functional perspectives* (pp. 196–219). London: Continuum.

Halliday, M. A. K. (1975). *Learning how to mean: Explorations in the development of language*. London: Edward Arnold.

Halliday, M. A. K. (1978). *Language as social semiotic*. London: Hodder-Arnold.

Halliday, M. A. K. (1994). *An introduction to functional grammar*. London: Edward Arnold.

Halliday, M. A. K. (2003). *On language and linguistics*. London: Continuum.

Halliday, M. A. K. (2004). Three aspects of children's language development: Learning language, learning through language, learning about language. In J. J. Webster (Ed.), *The language of early childhood* (pp. 308–326). New York: Continuum.

Halliday, M. A. K., & Martin, J. R. (1993). *Writing science, literacy and discursive power*. Basingstoke, UK: Falmer Press.

Halliday, M. A. K., & Matthiessen, C. M. I. M. (2004). *Introduction to Functional Grammar,* (3rd ed). London: Edward Arnold.

Halliday, M. A. K., & Matthiessen, C. (2006). *Construing experience through meaning: A language-based approach to cognition*. London: Continuum.

Hamp Lyons, L. (1991). Reconstructing academic writing proficiency. In L. Hamp-Lyons (Ed.), *Assessing L2 writing in academic contexts* (pp. 127–153). Norwood, NJ: Ablex.

Hannan, A., & Silver, H. (2000). *Innovating in higher education: Teaching, learning and institutional cultures*. Berkshire, UK: The Open University Press.

Hao, J., & Humphrey, S. (2012). The role of "coupling" in biological experimental reports. *Linguistics and the Human Sciences*, *5*, 169–194.

Hasan, R. (1996). Literacy, everyday talk and society. In R. Hasan & G. Williams (Eds), *Literacy in society*. London: Addison Wesley Longman.

Hasan, R. (2005). *Language, society and consciousness*. London: Equinox.

Hasan, R. (2009). The ontogenesis of decontextualised language: Some achievements of classification and framing. In J. Webster (Ed.), *Semantic variation: Meaning in society and sociolinguistics* (pp. 403–432). London: Equinox.

Hasan, R. (2011). *Language and education: Learning and teaching in society*. London: Equinox.

Herring, S. C. (2012). Grammar and electronic communication. In C. Chapelle (Ed.), *Encyclopedia of applied linguistics* (pp. 2338–2346). Hoboken, NJ: Wiley-Blackwell.

Hewings, A. (2004). Developing discipline-specific writing: An analysis of undergraduate geography essays. In L. Ravelli & R. Ellis (Eds.), *Analysing academic writing* (pp. 131–152). London: Continuum.

Hewings, A., Coffin, C., & North, S. (2007). Supporting undergraduate students' acquisition of academic argumentation strategies through computer conferencing. *Higher Education Academy Research Report*. Retrieved from http://www.heacademy.ac.uk/ourwork/research

Hodge, B., & Kress, G. R. (1988). *Social semiotics*. Cambridge, UK: Polity Press.

Hoey, M. (1995). *On the surface of discourse*. Nottingham, UK: University of Nottingham.

Hood, S. (2004). Managing attitude in undergraduate academic writing: A focus on the introductions to research reports. In L. Ravelli & R. Ellis (Eds.), *Analysing academic writing: Contextualised frameworks* (pp. 24–44). London: Continuum.

Hood, S. (2006). The persuasive power of prosodies: Radiating values in academic writing. *Journal of English for Academic Purposes*, *5*, 37–49.

Hood, S. (2008). Summary writing in academic contexts: Implicating meaning in processes of change. *Linguistics and education*, *19*, 351–365.

Hood, S. E. (2010). *Appraising research: Evaluation in academic writing*. London: Palgrave Macmillan.

Humphrey, S. (2008). *Adolescent literacies for critical social and community engagement*. Unpublished doctoral dissertation, University of New England, New South Wales, Australia.

Humphrey, S., & Dreyfus, S. (in press). What's the point? Exploring the interpretive genre in applied linguistics. *Functions of Language*.

Humphrey, S., & Hao, J. (in press). Becoming a researcher in science: From laboratory report to research report in an undergraduate biology degree. *Linguistics and Human Sciences*.

Humphrey, S. L., & Macnaught, L. (2011). Revisiting joint construction in the tertiary context. *Australian Journal of Language and Literacy*, *34*, 98–116.

Humphrey, S. L., Martin, J. R., Dreyfus, S., & Mahboob, A. (2010). The 3×3: Setting up a linguistic toolkit for teaching academic writing. In A. Mahboob & N. Knight (Eds.), *Appliable linguistics* (pp. 185–199). London: Continuum.

Hyland, K. (2004). *Genre and second language writing*. Ann Arbor: University of Michigan Press.

Hyland, K. (2009). *Academic discourse*. London: Continuum.

Hyland, K., & Hamp-Lyons, L. (2002). EAP: Issues and directions. *Journal of English for Academic Purposes*, *1*, 1–12.

Ivanič, R., & Lea, M. R. (2006). New contexts, new challenges: The teaching of writing in UK higher education. In L. Ganobcsik-Williams (Ed.), *Teaching academic writing in UK higher education: Theories, practices and models* (pp. 6–15). Basingstoke, UK: Palgrave.

Jewitt, C., & Kress, G. (Eds.). (2003). *Multimodal literacy*. New York: Peter Lang.

Johns, A. M. (1997). *Text, role, and context*. London: Cambridge University Press.

Kachru, B. B. (1985). *Standards, codification and sociolinguistic realism: The English language in the outer circle*. Cambridge, UK: Cambridge University Press.

Jones, J. (1991). Grammatical metaphor and technicality in academic writing—An exploration of ESL (English as a second language) and NS (native speaker) student texts. In *Literacy in Social Process*, papers from Inaugural Australian Systemic Linguistics Conference, Deakin University.

Jones, J. (2004). Learning to write in the disciplines: The application of systemic functional linguistic theory to the teaching and research of student writing. In L. Ravelli & R. Ellis (Eds.), *Analysing academic writing: Contextualized frameworks* (pp. 254–274). London: Continuum.

Jones, J. (2007). Multiliteracies for academic purposes: Multimodality in textbook and computer-based learning materials in science at university. In A. McCabe, M. O'Donnell, & R. Whittaker (Eds.), *Advances in language and education* (pp. 103–121). London: Continuum.

Kearney, N. (2013). *Literacy in a digital world: Searching for common understandings*. Unpublished doctoral dissertation, The Open University, Berkshire, UK.

Kress, G. (2013). *Multimodality: A social semiotic approach to contemporary communication*. London: Routledge.

Lander, J. (2013). *Negotiating community and knowledge in asynchronous online discussions in higher education*. Unpublished PhD thesis, University of Sydney.

Laurillard, D. (2002). *Rethinking university teaching: A conversational framework for the effective use of learning technologies* (2nd ed.). London: Routledge Falmer.

Laurillard, D. (2012). *Teaching as a design science: Building pedagogical patterns for learning and technology*. London: Routledge.

Lave, J., & Wenger, E. (1991). *Situated learning: Legitimate peripheral participation*. New York: Cambridge University Press.

Lea, M. R. (2008). Academic literacies in theory and practice. In N. Hornberger (Ed.), *Encyclopedia of language and education* (2nd ed.; pp. 227–238). New York: Springer.

Lea, M. R., & Street, B. (1998). Student writing in higher education: An academic literacies approach. *Studies in Higher Education, 23*, 157–172.

Ledwith, M. (2011). *Community development: A critical approach*. Bristol, UK: Policy Press.

Lee, S. H. (2010a). Attribution in high- and low-graded persuasive essays by tertiary students. *Functions of Language, 17*, 181–206.

Lee, S. H. (2010b). Command strategies for balancing respect and authority in undergraduate expository essays. *Journal of English for Academic Purposes, 9*, 61–75.

Lemke, J. (1985). Thematic analysis: Systems, structures and strategies. *Semiotic Inquiry, 3*, 159–187.

Lemke, J. (1990). *Talking science: Language, learning, and values*. Norwood, NJ: Ablex.

Lillis, T. (2001). *Student writing: Access, regulation, desire*. London: Routledge.

Lillis, T. (2003). An "academic literacies" approach to student writing in higher education: Drawing on Bakhtin to move from "critique" to "design." *Language and Education, 17*, 192–207.

Macken-Horarik, M., Devereux, L., Trimingham-Jack, C., & Wilson, K. (2006). Negotiating the territory of tertiary literacies: A case study of teacher education. *Linguistics and Education, 17*, 240–257.

Mahboob, A., Humphrey, S., Webster, J., Wong, E., Wong, C., & Chan, A. (2010). Genre pedagogy meets e-learning: An introduction to the language companion course. In L. Lan & D. Qian (Eds.), *English language education in Asian universities: Classroom practices and research issues*. Hong Kong: The Hong Kong Polytechnic University Press.

Malcolm, K. (2010). *Phasal analysis: Analyzing discourse through communication linguistics*. New York: Continuum.

Malinowski, B. (1923). The problem of meaning in primitive languages. In C. K. Ogden & I. A. Richards, *The meaning of meaning: A study of the influence of language upon thought and of the science of symbolism* (pp. 296–336). New York: Harcourt, Brace Jovanovich.

Martin, J. R. (1992). *English text: System and structure*. Amsterdam: John Benjamins.

Martin, J. R. (1999). Mentoring semogenesis: "Genre-based" literacy pedagogy. In F. Christie (Ed.), *Pedagogy and the shaping of consciousness: Linguistic and social processes* (pp. 123–155). London: Cassell.

Martin, J. R. (2009). Genre and language learning: A social semiotic perspective. *Linguistics and Education, 20*, 10–21.

Martin, J. R., & Rose, D. (2007). *Working with discourse: Meaning beyond the clause* (2nd ed.). New York: Continuum.

Martin, J. R., & Rose, D. (2008). *Genre relations: Mapping culture*. London: Equinox.

Martin, J. R., & White, P. R. R. (2005). *The language of evaluation, appraisal in English*. London: Palgrave Macmillan.

Marton, F., Hounsell, D. J., & Entwistle, N. J. (Eds). (1997). *The experience of learning* (2nd ed.). Edinburgh, Scotland: Scottish Academic Press.

Maton, K. (2014). *Knowledge and knowers: Towards a realist sociology of education*. London: Routledge.

Maton, K., Hood, S., & Shay, S. (Eds). (in press). *Knowledge-building: Educational studies in legitimation code theory*. London: Routledge.

McNamara, M. (2010). What lies beneath? The underlying principles structuring the field of academic nursing in Ireland. *Journal of Professional Nursing*, *26*, 377–384.

Meyer, J. H. F., & Land, R. (2005). Threshold concepts and troublesome knowledge (2): Epistemological considerations and a conceptual framework for teaching and learning. *Higher Education*, *49*, 373–388.

Moore, T. (2007). The "processes" of learning: On the use of Halliday's transitivity in academic skills advising. *Arts and Humanities in Higher Education*, *6*, 50–73.

Mort, P., & Drury, H. (2012). Supporting student academic literacy in the disciplines using genre-based online pedagogy. *Journal of Academic Language & Learning*, *6*(3), A1–A15.

Nesi, H., & Gardner, S. (2012). *Genres across the disciplines: Student writing in higher education*. Cambridge, UK: Cambridge University Press.

North, S. (2005). Different values, different skills? A comparison of essay writing by students from arts and science backgrounds. *Studies in Higher Education*, *30*, 517–533.

North, S., & Hewings, A. (2006). Emergent disciplinarity: a comparative study of Theme in undergraduate essays in geography and history of science. In R. Whittaker, M. O'Donnell, & A. McCabe (Eds.), *Language and Literacy* (pp. 264–281). London: Continuum.

Northedge, A. (2003a). Rethinking teaching in the context of diversity. *Teaching in Higher Education*, *8*, 17–32.

Northedge, A. (2003b). Enabling participation in academic discourse. *Teaching in Higher Education*, *8*, 169–180.

Northedge, A. (2005). *The good study guide*. Berkshire, UK: The Open University Press.

O'Halloran, K. L. (2008). Systemic functional-multimodal discourse analysis: Constructing ideational meaning using language and visual imagery. *Visual Communication*, *7*, 443–475.

Orr, J. (1998). *Contemporary cinema "The Road to Nowhere."* Edinburgh, UK: Edinburgh University Press.

Parsons, T., & Bales, R. (1956). *Family, socialization and interaction process*. London: Routledge and Kegan Paul.

Percy, A., & Skillen, J. (2007). *A systemic approach to working with academic staff: Addressing the confusion at the source*. Wollongong, Austalia: University of Wollongong Research Online.

Portman, D. (2014). *Walking a linguistic tightrope: Learner development in writing job application letters*. Unpublished doctoral dissertation, The Open University, Berkshire, UK.

Pratt, M. L. (1998). Arts of the contact zone. In V. Zamel & R. Spack (Eds.), *Negotiating academic literacies: Teaching and learning across languages and cultures* (pp. 171–185). Hillsdale, NJ: Erlbaum.

Ravelli, L. (2004). Signalling the organization of written texts: Hyper-themes in management and history essays. In L. Ravelli & R. Ellis (Eds.), *Analysing academic writing: Contextualised frameworks* (pp. 104–130). London: Continuum.

Rose, D., & Martin, J. R. (2012). *Learning to write, reading to learn: Genre, knowledge and pedagogy in the Sydney school*. London: Equinox.

Rose, D., Rose, M., Farrington, S., & Page, S. (2008). Scaffolding academic literacy with indigenous health sciences students: An evaluative study. *Journal of English for Academic Purposes*, *7*, 165–179.

Saljo, R. (1988). Learning in educational settings: Methods of enquiry. In P. Ramsden (Ed.), *Improving learning: New perspectives* (pp. 32–48). London: Kogan Page.

Schleppegrell, M. J. (2004). *The language of schooling: A functional linguistics perspective*. Hillsdale, NJ: Erlbaum.

Scouller, K., Bonanno, H., Smith, L., & Krass, I. (2008). Student experience and tertiary expectations: Factors predicting academic literacy amongst first-year pharmacy students. *Studies in Higher Education*, *33*, 167–178.

Shor, I. (1987). *Freire for the classroom: A sourcebook for liberatory teaching*. Portsmouth, NH: Boynton.

Shrestha, P. (2011). *Dynamic assessment of academic writing for business studies*. Unpublished doctoral dissertation, The Open University, Berkshire, UK.

Swain, E. (2007). Constructing an effective “voice” in academic discussion writing: An appraisal theory perspective. In A. McCabe, M. O’Donnell, & R. Whittaker (Eds.), *Advances in language and education* (pp. 166–184). London: Continuum.

Swales, J. (1990). *Genre analysis: English in academic and research settings*. Cambridge, UK: Cambridge University Press.

Tanguay, E. (2012). *Breaking the mould: Generic chunking and hybridity in postgraduate academic seminar discussions*. Paper presented at the 23rd European Systemic Functional Linguistics Conference and Workshop, Bologna University, Italy.

Taylor, C., & Drury, H. (2007). An integrated approach to teaching writing in the sciences. In A. Brew & J. Sachs (Eds.), *Transforming a university: The scholarship of teaching and learning in practice* (pp. 117–125). Sydney, Australia: Sydney University Press.

Thompson, G. (2014). *Introducing functional grammar* (3rd ed.). Oxon, UK: Routledge.

Thurlow, C., & Mroczek, K. (Eds.). (2011). *Digital discourse: Language in the new media*. New York: Oxford University Press.

Twiner, A. (2012). *Sociocultural understandings of technology-mediated educational practices: Improvable objects and meaning-making trajectories in the ICT-literate classroom*. Unpublished doctoral dissertation, The Open University, Berkshire, UK.

Twiner, A., Coffin, C., Littleton, K., & Whitelock, D. (2010). Multimodality, orchestration and participation in the context of classroom use of the interactive whiteboard: A discussion. *Technology, Pedagogy and Education*, *19*, 211–223.

Unsworth, L. (2011). *Multimodal semiotics: Functional analysis in contexts of education*. London: Continuum.

Vygotsky, L. S. (1978). *Mind in society: The development of higher psychological processes*. Cambridge, MA: Harvard University Press.

Vygotsky, L. S. (1981). The genesis of higher mental functions. In J. V. Wertsch (Ed.), *The concept of activity in Soviet psychology* (pp. 144–188). Armonk, NY: Sharpe.

Vygotsky, L. S. (1987). Thinking and speech (N. Minick, Trans.). In R. W. Rieber & A. S. Carton (Eds.), *The collected works of L.S. Vygotsky, Volume 1: Problems of general psychology* (pp. 39–285). New York: Plenum.

Vygotsky, L. S. (1999). Tool and sign in the development of the child. In R. W. Rieber (Ed.), *The collected works of L. S. Vygotsky, Volume 6: Scientific legacy* (pp. 3–68). New York: Kluwer Academic/Plenum.

Wallace, C. (2003). Local literacies and global literacy. In S. Goodman, T. Lillis, J. Maybin, & N. Mercer (Eds.), *Language, literacy and education* (pp. 89–107). Milton Keynes, UK: The Open University Press.

Webb, C., & Bonanno, H. (1995). Assessing the literacy skills of an increasingly diverse student population. *Research and Development in Higher Education*, *17*, 784–790.

Webb, C., English, L., & Bonnano, H. (1995). Collaboration in subject design: Integration of the teaching and assessment of literacy skills into a first year accounting course. *Accounting Education*, *4*, 335–350.

Wells, G. (1981). *Learning through interaction: The study of language development*. Cambridge, UK: Cambridge University Press.

Wells, G. (1986). *The meaning makers: Children learning language and using language to learn*. Portsmouth, NH: Heinemann.

Wenger, E. (1998). *Communities of practice: Learning meaning and identity*. Cambridge, UK: Cambridge University Press.

Wignell, P. (2007). *On the discourse of social science*. Darwin, Australia: Charles Darwin University Press.

Wilkinson, R. (Ed.). (2004). *Integrating content and language: Meeting the challenge of multilingual education*. Maastricht, Netherlands: University of Maastricht.

Wilkinson, R., & Zegers, V. (Eds.). (2008). *Integrating content and language: Realizing content and language integration in higher education*. Maastricht, Netherlands: Maastricht University.

Williams, P. (2002). The learning web: The development, implementation and evaluation of internet-based undergraduate materials for the teaching of key skills. *Active Learning in Higher Education*, *3*, 40–53.

Wingate, U. (2006). Doing away with study skills. *Teaching in Higher Education*, *11*, 457–465.

Woodward-Kron, R. (2002). Critical analysis versus description? Examining the relationship in successful student writing. *Journal of English for Academic Purposes*, *1*, 121–143.

Woodward-Kron, R. (2004). Discourse communities and "writing apprenticeship": An investigation of these concepts in undergraduate education students' writing. *Journal of English for Academic Purposes*, *3*, 139–161.

Woodward-Kron, R. (2005). The role of genre and embedded genres in tertiary students' writing. *Prospect*, *20*(3), 24–41.

Woodward-Kron, R. (2007). Negotiating meanings and scaffolding learning: Writing support for non-English speaking background postgraduate students. *Higher Education Research and Development*, *26*, 253–268.

Woodward-Kron, R. (2009). This means that: A linguistic perspective of writing and learning in a discipline. *Journal of English for Academic Purposes*, *8*, 165–179.

Index

Index